The Legalization of Prostitution

A sociological inquiry into the laws relating
to prostitution in India and the West.

JEAN D'CUNHA

WORDMAKERS, Bangalore
for the
Christian Institute for the Study of Religion
and Society

The Legalization of Prostitution

A sociological inquiry into the laws relating to prostitution in India and the West.

JEAN D'CUNHA

Published by
WORDMAKERS
18/1 Ali Asker Road
Cunningham Road Cross
Bangalore - 560 052

for the

**Christian Institute for the Study
of Religion and Society**
P.O.Box 4600, 73 Millers Road, Bangalore - 560 046

ISBN 81 - 85447 - 00 - 4 (PB)
ISBN 81 - 85447 - 01 - 2 (HB)

First printing 1991

Cover Design: M.S. Dileepan
Typeset by WORDMAKERS

To

Cynthia, My Mother

To

Loy, My Husband

And

To

All Women in Prostitution

Acknowledgements

Many people have helped me with this book. Though I cannot mention all of them, I wish to thank each one.

I am deeply indebted to the women in prostitution, who so candidly shared their feelings and exprteriences with me. I thank Mrs. Lawate, former medical social worker at Dr. Kotnis Arogya Kendra, a semi-government hospital in Pune, for introducing me to and allowing me to speak with women visiting the hospital. I wish to thank ex-superintendents of rehabilitative homes, and social workers, especially Anjali Dave, Shobhana Manadier and Preeti Pai, for their invaluable insights and help in meeting women in prostitution in Bombay. I am also grateful to the police of the Vigilance Branch, C.I.D., Bombay, for the information provided to me; to the librarians of Tata Institute of Social Sciences, S.N.D.T. Women's Research Unit, Centre for Education and Documentation (Bombay), the Centre for Informal Education and Development Studies, Bangalore and Mr. Jan Wisser of the Documentation Centre on Prostitution, Amsterdam, for giving me free and easy access to reading material. I thank Bombay-based advocates Ms. Indira Jaisingh and Ms. Gayatri Singh, for their clarifications and insightful comments on the law. I am very grateful to Dr. Neera Desai, former Director and Dr. Maitreyi Krishnaraj, Director of the S.N.D.T. Women's Research Unit, Bombay, for commissioning and guiding me on a project on *Prostitution and the Law in India*, without which this book on legalization of prostitution might not have been conceived. I am immensely grateful to Ms. Jyotsna Chatterji of the J.W.P. Delhi for assigning this project to me and the Tata Trust, Bombay and Misereor, Germany, for making possible my study travel to Europe.

I would also like to thank the typist for his excellent typing work, and last but not least, I wish to thank my mother and husband for their unflinching support and encouragement.

September 1989   **Jean D'Cunha**

Foreword

The Joint Women's Programme of the CISRS and the William Carey Study and Research Centre has been concerned about prostitution as part of its study and action programme on women's problems. It carried out studies of the Devadasi system and trafficking in women and children for prostitution which brought the evils to public notice. It was realised in course of time that there was need to take a look at the current laws relating to prostitution and study their working as they still violate justice for women and favour pimps, looking upon prostitutes as criminals. It was felt that we must examine the whole situation and see where changes are needed in the laws. Hence this study by Ms. Jean D'Cunha who has recognised experience of research in this field. We hope this will prove helpful to all those working in the interests of exploited women.

New Delhi
December 1990.

Jyotsna Chatterji
Associate Director,
Joint Women's Programme

Contents

Part I

Chapter 1 : Introduction

Prostitution is not a world apart. It is bound up with wider social processes and permeated by assumptions current in society at large. The institution of prostitution has thus existed in one form or another in all class-based patriarchal societies. India is no exception.

In ancient India, female prostitution was closely related to religious practices and was endorsed by religion as such. The Devadasi system and the singing and dancing girl tradition have become a familiar and accepted part of the Indian ethos. Although the Devadasi system still exists, particularly in parts of South India, the development of industrial capitalism has led to the breakdown of this system and the singing and dancing girl tradition. These traditions are now giving way to common prostitution both in rural and in urban areas. Prostitution in modern India, as in other parts of the world, is now socially condemned and penalized by law.

Categories of Prostitutes in Urban India

Prostitution in urban India as elsewhere is hierarchically structured. There are three main classes of female prostitutes categorized on the basis of the structure within which they operate, the degree of mobility and control over their lives, their earnings and their amenities.

At the lowest end of the scale are the street-walkers and the brothel-owned prostitutes. The street-walkers may function independently or may have pimps. Without pimps, they are very vulnerable to harassment from clients, the police and thugs, with little or no way of combating them. Clients may even refuse to pay. Having a pimp is not much better. They exploit them economically, emotionally, physically and sexually. Street-walkers may earn anything between 50 p. and Rs. 20 a day and there are days on which they earn nothing (D'Cunha, Jean; 1984)[2].

The cage-brothel prostitute is attached to and housed in a brothel, which has a landlord who rents the premise, a brothel-keeper who runs the brothel, pimps, procurers and a retinue of thugs. The cage-brothel prostitute is strictly confined to the brothel in the first few years of entry into the profession, lest she escapes. Her earnings may, on average, range from Rs. 10 to Rs. 50 a day with nearly half to three-fourths being appropriated by the brothel-keeper. Daily earnings of the prostitutes fluctuate and they are often in debt (D'Cunha, Jean; 1984)[2].

Not only does there exist a class hierarchy in prostitution, but a caste stratification as well. In a survey of prostitutes in Pune by Vilas Wagh, a Pune-based researcher, it was discovered that more than 60% of the women were dalits. There was not a single prostitute from the Brahman, Maratha, Jain or Lingayat castes. Girls from the so-called higher castes or upper classes do practise prostitution, but instead of becoming brothel-bound prostitutes, they operate as independent call girls. As one dalit student told Wagh, 'Lower caste women may earn Rs. 4 a day but the upper class women may earn Rs. 400 a day, as caste and class divisions prevail here' (Omvedt, Gail; 1983)[11].

The second category of prostitutes is the independently operating lower middle-class women. They may have pimps. Many of them hold regular jobs and may resort to prostitution regularly or intermittently, as a way of supplementing their meagre incomes. These women may also operate through massage parlours, health clubs, dancing schools or meet clients through jobs as waitresses or bar girls.

The third category of prostitutes is the upper middle-class clandestine call girls who may own apartments with telephone and other amenities. They either operate independently or through a 'contact' and may have a regular clientele who pay exorbitant fees of Rs. 500 or more per night.

Regardless of the cultural specificities of each country or urban-rural specificities in the same society, female sexuality carries an economic value, around which different institutions providing female sex services are formed. These institutions interact with and are conditioned by changes in the economic substructure and transform themselves accordingly. There have been dramatic changes in female prostitution in India and South-East Asia in the last three decades. Not only has the scale enlarged, but the forms, transaction arrangements and institutions within which the phenomenon manifests itself have also become highly differentiated. A new phenomenon witnessed in South-East Asian countries like Thailand, Philippines and Korea, is the growing link between prostitution and the tourist industry. In cases where prostitution has developed into a highly organized trade, it has been suggested that it contributes to the process of economic development at the national level through foreign exchange earnings and at a regional level through the prostitute's income remittances (Truong, Thanh-Dam; 1985)[18]

Despite several new and important dimensions which the phenomenon has acquired, prostitution as an institution together with the new forms in which it manifests itself has received scant analytical attention.

Literature Survey of Prostitution in India

With the development and consolidation of the social sciences in India, several social and historical studies on prostitution have been undertaken in various parts of the country. These studies tend to be disparate and address themselves to specific aspects of the phenomenon such as, types of prostitution, the lifestyle and living conditions of prostitutes, etc.

Significant among these works are J.N. Ghosh's research on the economic life of prostitutes and brothel-managements in Calcutta in 1923,[3]; Studies on Prostitutes and Prostitution by S.N. Mukherjee and J.N. Chakraborty in Calcutta in 1933,[10]; Correira, Alberto and Germano in Portuguese India in 1938,[1]; Gokhale in Pune in 1955,[4]; Agnihotri Vidhyadhar in Kanpur 1955,[19]; S.D. Punekar and Kamala Rao in Bombay in 1962,[12]; A.S.Mathur and B.L. Gupta in Lucknow in 1965,[9]; M. Rangarao and R. Rao in Hyderabad in 1969,[14]; Swarnalata Hooja in Rajasthan in 1970,[5]; B. Joardar in Vizag in 1974,[6]; and in an industrial area of West Bengal in 1976,[7]; Promila Kapur's *Call Girls of India* in 1978,[8]; and *Trafficking in Women and Girls for Prostitution* by Sr. R. Rozario in 1988,[15].

As an illustration of the nature of most of the above studies or aspects covered in them, the author dicusses S.D. Punekar and Kamala Rao's study entitled *Prostitutes of Bombay*, 1962. The study covers 350 prostitutes in Kamatipura, a red light area in the metropolitan city of Bombay.

It examines the socio-economic background of common prostitutes in terms of place of origin, religion, caste, family background, marital status and abilities of the woman. It also highlights the Devadasi origins of several of the prostitutes.

Another aspect that the study explores are the causes of prostitution. Here the "action and interaction of various forces and the cumulative experience" of the individual is stressed. The authors distinguish between the two types of causes. Twenty-six distinct reasons for entry into prostitution are listed under six groups divided under the two-fold classification of predisposing and direct precipitatory causes. The study concludes that the death of guardians and ill-treatment by relatives is the largest predisposing cause for prostitution, with poverty and destitution ranking second. Connivance of relatives, deception, kidnapping, heredity and environmental influences constitute, according to the study, the largest incidence of direct precipitatory causes.

The study also focuses on the life-style of common prostitutes in terms of their life-span in the profession, income and savings, clientele, living conditions (food, clothing, sanitation, health, relationship with the brothel management and police) and attitude towards the profession and so on. (Punekar, S.D. and Rao, Kamala; 1962; 2nd ed. 1967).[12]

It will be observed that the above mentioned studies tend to be disparate, descriptive, empirical works. They highlight specific aspects of prostitution, rather than provide a coherent analytical framework of the institution, wherein the patriarchal and macro-level socio-economic base of prostitution as an institution is examined.

Also as far as it is possible to discern, most of these studies tend to be structural-functionalist in their approach, while a few reveal no clear theoretical assumptions, but tend to emphasize individual motives, attitudes and behaviour.

The former is perhaps because of the positivist orientation of the social sciences in India, particularly Sociology, wherein structural functionalism has been a dominant theoretical tradition.

The disparate character of the studies may be the result of controversies embodied in the issue of prostitution itself.

There are three conflicting views on prostitution — the moralist's, the institutionalist's and the feminist's. The first two refer to street and brothel prostitution, while the third and recently emerging view refers to the social conditions of all women. The moral view maintains that prostitution is immoral and hence undesirable. They say that severe penal measures should be used to eradicate it. The institutional view argues that the phenomenon is 'as old as human civilization' itself, it is an inevitable social evil, and in the past it has only been possible for the state to introduce some mechanisms of control (while collecting taxes) in order to safeguard public health and to limit the incidence of excessive exploitation. These two views have been advocated from the point of view of policy-making and are based on the assumption that social activities can be regulated for the benefit of all, and that regulations can be designed and executed by a neutral body of executives. The third view recently reflected in feminist circles in India, but not yet significantly embodied in Indian studies on prostitution, challenges the two above-mentioned positions. It maintains that prostitution reflects the prevailing double standards of unequal relations between men and women. The institution of prostitution, it is said, has the fundamental purpose of maintaining male supremacy. Thus prostitution as a social phenomenon will survive as long as the social structures surrounding it prevail. Neither sanctions nor moral condemnation will change the situation. Meanwhile the legal status of prostitutes and the social stigmatization they must endure, isolate them from the rest of humankind and expose them to various forms of exploitation by pimps, the police and clients. (Truong, Thanh-Dam; 1985).[18]

Studies on the Devadasi System

No picture of the studies on prostitution in India is complete, without consideration of the research work on the Devadasi system in India. Several studies on the Devadasi system have been undertaken.

A research project undertaken by researcher-activist Gail Omvedt in 1983, examines the origins and the caste-class basis of the Devadasi system. It also records and briefly analyses the protest actions against the system. (Omvedt, Gail; 1983).[11]

A study by Amrit Srinivasan published in 1985, presents the life-style and status of the Devadasi community before it was banned, in the context of a changing socio-economic political system. It also discusses the anti-Devadasi movement and the cultural revival movement of the Devadasi dance form — Bharatnatyam (Srinivasan, Amrit; 1985).[17]

Another study by Savli, a group working among Devadasis in Belgaum, explores the historical origins of the phenomenon, the legendary justifications, the life-style and status of the Devadasis and the changes in the same, the methods of recruitment and welfare measures for Devadasis (Savli; 1985).[16]

Yet another study in Karnataka undertaken by the Joint Women's Programme and published in 1985, highlights the oppressive conditions of Devadasi women and examines the socio-economic basis of the system (Ramesh, Asha and Philomena, H.P. 1985)[13]

Studies on Prostitution and the Law

It is pertinent to observe that there are scarcely any studies on state control and regulation of prostitution through the law in India.

This author has however completed a comprehensive three-year research project for the Research Unit on Women's Studies, SNDT University, Bombay, on prostitution laws in India. The study is entitled *"The Suppression of Immoral Traffic in Women and Girls Act 1956 (SIT Act of 1956) : A Critical Review."*[2a]

Rationale of the Present Study

Given the complexity of the phenomenon of prostitution, given the fact that female prostitution has become an internationalized industry and given the gaps in information, study and research on prostitution laws, there is a pressing need to delineate policy issues and discuss them within an analytical framework, with special reference to women. As mentioned earlier, this author therefore undertook a research project for the SNDT Women's Research Unit, Bombay, on the state control of prostitution through law. It took concrete shape in the form of a critical evaluation of the law governing prostitution in India. The project was entitled, *"The*

Suppression of Immoral Traffic in Women and Girls Act 1956; (SIT Act of 1956) : A Critical Review".   In the course of this study one learnt of legalization as a system of law in other countries and its prevalence in 19th century India.

The last decade witnessed attempts by the Indian Government to explore alternatives or remedies to SITA, as it failed to meet its objectives.   More recently several news items reported the desire of various   state governments to legalize and licence prostitution as an alternative to the SITA.   The debate on whether or not to legalize prostitution acquired a special significance in the wake of the AIDS scare, which whipped up a fear phychosis.   It led to frequent assertions on the part of certain state governments (Maharashtra and Karnataka for instance), that legalization and licensing prostitution (thereby regulating the health conditions of the prostitutes, in an effort to curb sexually transmitted diseases (STDs) and AIDS and thus protect and preserve public health) was a necessity.

The demand for prostitution to be recognised as a legitimate form of work was also being raised by certain prostitutes' rights groups and women's groups in the West.   Strains of such thinking are also current among certain liberal sections in India.

The Central Government finally passed the Immoral Traffic in Persons Prevention Act 1986 which is basically an amendment to the SIT Act (SITA).

It is against this background and the paucity of research on an assessment of prostitution laws in India that this author has chosen this area of study.

A study assessing the impact of legalisation of prostitution as a system of law for India also assumes significance in the light of policy rethinking and reformulation and can provide some pointers for legal reform.   More importantly, such policy issues need to be discussed with reference to their specific impact on women.

Content of the Study

The study makes a modest attempt at evaluating the desirability of legalization of prostitution from the ideological point of view, its feasibility in implementation and whether or not prostitutes will benefit from the system.   An understanding and evaluation of the legalization has been made within the context of the micro-socio-economic power linkages between prostitution racketeers and implementing authorities and within a larger understanding of the institution of prostitution in terms of its causes and emergence, patriarchal and macro-level socio-economic bases in modern capitalist societies and the specific experiences of alienation of women in prostitution. The experience of western countries that have legalized prostitution has also been drawn upon to assess the feasibility of legalization. Recommendations for legal reform have also been advanced.

Structure of the Study

The study is organized as follows:

Part II: Chapter 2 deals with an analytical framework of the institution of prostitution, within which the legalization debate is located.

Part III: Chapters 3 & 4 deal with the law governing prostitution in India. Chapter 3 deals with the Suppression of Immoral Traffic in Women and Girls Act 1956 (SITA) and Chapter 4 deals with the amendment to the SITA — The Immoral Traffic in Persons Prevention Act 1986. These Acts are dealt with in terms of their shortcomings in scope, formulation, basic ideological assumptions, implementation and the need to explore legal remedies.

Part IV: Chapters 5 & 6 deal with the debates on legalisation of prostitution. Chapter 5 discusses legalisation as an alternative to the SITA, as advanced by certain state governments and social welfare organizations in India, while Chapter 6 highlights the debates on legalization in the West. Historical and scientific evidence has been used in these chapters to assess the arguments in favour of legalisation.

Part V: Chapters 7, 8, 9 & 10: These chapters explore the experience of those countries that have legalised prostitution. Chapters 7 and 8 deal with legalisation in 19th century England and India respectively. Chapter 9 discusses the experience of legalized prostitution in the state of Nevada in the U.S.A. and Chapter 10 deals with the experience of West Germany.

Part VI: Chapter 11: This chapter suggests pointers in the direction of legal reform and progressive and human socio-economic support structures.

Scope of Study

Although the study has an all-India applicability, data collection on a detailed implementation of the SITA and interviews with Indian prostitutes have been restricted to the cities of Bombay and Pune. A less detailed statistical breakup of the implementation of SITA at an all-India level has also been presented.

Data was also gathered from UK, USA, Belgium, Holland and Germany in the course of participation in an International Congress on Prostitution, Human Rights and Feminism in Brussels in 1986, followed by a study tour in Europe. Data collected pertains to legal provisions in these countries and in-depth interviews with prostitutes and prostitutes' rights groups.

The study is restricted to prostitution under capitalism.

Techniques of Data Collection

The study is a qualitative one, based on primary as well as secondary sources of data.

Secondary sources were relied on for an understanding of the laws governing prostitution in India and abroad, their historical background and an analytical framework of the institution of prostitution.

Reliance has also been placed on primary data. This consisted of compiling and organizing raw statistical data from police records and case files.

Prostitutes in Pune were interviewed at the STD Clinic of Dr. Kotnis Arogya Kendra Hospital, Pune, a semi-government hospital, through the good offices of a medical social worker. Prostitutes in Kamatipura, a red light area in Bombay, were interviewed through the assistance of a social worker in the area.

Detailed interviews were also held with brothel-keepers, police officials from the Vigilance Cell Crime Branch, Bombay, politicians, lawyers, social workers, protective home authorities and women activists.

In-depth discussions were conducted with European and Third World prostitutes, researchers, lawyers, social workers and women activists who participated in the Brussels Congress in 1986.

Problems in Data Collection

There were several problems in data collection and tabulation. Firstly, access to Indian prostitutes, whether brothel-attached or independent was difficult. Tight links with the underworld and suspicion of outsiders blocked communication. A purposive quota sample of prostitutes was used for lack of choice.

This together with the low level of literacy and legal knowledge of prostitutes led to the collection of information mainly about how Indian prostitutes saw themselves, their life and trade, clients, police, courts and the possibility of compulsory health checks in the context of legalization.

By contrast, the European prostitutes were candid and insights were easier to obtain. They had a higher degree of literacy. Most of them were independently operating prostitutes. Several of them belonged to prostitutes' rights organisations in Europe. They also vehemently asserted that prostitution was a legitimate form of work and were therefore unashamed to identify themselves as prostitutes as they believed this to be the first step towards recognizing a prostitute as a worker and erasing the social stigma attached to prostitutes' and prostitution.

Problems in Data Collection with respect to Interviews with Prostitutes

Interviews with prostitutes were open-ended, in-depth personal discussions, which explored the alienation they faced in the context of the desirability of legalization from an ideological point of view. It was difficult to quantify and tabulate such emotions and perceptions.

References

1. Correira, Alberto S. and Germano, C.; (1939): "Indian Portuguesa; Prostitution e Profilaxia, Anti-Venera-Historica, Demografia, Ethnographe, Higiene e Profilaxia - Tipographia Rangel Bastora". -

2. D'Cunha, Jean; (1984): "Voices in the Dark"; *Eve's Weekly.*

2a. D'Cunha, Jean; (1984): "The Suppression of Immoral Traffic in Women and Girls Act (1956): A Critical Review"; Research Unit on Women's Studies, S.N.D.T. University, Bombay, India.

3. Ghosh, J.N.; (1923): *Social Evil in Calcutta*; (Booklet); City Press, Calcutta.

4. Gokhale, B.B.; (1955): "Study of Prostitution in Pune"; Paper published in *Samaj Seva*; January.

Part II

Chapter 2 : Towards an Understanding of the Institution of Prostitution

Introduction

Prostitution has by and large, been conventionally viewed throughout history as a female phenomenon, despite the existence of male prostitution. This is partly the product of structural and cultural factors, which account for gender role and gender trait stereotypes in society and in crime. Women are defined by characteristics which are often sexual and this is reflected in criminology, where deviations from socially prescribed norms of sexual behaviour by women are treated as crimes (Leonard, B. Eileen; 1982)[9]. Male prostitution often goes unaddressed because it is perhaps more limited, less varied and institutionalized, compared to female prostitution.

Female prostitution as manifested in India and several other Asian countries cannot be studied in isolation, with reference only to certain culture specific variables. It must be understood within a complex context which has two important dimensions — "(a) structural aspects rooted in the historical development of gender relations which cause prostitution in most societies and (b) conjunctural aspects resulting from certain state policies, adopted at particular historical junctures, which exacerbate the phenomenon". Prostitution as an institution therefore cannot be understood as originating from the contradictions of a moral system. It has a definitive economic base which interacts with and is intrinsically related with the

5. Hooja, Swarnalatha; (1970): "Prostitution in Rajasthan: Then and Now", *Indian Journal of Social Work*: Vol. XXXI, No.2: July.

6. Joardar, B.; (1974): "A Social Study of Prostitutes in Vizag"; *Bulletin of Anthropological Survey of India*, Government of India, Vol. XXIII, Nos.1-2.

7. Joarder, B.; (1976): *A Study of Prostitution in the Industrial Area of West Bengal.*

8. Kapur, Promila; (1978): *Life and World of Call Girls of India*; Vikas Publishing House Private Limited, New Delhi.

9. Mathur, A.S. and Gupta, B.L.; (1965): *Prostitutes and Prostitution*, published by Ramprasad and Sons.

10. Mukherjee, S.N. and Chakraborty, J.N.; (1933): *Prostitution in India.*

11. Omvedt, Gail; (1983): "Devadasi Custom and the fight against it"; *Manushi: No.19.*

12. Punekar, S.D. and Rao, Kamala; (1962): *Study of Prostitutes in Bombay*; Lalwani Publishing House; 2nd Edition 1967.

13. Ramesh, Asha and Philomena, H.P.; (1985): *Devadasi System in North Karnataka*; Preliminary report of the study conducted by the Joint Women's Programme team in North Karnataka.

14. Ranga Rao, M. and Rao, R.; (1969): *A Study of Prostitutes and Prostitution in Hyderabad City;* published by the Association for Social Health in India, Andhra Pradesh Branch.

15. Sr. Rozario, M. Rita R.G.S. assisted by Mr. Rasool, Javed and Mr Kesari, Pradeep; (1988): *Trafficking in Women and Children in India (Sexual exploitation and sale)*; A Joint Women's Programme Publication: Uppal Publishing House, New Delhi.

16. Savli; (1985): "Devadasis - Victims of Social Slavery", an article presented to the Working Group of the Human Rights and Anti-Slavery Commission of the UN, Geneva; July 29 - August 2.

17. Srinivasan, Amrit; (1985): "Reforms and Revival : The Devadasi and her Dance"; *Economic and Political Weekly*; Vol. XX, No. 44, November 2.

18. Truong, Thanh-Dam; (1985): "Virtue, Order, Health and Money Towards a Comprehensive Perspective on Female Prostitution in Asia"; Paper prepared for Workshop of Experts on Prevention and Rehabilitation Schemes for Young Women in Prostitution and Related Occupations, ESCAP: Bangkok, June 17-21.

19. Vidhyadhar, Agnihotri; (1955): *Fallen Women, a Study with Special Reference to Prostitution in Kanpur, the Industrial Metropolis of Uttar Pradesh*; Maharaja Printers, Janvala Bhavan, Pune, India.

rest of the economic system, making it a crucial part of the labour transformation process, rather than a moral issue. The degree of interaction between prostitution and the economy determines the extent to which vested interests get entrenched and consolidated within the institution. It also determines the extent of challenge to policy makers who intend to rectify the situation (Truong, Than-Dam; 1985).[20] In this context, policies aimed at transforming the situation must primarily be geared towards restructuring socio-economic conditions, work conditions of women and men in general, and prostitutes in particular, tackling vested interests in the sex industry and rethinking our patriarchal value system.

This chapter is therefore a modest attempt at elaborating an analytical framework to understand the institution of female prostitution in terms of its causes, emergence, patriarchal and micro/macro level socio-economic bases in modern capitalist societies, linkages between the exploitation and oppression of all women under capitalism and the specific alienation of women in prostitution. It is against this background that the study attempts an evaluation of the desirability of legalizing prostitution as a measure of state control, from the ideological point of view, its feasibility in implementation and whether or not prostitutes will emerge beneficiaries of such a system.

The Exploitation of Women under Capitalism

The capitalist social system has consolidated itself at a global level. Its hallmark is generalized commodity production, in which labour power itself becomes a commodity for the generation of surplus value. Women as components of the labour force, sell their labour power together with men in the labour market and are thus exploited as wage workers. The sexual division of labour in employment and lower wages paid to women *vis-a-vis* men, for work of the same or similar nature, are other means of exploiting women to augment surplus value. All this takes place at the point of production and constitutes one dimension of capitalist production relations.

But capitalism is also concerned with the maintenance and reproduction of surplus value on which the system thrives. The system resorts to a generalized sexual division of labour in society. It assigns to women the primary task of maintaining and reproducing labour power for capital. Maintenance and reproduction of labour power include all forms of domestic work that replenish and revitalize the worker for the next day's work. It also involves the activities of child-bearing and child-rearing to ensure a stable and legitimate supply of labour power for the production of capital. Women are thus directly linked to capital and play a vital function, the non-performance of which would bring the system to a halt. However, this linkage is blurred by the privatized and isolated nature of this activity under capitalism. It remains invisible and unpaid. Maintenance and reproduction of labour power is considered non-economic and unproductive. Domestic work and women, its performers, are thus accorded a secondary and subservient status.

Capitalist production, like any other form of production, is organically linked with all other spheres of social life which make possible the existence, perpetuation, extension and expansion of the sphere of production. An ideological system is thus created to justify and explain the above-mentioned exploitation of women under capitalism. It also provides scope for action within the capitalist framework.

Patriarchy: Definition

Patriarchy is defined as man's control over woman's sexuality, fertility/reproduction and labour power.

"Sex is power, is its foundation and patriarchy is rule by male right, thus giving rise to male authority" (Barry, Kathleen; 1979).[3]

These rights established through the 'sex is power' ethic are institutionalized into the socio-economic, political order and are manifested in the discrimination, inferiorization, subservience, objectification, dehumanization and degradation of women in every sphere of life — social, cultural, economic and political.

The activity of maintaining and reproducing labour power and the need for its continuation gives rise to a set of gender-trait and gender-role stereotypes. Women are thus primarily defined as reproductive units and/or sexual entities, responsible for sex services.

The gender-stereotyped role images of women that have thus emerged to serve the needs of capital are: (a) Woman the child-bearer; (b) woman the child-rearer;(c) woman the domestic/housewife; (d) woman the sex object. Associated gender-trait stereotypes of woman, "the weak, docile, passive, self-sacrificing, subservient" controlled by man.

The Monogamous Patriarchal Family: The Woman's Position in it and its Relation to Prostitution

The institution within which the maintenance and reproduction of labour power is made possible, to ensure a steady and legitimate workforce for capitalism, is the patriarchal monogamous family unit. However, monogamy is by and large directed only towards the woman. The property concerns of the dominant classes and the desire to trace descent and inheritance through the male line, make the undisputed determination of paternity essential.

Two categories of moral systems therefore emerge under patriarchy, one applicable to each sex, with each moral system based on concepts of honour.

A woman's honour is intrinsically linked to her body and sexuality. The various facets of female sexuality, that is, the reproduction of labour power and the production of pleasure are defined by their relationships with men and according to male interests. Thus, as mothers and wives, women bear children for men and nurture their families. To enjoy these rights they must be legally wedded and to be legally wedded they must have certain socially prescribed criteria, namely, chastity, capacity to labour and/or wealth. So chastity of a woman before marriage and faithfuless to her husband after marriage became cherished feminine traits and values, whose degree of significance is determined by the class structure and particular historical period (Truong, Thanh-Dam; 1985).[20] Thus a woman becomes the private property of her husband and therefore his sexual property. A man owns his wife's entire being, controlling her earnings, thoughts, reproduction and sexuality. Women who fail to meet the criteria for ideal wifehood/motherhood, fall into the role of producing pleasure for men without the legal sanction of marriage. If they reject this, they can pursue the life of an ascetic, unless this is prohibited by religion.

Such patriarchal control permeates all individual man-woman relationships. It is internalized by all classes of men and women, including the working class. The oppressed usually internalize the organizational formats and ideological articulations of the oppressor until they realise their situation and start to rebel. The male worker is at one level antagonistic towards the bourgeoisie and at another level becomes the gendarme of the bourgeoisie by exercising his own male power and control over woman. This helps to stabilize the system and diffuses the sense of alienation and powerlessness that the male worker feels at his workplace. But for women it is a manifestation and reinforcement of the fragmentation of the working class. It represents a greater sense of alienation, slavery and terror.

The authority of the working class male is, however, restricted by the ruling class male who commands the working woman's labour, appropriates the surplus value she creates, controls her children for work and encroaches on her sexuality by right.

The double standards of male sexual morality extend to all males as an expression of class and/or male power. Patriarchal society defines male honour in terms of his conduct in public life and permits him the freedom to formulate his own rules in matters of sexuality. It allows him access to sexual pleasure in varied forms and with several women. While a woman is severely condemned for allowing more than one man access to her body, man by contrast is praised for proving his virility regardless of the basis, be it love, money or force. While being sexually 'serviced' by wives within marrage, men are allowed by society to find sexual pleasure elsewhere. Society goes so far as to create the institution of prostitution outside marriage, which caters to man's so-called diverse sexual needs, 'natural' sexual virility and aggressiveness, all of which cannot or may not be fulfilled by his wife.

A group of women are set aside to provide such sexual services for men. This institution of prostitution is the other side of male domination and class oppression of women.

Patriarchal society thus morally fragments women into 'madonnas' and 'whores', each having a specific function. The former represents the chaste, faithful wife, the private property of her husband, the reproducer of a stable and legitimate workforce for capital, the producer of her husband's children, who will carry on his line of descent and inheritance. The prostitute, on the other hand, is the shared property of several men. She is denied chastity and exclusivity. She has to sell sexual services. There is therefore less social interest in her

(Barnett, C. Harold).[2] Such moral fragmentation and functional division between women, creates a social hierarchy between them and serves to control their lives at all levels. Further, while society on one hand createss the institution of prostitution, on the other it castigates the prostitute as a 'fallen' woman.

Elements of a Definition of Prostitution

Prostitution has been variously defined. Social scientist Thanh-Dam Truong examined definitions of prostitution beginning with the Latin word *prostituere*; the definition was elaborated in the *Encyclopedia of Social Sciences* (1933) and that by sociologist K. Davis (1961), Polsky (1967), Gagnon (1968), and Kathleen Barry (1979). Finding these inadequate Kathleen Barry gives guidelines for a new definition of prostitution which can be applied cross-culturally and historically. She defines prostitution as "the provision of sexual services in exchange for material gains. This provision may be induced by one or more of a variety of conditions: physical coercion (abduction, seduction) socio-economic coercion (sexual abuse, poverty); acquisition by purchase; individual decision". Prostitution may be organized in different ways depending on the number of men to whom the services are provided, the nature of payment and the institutions. Different forms of prostitution are condoned or condemned throughout history.

"At one extremity, prostitution may be disguised in the legal institution of marriage, through which a woman is contracted to be sold or contracts to sell herself to a man in exchange for social acceptance, economic security, etc. Sexual services form only a part of the relationship. At the other end, prostitution is a practice involving the exclusive provision of sexual services, on a relatively indiscriminate basis similar to the sale of unskilled or semi-skilled labour power. Between, there are the others who provide sexual services to a select number of partners as a form of erotic art, and generally against payment ranging from money, gifts and/or opportunities for social mobility. There is also the mistress or the hired wife whose partner maintains her in exchange for occasional sexual services, without a binding marriage contract and its legal implications. The social conditions of the women in prostitution are determined by the institutional structure within which they operate. The institutions themselves vary according to socio-economic changes." (Truong, Thanh-Dam; 1985).[20]

There are five important issues that emerge from this definition.

(1) Sexual services in prostitution may not be limited to sexual intercourse but include various other sexual acts. Further, the services that prostitutes provide may include companionship, care and nourishment, as professionals and as women.

(2) Payments may not merely refer to money and gifts, but must be perceived in terms of capacity for social mobility as well, both for the individual and the organization, setups, as the latter benefits greatly from prostitution.

(3) Conditions of women in prostitution must be understood and assessed more widely than those in conditions of slavery and bondage. They must include other forms of prostitution. This is because each institution is governed by a separate set of social relations which determine the conditions and status of the prostitute.

(4) The act of prostitution is not just the result of individual motives but must be understood in the context of socially structured gender relations and the class structure of society.

(5) Social conditions of individual prostitutes change, depending on several factors with personal and institutional dimensions. The former includes physical attributes or consciousness of the individual prostitute, the latter the socio-economic-legal system within which she operates (Truong, Thanh-Dam; 1985).[20]

Basis of Institution of Prostitution: Ideological/Economic

The definition of prostitution and issues raised therefrom, highlight the ideological and socio-economic basis of the institution of prostitution.

Ideological Roots: The primary ideological assumption underpinning the institution of prostitution is that sex is a male

right and further that sex and women's bodies are commodities (under capitalism) that can be packaged and sold by women themselves or by pimps and procurers to clients. This is true, regardless of whether an individual woman practises prostitution 'voluntarily' or is forced or coerced into it (ed. Barry, Kathleen; Bunch, Charlotte; Castley, Shirley; 1983).[4]

Economic Aspects: While being a cultural phenomenon, rooted in masculine and feminine images current in society, prostitution has economic dimensions as well, mostly related to its ideological assumptions. In a commodity-oriented social system, prostitution is very lucrative, the merchandise involved being physical intimacy with women and/or girls (ed. Barry, Kathleen; Bunch, Charlotte; Castley, Shirley; 1983).[4]

It is pertinent to note that the ideological assumptions of the institution of prostitution have rarely been analysed. "Traditionally prostitutes have always been equated with prostitution. Patriarchies have never distinguished between the individual, that is, the woman in prostitution, and the institution, that is, the commodity-based market of prostitution. The individual woman has been perceived as the institution and the commodity, while the pimps have been seen as the market. The practices of procuring, "seasoning" and prostituting thus become invisible (ed. Barry, Kathleen; Bunch, Charlotte; Castley, Shirley; 1983).[4] With no distinctions between the individual and the institution all prostitutes are seen as victims or criminals; it blurs the hierarchy in the sex industry and conceals the heterogeneity within the prostitute population. It also conceals the complex relationship between prostitution and the economy and ultimately leads to prostitution being surrounded by a cloud of inevitability, leaving the basis of the institution unchallenged.

Nature of Prostitution as an Economic Activity

Many countries around the world prohibit prostitution as an economic activity. In several others, the act of prostitution, brothel-keeping, encouraging and living off the earnings of prostitution etc., are prohibited. The definition of encouragement, however, only relates to one individual encouraging another and not to direct or indirect encouragement by large establishments and state institutions like the media, the tourist or entertainment industry.

In the actual implementation of these laws, prostitutes are

overwhelmingly treated like criminals and punished while prostitution racketeers are allowed to thrive.

This leads to the moral condemnation and legal isolation of women in prostitution. Such isolation and stigma lead to discreet/clandestine operations — survival strategies to hide their identities in order to gain social acceptance. A woman's level of discretion is largely dependent on several factors — the tolerence level of the community and the extent of her own desire for social acceptance as a normal human being and a citizen with full rights. This also determines the degree to which she must depend on other individuals or institutions to advertise her services, while simultaneously concealing her identity and operating from a place from where she has a movable control over her conditions of service (Truong, Thanh-Dam, 1985).[20]

The public outcry against prostitution, the fact that a person living with a prostitute can be booked for pimping, and/or the inability of a woman in prostitution to afford an establishment from which she can operate, force many women to depend on institutes, like brothels, entertainment or health parlours. These are regarded as market places, where their services are advertised and they can find clients. Prostitutes may also solicit in the street where they have a relatively greater degree of independence, but where they are exposed to the public eye and to greater violence and danger (Truong, Thanh-Dam).[20]

Conditions in these institutions are horrendous. The women are enslaved, bonded, confined and concealed. Their earnings are appropriated by the brothel management. The degree of exploitation depends on the conditions of entry into prostitution, physical assets and so on. Torture in the form of physical and mental coercion and abuse, kidnapping and debt bondage turns the woman or girl into an object of slave labour. Her physical assets are used to produce pleasure for the client, while she is deprived of any rewards.

In cases of socio-economic pressure, the woman must compete with other women in the business and effectively advertise and crudely expose herself to attract clients. Women must invest in accessories to maintain their market value. They determine their mobility within the hierarchichally structured sex industry; and the institution through which they provide their services determines their income and the number of clients they must entertain per day. For example in institutions like escort services, which are at the apex of the sex industry, women may not take more than one client a night, but in most brothels, they are forced to entertain numerous clients during the same time span. There are also institutions charging varying amounts for rent or bar fines. Here the number of clients that a woman must entertain depends not only on the availability of clients, but also the rent she must pay so that she can continue to use the premises and thence have access to the market. The numerous clients, physical abuse, long and irregular hours of work, insanitary living conditions and poor nutrition are factors that adversely affect the woman's health and the length of her working life. Also, social stigma, health problems such as repeated abortions and venereal diseases, the rapid deterioration of her physical condition and appearance, and physical violence often lead to mental depression and the use of drugs or alcohol.

There are escort and call girls in the higher echelons of the sex industry and they do not suffer the same conditions. They buy the services of their agents who advertise what the women have to offer and mediate with the buyers.

Women in escort services have a greater degree of control over their earnings and individual bargaining power, depending on their skills, physical attractiveness and client taste, largely because merely escorting someone is not a moral or legal crime. As clients are generally top executives on business trips, women in escort services are able to maintain a high market value. They are able to earn high incomes without having to take on many clients. They have a greater degree of social mobility.

Women who work as escorts generally meet their clients in their hotels to provide sexual services, thus avoiding the stigma attached to a 'common prostitute' or a 'call girl' operating from her residential premises — a stigma that can lead to legal problems and a decline in market value.

Escort girls are usually educated, physically attractive and multilingual. It is a well known fact that the escort network has reached international dimensions, involving women from diverse races and that escort agencies are integrated into tourism-linked services which form part of the hospitality offered by local companies to travelling businessmen.

By contrast, most call girls use their homes or places rented on a long term basis for their work. Although relatively financially independent, a large majority of them are those who can no longer compete in the escort market and hence cannot afford to be too selective. They advertise their services through daily newspapers as cheaply as possible and always have a contact phone number. Where access to a phone is limited, they usually rely on casual informants like shop-keepers, street vendors, hoteliers, cabbies and bartenders to negotiate for them in exchange for a small fee. Many call girls may also have a pimp with whom they share their income. They may even frequent bars, not just as consumers but to meet potential clients. Call girls run a greater risk of bearing the stigma attached to prostitution, but their chances of being arrested are limited as they operate from their homes. They are generally tolerated by the community because they keep to themselves and contribute to the economic activities of shopkeepers, beauty parlours, restaurants and the like in the area (Truong, Thanh-Dam; 1985).[20]

Although escort girls and call girls are better placed in the sex industry than street prostitutes or prostitutes living in conditions of slavery and bondage, they do not entirely escape customer violence, control and violence of pimps or police harassment when their identity is discovered.

In conclusion it can be said that, unlike most other economic activities, prostitution is characterized by legal isolation, moral alienation, severe mental and physical health hazards, and vulnerability to economic exploitation because of the lack of bargaining power and a dependence on their institutions and those who can manipulate the legal system.

The illegality of prostitution ensures the thriving of its economic base and the proliferation of brothel managers and entrepreneurs in the service sector. They create a highly organized trade, well enmeshed in the economy.

The degree of prostitutes' mobility within the hierarchically structured sex industry is largely dependent on sustained physical attractiveness, market fluctuations, the amount saved, the degree of freedom allowed by the institutions where they operate, knowledge and experience of the market rules and contacts within the profession enabling them to work independently. While in other professions accumulation of experience leads to an increase in the market value of the labour, it is the reverse in prostitution. Prostitution requires physical attractiveness, but the nature of the work leads to a deterioration in the woman's appearance and health. This results in a decline in the value of a prostitute's labour power. The international market for prostitution, particularly in Asian countries, is characterized by a demand for freshness, sweetness and virginity. But a woman has lost her health, youth and beauty by the time she has acquired experience and knowledge of the market for upward mobility and the opportunity to operate independently.

The decrease in value of her physical assets renders her unable or less able to compete in a market where there is a fresh and fast turnover of women and girls. Establishment managers are always on the lookout for new girls because of the keen competition among brothels for clients. The dynamics of the institutions demand that new women be dragged into prostitution. So, while institution owners depend on procurers and recruiters for the supply of women and as the market expands, more women are disposed off.

Causes of Prostitution : Demand and Supply Forces

Demand and supply factors in prostitution are largely conditioned by the process of capitalist development.

Demand Factors

Four factors may be distinguished as conditioning male demand for heterosexual prostitution services:

(a) Conditions preventing the establishment of a regular sexual relationship.

(b) Prescribed norms of sexual conduct: The double standards of male sexual morality.

(c) Lack of satisfaction within an existing relationship, which may include the desire to command the services of several women.

(d) Demand created by the tourist industry.

(a) Conditions preventing regular sexual relations

Lack of opportunity to establish a regular relationship occurs during prolonged separation and alienation from home and peer groups, for example businessmen, migrant labourers, seamen or military men whose jobs involve extensive travelling. Some of these circumstances are created and intensified by the internationalization of capital leading to transnational economic and political linkages, national and international division of labour, civil and international wars for capitalist economic expansion and political domination.

Furthermore, military bases have also 'approved' the demand for prostitutes. In the late 1960s, for example, about 40,000 US Servicemen were stationed at air bases in Thailand and nearly half a million were stationed in Vietnam. Entertainment centres grew up around these military bases forming a service infrastructure. In the case of Vietnam, most of these have disappeared following the American withdrawal but they have been maintained in Thailand and now serve the needs of a different category of visitor - the tourist. Similarly, in the Philippines, prostitution has flourished in places with a heavy concentration of foreigners. Olongapo near the US naval base in Subic Bay, for example, is popularly known as 'Liberty City' of the US Seventh Fleet, with 500 clubs, bars, restaurants, sauna baths and massage clinics (Truong, Thanh-Dam; 1983).[19]

More generally, in developing countries the lack of opportunity to establish a regular sexual relationship is not just geographical mobility, whether imposed by economic or military circumstances. Many men due to their age and/or stage in their life cycle (e.g. young men awaiting land rights) or those with family commitments cannot afford to marry. In societies where the demographic balance is weighed against females, there are men for whom female partners are simply not available (Truong, Thanh- Dam; 1983).[19] All these categories of men may demand the services of women in prostitution.

(b) Prescribed norms of sexual conduct : The double standards of male sexual morality

The double standards of male sexual morality reinforce and reflect the demand for prostitution. In many societies, while strict rules of sexual conduct are applied to women, men can maintain their sexual freedom, promiscuity often being considered as a proof of manhood. This leads to the familiar stereotyped segregation of women into the 'pure and virtuous' versus the 'impure and vicious'. The 'impure and the vicious' are assigned to sexually satiate 'uncontainable' male sexuality.

(c) Dissatisfaction with an existing relationship

For present purposes, it suffices to note that disparities between partners' sexual needs and views or forced abstinence in the context of power struggles between partners, can lead to dissatisfaction within an existing relationship. With the sexual revolution and the rise of feminism, sex becomes as Germaine Greer writes, 'the arena of confrontation in which new values must be hammered out'. Often this confrontation provides an additional reason for seeking extra-marital relationships between both men and women. In western societies where sexual norms are less stringent, this does not always imply a demand for prostitution, except in very specific forms. As Mead states, 'for sex satisfaction, it is no longer necessary to choose between marriage and prostitution. For most of those without religious scruples, sex is available on a friendly and amateur basis and without responsibility' (Truong, Thanh-Dam; 1985).[20]

However, a demand may arise among men who feel they are losing out in the power struggle between the sexes, and who need to restore their feelings of masculinity, but cannot find partners suitable for this. There are cases of sex excursions to South East Asia in search of a 'lost paradise' of traditionally submissive women and the 'mail-order bride' business selling catalogues stresses the obedience and devotion of Asian women.

Though the 'sexual revolution' in the West may have created the possibility for forms of sexual relationships outside the framework of marriage, the demand for services of women in prostitution has not declined (Truong, Thanh-Dam; 1985).[20]

(d) Demand created by the tourist industry

In a commodity-oriented social system in which technological growth, modernization in the field of transport and accommodation services, concentration of capital, integration of production and diversification of products has become the order of the day, corporate giants in the transport and hotel business have, with government support, promoted the tourist industry as one of the largest foreign exchange earners in some of the developing countries. Utilizing the already mentioned demand factors for women in prostitution, the tourist industry has successfully incorporated the 'hospitality industry' — a euphemism for prostitution.

Prostitution for the 'Inclusive Tour' and 'Rest and Recreation' markets has been well documented. For instance, Dutch, German, French and Australian tour operators have openly included prostitution as part of their tours. Firms like Casio Computer Company and Toyota automobiles have sponsored sex tours for their employees to various Eastern and South East Asian countries like South Korea, the Philippines, Taiwan and Thailand (Association of Anti-Prostitution Activity; 1984).[1]

Finally, as mentioned earlier, there is an increasing consolidation of prostitution tied up with the establishment of military bases and regular military joint exercises. Governments have provided tacit consent to this form of prostitution largely because military expansionism is a politically sensitive issue, benefiting super power expansionist interests and the interests of the local governments. Military-linked prostitution may also be a foreign exchange earner for the host countries and, lastly, patriarchal governments believe that estranged servicemen must have sexual access to women so as to increase or maintain their military efficiency. This has resulted in a boom in the 'Rest and Recreation' market.

It was reported that the American withdrawal from Indo-China led to a decline in the Thai tourist industry. The market has since been boosted by tourists from Europe, Japan, Malaysia, Singapore, Australia and, more recently, from the Middle East, 90% of whom come for the night life (Truong, Thanh-Dam; 1985).[20]

While there is a lack of reliable data on prostitutes and their clients to posit a definite analysis on the relationship between tourism and prostitution, there is sufficient documentation suggesting that tourism and prostitution (which historically existed independently in the form of small scale enterprises) have been amalgamated into a large scale network of enterprises. The structure of the international tourist industry is one of the factors that has contributed to the merger of tourism and prostitution into a well organised trade. This process has also resulted in a change in the very concept of leisure itself. The character of leisure has been transformed. There is a commodity that can be readily purchased on the market. Further, it is the persuasive media serving the marketing strategies of tourist firms that is increasingly defining leisure (Truong, Thanh-Dam; 1985).[20]

National tourist campaigns have been selectively advertising traditional attributes relating to women. Officials in the department of tourism are even known to have explicitly marketed female sexuality as an economic asset in their endeavour to promote tourism.

To illustrate the above, the Berlitz Travel guide reads: "From Munich to Melbourne the name 'Pat-Pong' evokes the image of go-go bars and massage parlours. As a sociological phenomenon, 'Pat-Pong' ought to be seen if not sampled. "The 'Pat-Pong' areas symbolize what great numbers of young and not so young males come to Thailand for — girls" (Truong, Thanh-Dam; 1985).[20]

A similar trend is emerging in Goa in India, where the Goa government and five-star hoteliers are about to sell Goa as a tourist package, in order to increase foreign exchange reserves and the income of the hoteliers. An advertisement marketing the five-star hideout, Majorda, on Goa's Majorda beach, has a graphic visual of bikini clad women with the caption below reading: "Majorda Beach Resort: The therapy for jaded nerves and tired eyes". The tourism department of Goa and the big hoteliers have been using bikini clad women in their advertisements and brochures to woo tourists to come for 'sun, sea and sex'.

In February 1987, the same Majorda Beach Resort advertised for masseuses between 18 to 25 years of age, and at another time for masseuses below 28 years of age. This appears to be a front for prostitution. That some of these five-starred hotels maintain albums containing photographs of prostitutes from which tourists can choose, is further evidence of this trend (Tourism - its effects on women in Goa; 1988).[18]

Such perceptions and marketing of female sexuality by local governments and officials have encouraged several foreign firms to explicitly promote sex tours. Some tour operators have also used this to justify promotion of sex tourism as a form of development aid (Truong, Thanh-Dam; 1985).[20]

Because of the above it can be seen that the demand for sexual services was brought into existence by all these categories of men who have the power to purchase sex for a price. They create a large market for women's bodies, a market that is constantly kept supplied through procurers and gangs that traffic in women and children for prostitution. There are financial gains for pimps, procurers and brothel-keepers. There are economic and political interests of governments, police and courts and other authorities leading to their collision with prostitution racketeers. There is the sexual gratification of clients. There are social attitudes tolerating the abuse and enslavement of women and the reinforcement by governments by virtue of their neglect, toleration, sanction, suppression of evidence and complicity. This is the social structure that creates the conditions for prostitution (Barry, Kathleen; 1979).[3]

Supply Factors

Women are one of the most vulnerable sections in society, socially and economically. As a result, they are often put into prostitution by the coercion, and deceit of prostitution racketeers. Alternatively, prostitution is also perceived by some women as a means for survival, given the lack of available options.

Studies on prostitutes and prostitution both in India and other parts of Asia, indicate three crucial issues responsible for a woman's entry into prostitution:

(a) the unequal nature of gender relations

(b) widening socio-economic disparities within the population and government policy that exacerbates this, creating conditions for prostitution.

(c Socio-religious factors.

(a) The Unequal Character of Gender Relations

Empirical studies highlight several causes of prostitution which can be classified under categories regarding relationships between men and women. They are: unwed motherhood, demands for dowries, child marriages, desertion by husbands, divorces or separations, ban on widow remarriages, loss of virginity to boy- friends or lovers, victims of procurers who use physical and emotional coercion, child abuse by male relatives including father/step fathers, forced sale of virginity by parents (usually step father) and the practice of dedicating virgin girls to the temples and their 'deflowering' by rich village patrons, given socio-religious sanction in India because of the Devadasi system.

The percentage of such cases varies between studies. However the findings indicate an important paradox in gender relations, namely, the control of female sexuality by men and the commercial availability of female sexuality created by men. This control is manifested both at the moral and economic levels (Truong, Thanh- Dam; 1985).[20]

Oppression within marriage: As mentioned earlier, a considerable stress has been laid on the economic function of the cultural subordination of women in ensuring the reproduction of labour power. This subordination is first and foremost reinforced by sexual codes of conduct established to ensure the undisputed paternity of the children. Together these two elements have substantially contributed to the social retardation of women. By contrast, males enjoy the freedom to define their own rules and norms in matters of sexuality, their social conditions being unaffected by permissive sexual conduct. In fact in several societies, the greater the access males have to women and women's bodies, the higher is their social status.

Under the prevailing traditional marriage customs, women are explicitly exchanged for economic gains, thus denying them the free choice of partners; or they are forced to enter into matrimony to gain social acceptance and limited rights. Although the situation is changing for some, many still do not have access to the means of controlling their own lives. The male functions as a 'protector and/or controller' of his wife's entire being to the point of exercising his power and control to brutalize her psyche and body. While enjoying sexual access to other women after marriage, he also enjoys the freedom to desert, divorce or separate from his wife for another woman, without blame. By contrast, as well as numerous forms of confinement and control, a woman is socially condemned for allowing more than one man access to her body.

In these circumstances, women who are victims of such exploitation may be forced to turn to their last resort, namely their bodies, as a means of survival, either consciously or because they have inadvertently succumbed to unscrupulous elements who have coerced or tricked them into prostitution.

Moreover, as a strategy for survival prostitution is not simply a matter of rejecting traditional customs or of being victimized by them, it also reflects the female social retardation which renders women ill-equipped to be absorbed into other productive spheres (Truong, Thanh-Dam; 1983).[19]

According to D'Souza, child marriage, the dowry system, social taboos on widow remarriage and drastic sanctions against female infidelity have all been factors contributing to prostitution (D'Souza; 1973).[6] In a study of several villages near Mamfe in Cameroun, Lagerberg and Wilms report that young women sometimes shirk forced marriages by migrating to the nearest city, and that to attain and sustain economic independence about 70% of them engage in prostitution (Lagerberg and Wilms; 1972).[8] Case studies of the Philippines, Thailand and India indicate similar factors which lead women into prostitution, namely, dire poverty, unhappy marriages, abandonment by husbands and single motherhood (Truong, Thanh-Dam; 1985).[20]

Deserted, separated, divorced women: A deserted, divorced or separated woman, who is in effect a victim of sexual politics is socially castigated, unfairly blamed for her inability to persevere with or hold on to her husband in her socially prescribed role of wife and mother. In the absence of a 'protector or controller', she is perceived as 'free', 'loose' and vulnerable to other males. In the context of her economic dependence on her husband within marriage and the absence or lack of employment opportunities for financial sustenance after a desertion, or separation, she may well be vulnerable to prostitution either because she is deceived or coerced or because prostitution is the only option for survival.

Widowed Women: The same is true for widows, particularly in Indian society. A widow is socially enjoined to remain so, especially among the upper castes or classes as an expression of her everlasting chastity and fidelity to her husband, for reasons of maintaining purity of race and descent. Paradoxically, she is also perceived as an ill-omen responsible by virtue of her sinful behaviour for her husband's death. She is hidden within the family, burdened with all kinds of manual tasks, and forced to repudiate anything that would stimulate her sexuality or enhance her physical appearance. Also, the institution of Niyoga which prevails in certain parts of India, compels a widow to have sexual liaisons with her husband's eldest brother, as well as enduring all the other forms of confinement and control imposed on her. Documentation on the status of women in India through the ages suggests that being a widow in pre-British and British India were so appalling, (this does not imply that the situation has drastically changed) that several high caste widows ràn away from their families to escape family oppression. Naivety or the marginalization of women from employment drove many of them to succumb to prostitution, allowing the economic base in prostitution to thrive (Liddle, Joanna and Joshi,Rama; 1985).[10]

The cult of virginity and prostitution: In societies where a cult of virginity exists, accompanied by the belief that virgins can biologically enhance male sexual potency or that sexual intercourse with virgins can cure sexually transmitted diseases in males, there exists a lucrative trade in virgins. The virginity cult implies a rigid control on the sexuality of young girls and their consequent inaccessibility to males. On the other hand, the cult of male potency through the 'deflowering' of young girls attaches a market value to the sexuality of young girls. Interviews with prostitutes reveal that there is an increasing demand for virgin girls in the city of Bombay, particularly from Arab clientele. They want to experiment with 'freshness'. They desire 'clean sex' and believe that STDs can be cured by intercourse with virgins. A virgin girl can be sold to a Bombay brothel for as much as Rs. 7,500(D'Cunha, Jean; 1986).[5]

Case studies in Thailand reveal that a girl's virginity can be traded at prices ranging from 4000 baht (Thista; 1983)[17] to 8,000 baht depending on the clientele. According to a study in Thailand, 6% of the 50 women interviewed were still virgins when they entered the trade. Most of the girls got a very small share of the money earned from the sale of their virginity, and many were deceived and forced to continue in prostitution (Truong, Thanh-Dam; 1985).[20]

Sale of Virgin girls by parents into prostitution: In male dominated cultures where virginity is highly valued, it is assumed that the father or other male family members have absolute moral and legal rights to control the lives and destinies of their female children. One form is a rigid control over the girl's sexuality before marriage, as virginity increases her value in the marriage market. Among certain socio-economic strata, where parents may be forced to sell their daughters into prostitution, this high premium on virginity is a double edged sword, as virginity increases the girl's market value in prostitution.

Rape as a predisposing factor for prostitution: The high demand for virgins in certain areas, also increases the vulnerability of young girls to rape, seduction and disposal by males who are unwilling or unable to purchase virginity on the market or are incapable of maintaining a wife financially or assuming the legal responsibility of being a husband. The loss of virginity implies the loss of their value as women in the eyes of society, as well as the loss of their own self esteem. Rape, including gang rape, is thus also used as an explicit strategy to break a woman's will, ego and resistance and force her to succumb to prostitution. This contradiction between the cult of virginity and the cult of male potency therefore allows the economic base in prostitution to develop and flourish as pointed out by Barry (1981; p. 121):

"Contrary to the prevalent assumption that women and girls end up or 'fall into' prostitution, the markets and networks of this system are maintained because of specific strategies of pimps who traffic women into prostitution. Those strategies play on women's economic and emotional vulnerability".

Unequal gender relations - In conclusion: In conclusion it may be said that the dual system of morality that circumscribes male-female relationships fragments female sexuality into numerous dimensions, resulting in a hierarchichal divide and distantness between women. It is this fragmentation that permits the coexistence and interaction between the control of female sexuality on one hand and its commercialization on the other.

(b) Economic Disparities within Populations and its Exacerbation by Government Policies

Unequal gender relations apart, prostitution studies point to the widening socio-economic disparity and deprivation within population groups, both at a macro and micro level, as laying the preconditions for prostitution as a survival mechanism. Such social processes are exacerbated by government policy.

The internationalization of capital, the international division of labour and corporate strategies of profit-maximisation have resulted in new ways of controlling labour, especially female labour and female sexuality, in the context of rapid economic development in various Asian and South East Asian countries. Diverse modes of institutionalized exploitation of women, accompanied by local methods of male domination have been systematized into modern productive enterprises in third world countries. This has resulted in new patterns of inequality in gender relations within the local population and a reinforcement of unequal relations between the host country and advanced capitalist countries (Ong, Aiwaha Dr.; 1984).[11]

Development strategies in the agrarian sector, female emigration and prostitution: The 1960s saw several Asian countries expanding commercialized agriculture and beginning to develop industrially with the participatiuon of foreign investors and international aid agencies.

The growth policies of these countries are usually most concerned with the export of agricultural commodities through large and medium scale mechanized agriculture, the establishment of export processing zones, the stimulation of small scale enterprises and the export of labour to oil producing countries in the Middle East. Though these policies have met with success if measured in terms of foreign exchange earnings, they have resulted in the dislocation of the local population and a disruption in their life styles.

Studies on the agricultural sector in the developing countries indicate that agricultural development programmes introducing modern technology for large scale farm operations have been decisively biased in favour of large and middle range farmers. Small farmers have been edged out of operation. They have been transformed into agricultural wage labourers and the viability of small scale farming has been drastically reduced. In addition, the absence of monetary compensation paid to them by the government, has driven many of them to a life below the poverty line. The increasing rural-urban wage differentials have resulted in migration to urban areas for employment, so as to sustain their families in the village.

Around 75% of women working in the entertainment industry in various Asian countries come from impoverished rural areas. The size of their families is above the average size of six, excluding other dependents like elderly relatives. In such situations prostitution is one of the family's survival options.

Income earned from prostitution is remitted to rural areas to help sustain families and farming activities. However the number of women who make an entrepreneurial move into prostitution is limited (Truong, Thanh-Dam; 1985).[20]

An analysis of migratory patterns of victims of sexual exploitation and sale, which forms part of a study on trafficking in women and children in India revealed that 326 out of 1100 women (29.64%) had migrated between states, 128 (11.64%) within their state, 149 (13.54%) from rural to urban areas and vice versa. Data was not available for 189, that is, 17.8% of the women (Rozario, M. Rita; 1988).[15]

So, contrary to the assumption that the high rate of rural emigration is predominantly male and that females only migrate when they marry, and when they join their families or for educational purposes, recent studies have revealed changes in migratory patterns indicating that there is an increasing amount of rural emigration of young women between the ages of 15-19 years to urban areas (Truong, Thanh-Dam; 1985).[20]

Employment of women in industry and prostitution: The process of female emigration is also the result of special industrial development policies which favour 'development' of women, that is, Free Export Processing Zones.

Though they carp about the social and physical attributes of young women, managements especially employ them in these industries because of the significant social and economic benefits. While the exploitation of women is mystified by stressing their manual dexterity, biological adaptation to repetitive tasks and docility under male supervision, we are seldom told that these varied forms of exploitation pave the way for their entry into the sex industry.

For instance, though many of these enterprises are operated by international high tech corporations, they treat the majority of their female labour force as a labour reserve to be employed at low wages, generally even lower than males for jobs of the same or similar nature. Many women are known to supplement their meagre incomes from also regularly or intermittently engaging in prostitution.

It has also been observed that industries employing a large number of young women have a high degree of turnover of the labour force, because firms prefer young and single women.

This enables them to keep the level of productivity high and minimize the social security costs. Thus after a span of time, when female workers have reached a certain age, when they get married or pregnant, they are disposed of by the firms. They are made permanently unemployed because, being unskilled, they cannot find jobs easily elsewhere. It must be noted that disposal occurs for other reasons too. It can result from the nature of market trends or industrial deployment policies. For example, in 1974-75, the market recession resulted in the laying off of thousands of women workers by electronics firms in Malaysia, Singapore and the Philippines. Women workers can also lose their jobs as a result of industrial deployment policies which break up complex production processes into smaller operations that can be easily shifted between geographical areas, in response to government incentives. Studies on prostitution reveal that many women who have entered prostitution or the entertainment industry have been disposed of by firms and have had to find other jobs (Ong, Aiwaha Dr.; 1984).[11]

Male international emigration, female-headed households and prostitution: Another emerging phenomenon is the increase in the number of female headed households. Though the causes of this phenomenon merit greater exploration and analysis, interviews with prostitutes and media reports indicate some co-relation between female-headed households and male international emigration.

The early 1970s witnessed several Asian countries adopting the policy of export of labour to the oil-rich Middle East, in order to earn foreign exchange for governments, through the income remittances of workers. However, income remittance has either been difficult or impossible for a large number of workers, due to the fraudulent practices of recruiting and employment agencies. On arrival they find no jobs available for them or are given inferior jobs compared to those promised to them or are paid salaries much less than those agreed. As a result they plunge into deep debt because most of them borrow money to pay recruiting agents for the necessary papers. This places an increased burden on the women supporting the other members of the household and may partly be responsible for the increase in female-headed households. The separation for long periods results in an estrangement between husband and wife, often leading to a permanent separation or divorce. Whatever the reasons, it is a fact that there has been an increase in the number of female-headed households and those women have to find ways to earn in order to maintain their households. Either they themselves or their daughters enter prostitution (Truong, Thanh-Dam; 1985).[20]

This author is unaware of any comprehensive Indian study showing the co-relation between the labour export of males and the increase in female-headed households, with respect to the effects on those women's survival strategies, with specific reference to prostitution.

(c) Socio-Religious Practices and Prostitution: The Devadasi System

Prostitution in certain oriental cultures, in parts of India for instance, is known to be related to religious practices, which sanction and reinforce prostitution. Traces of this in the form of the Devadasi system continue to exist in the states of Karnataka and Maharashtra, India.

The Devadasi system is traditionally a practice of dedicating girls to a god or goddess to serve the temple. The girl is considered married to the god and cannot contract a legal marriage in her lifetime.

While she performed temple duties and was maintained therein, temple priests began to use her sexually. With the ascent of Kshatriya royalty over Brahmin priests, the royalty began to patronize the Devadasi, not only for her artistic but also her erotic skills.

Nowadays, the landed gentry or rich patrons choose the young girls, pay for the dedication ceremony, deflower them and then maintain them economically for a period of time in exchange for sexual access to them. Although the males may be married or have sexual access to other women during the liaison period, the Devadasis cannot marry nor can they form relationships with other men. As the Devadasis are not legal wives and exist primarily as a source of pleasure for males, their children are illegitimate and do not enjoy the right of being legal heirs of the patrons.

This ritual prostitution has provided religious legitimacy to upper caste males for accepted and unfettered sexual access to lower caste women. In several cases a patron has kept several women, the number of females being the measure of his status. This is an articulation of his class and male power. It has been observed that when a woman grows old or is deserted by her patron, she may have no option but to become a prostitute either in the area in which she lives or in an urban area.

The Devadasi system also destroys the lower castes' sense of self respect in a society in which women are accorded a pedestal status.

The entry of women into the Devadasi system is not difficult to explain. Parts of northern Karnataka (India), is a chronic drought-prone region and has been neglected by successive governments even after independence. This together with the caste system has rendered the area socially and economically backward.

The girls entering the Devadasi system come from lower caste, pauperized small farmers or landless labour households. Payment and maintenance by rich patrons are economic incentives for initiation.

Besides serving as a licence for prostitution with a religious sanction, the practice makes women believe that they are doing a service to Goddess Yellamma. These women, therefore, do not bear a social stigma by becoming Devadasis. They are accepted by other castes and their children are not stigmatized. In fact, the Devadasi profession attains a certain respectability because Devadasis are called upon to be present at auspicious functions in upper caste households (Ramesh, Asha and Philomena, H.P.; 1985).[14]

What is pertinent to note is that the socio-economic impoverishment of the area, the gradual breakdown of the Devadasi system, the availability of young women and girls who could be dedicated, and the desertion of Devadasis by patrons have resulted in more women and girls from this area being recruited for prostitution in urban areas.

It is evident that the Devadasi system has an economic base linked to a moral system and interacts with it and the existent socio-religious system. It has, in recent times, become a feeder to urban prostitutes.

Conclusion

Against this background, commercialization of female sexuality and women involved in prostitution cannot be perceived as morally deviant. There exists a similarity between social processes that have intensified inequality, marginalization and deprivation especially in developing countries. Women are more affected by this than men. Women are marginalized from the workforce or severely discriminated against, within it. Social transformations in several Asian countries have increased the traditional burdens of women in maintaining households - burdens which drive an increasing number of women to perceive their sexuality as a form of marketable labour power. What is wrong with female prostitution is that it is unjust patriarchal systems that have created unequal gender relations and the institution of prostitution. Men are active participants as organizers, pimps and clients who coerce and exploit women into prostitution, but they are not the targets of social condemnation or the law.

References

1. Association of Anti-Prostitution; 1984; *Anti-Prostitution activities in Japan*.

2. Barnett, C.Harold: "The Political Economy of Rape and Prostitution"; *The Review of Radical Political Economics;* Vol.8, No.1.

3. Barry, Kathleen; (1979): *Female Sexual Slavery;* Prentice Hall, Inc., Englewood Cliffs, New Jersey.

4. Ed. Barry, Kathleen; Bunch, Charlotte; Castley, Shirley; (1983):"International Feminism - Networking against Female Sexual Slavery"; Report of the Global Feminist Workshop about Traffic in Women; Rotterdam, The Netherlands; April 16.

5. D'Cunha, Jean; (1986): "The Suppression of Immoral Traffic in Women and Girls Act 1956: A Critical Review"; Research project for Research Unit on Women's Studies, SNDT University, Bombay, India.

6. D'Souza, A.A.; (1973): "Prevention of Prostitution: A Strategy of Social Change"; *Social Action*; Vol. 23.

7. Harrod J.; (1985): *The Unprotected Worker: The Social Relations of Subordination*; New York: Columbia University Press.

8. Lagerberg, C.S.I.J. and Wilms, G.P.; (1972): *Profiel Van Cenhandelstad in West Cameroon; Verslagen en verant woording van een social antropologisch Onderzock in Kumba* (Tilburg Development Research Institute).

9. Leonard, B. Eileen; (1982): *Women, Crime and Society: A Critique of Theoretical Criminology*; Longman; New York and London.

10. Liddle, Joanna and Joshi, Rama; (1985): "Gender and Imperialism

in British India"; *Economic and Political Weekly*; Vol.XX, No. 43, 6th October.

11. Ong, Aihawa Dr.; (1984): "Industrialization and Prostitution in South East Asia": Paper for UNNGOsInvitational consultation on "Female Sexual Slavery and Economic Exploitation", held on October 24, 1984, San Francisco, California.

12. Phongpaichit, R.; (1980): "Rural Women of Thailand: From Peasant Girls to Bangkok Masseuses"; Geneva: ILO, World Employment Programme; Research Working Paper 14.

13. Phongpaichit; (1981): "Bangkok's Masseuses: Holding up the Family sky"; *South East Asia Chronicle*; Issue No. 78.

14. Ramesh, Asha and Philomena, H.P.; (1985): *Devadasi System in North Karnataka*: Preliminary report of the study conducted by the Joint Women's Programme Team in North Karnataka.

15. Rozario, M. Rita R.G.S.; assisted by Rasool, Javed and Kesari, Pradeep; (1988): *Trafficking in Women and Children in India: Sexual exploitation and sale*; (A Joint Women's Programme Publication) Uppal Publishing House, New Delhi.

16. Thista K.; (1980): *Providence and Prostitution*; London: Change.

17. Thista K; (1983): "Nuns, Mediums and Prostitutes in Chiengmai:A Study of some Marginal Categories of Women"; Women and Development in South East Asia; Occasional Paper; Elliot College, University of Canterbury.

18. *Tourism - Its Effects on Women in Goa: A report of the people*; Bailancho Saad, 1988; Goa: A Women's Collective.

19. Truong, Thanh-Dam; (1983): *The Dynamics of Sex Tourism: The case of South East Asia: Development and change*; Sage, London, Beverly Hills and New Delhi, Vol. 14.

20. Truong, Thanh-Dam; (1985): "Virtue, Order, Health and Money: Towards a Comprehensive Perspective on Female Prostitution in Asia"; Paper presented for Workshop of Experts on Prevention and Rehabilitation Schemes for Young Women in Prostitution and Related Occupations; ESCAP, Bangkok, 17-21 June.

Part III

Chapter - 3: The Suppression of Immoral Traffic in Women and Girls Act 1956 (S.I.T.A. India : 1956) : A Critical Evaluation

Introduction

Governments the world over have attempted to handle the issue of prostitution through the use of law. Three systems of law have been formulated and applied in various parts of the world with respect to prostitution. They are the Prohibitionist system, the Tolerationist system and the system of legalization of prostitution.

Let us briefly look at each system:

1. Prohibitionism

The Prohibitionist system as it exists in the U.S.A., (except in the state of Nevada), Japan and the like, bans prostitution *per se*. It therefore criminalizes the activities of all categories of people involved in prostitution, namely, brothel keepers, pimps, procurers, prostitutes and clients.

In its actual operation, however, it is discriminatorily enforced against the woman. It overwhelmingly penalizes the prostitute, while the men who derive profit and pleasure from prostitution (that is, pimps and clients) go scot free.

In 1983, 126,500 people were arrested for prostitution in the United States (figures from US Department of Justice, 1985). This is a 148.4% increase over the number arrested in 1973, the year that the prostitutes' rights movement began in the country (in comparison, arrests for all crimes increased by only 35.6%).

Although the law makes no distinction between men and women and in most states, and prohibits both sides of the transaction, the percentage of women arrested generally hovers around 70% (in 1979 it dropped to 67%, probably as a result of feminist pressure on police departments to arrest customers if prostitutes were going to be arrested, but in 1983, it was back up to 73%. About 10% of those arrested are customers (usually arrested in a series of raids over a period of a couple of weeks and then ignored the rest of the year). The remainder of the arrests are of transvestites and pre-op-transsexual prostitutes.

Related arrest records in San Francisco, USA, for the months of April and October 1976 reveal that the number of prostitutes arrested in April and October were 179 and 157 respectively. By contrast, the number of male clients arrested were 15 and 9 respectively and the number of male pimps arrested were 12 and 3 respectively. Similar trends are evidenced in New York City (Barry, Kathleen; 1979).[2]

Enforcement practices similarly discriminate on the basis of race and class. 85 to 90% of the prostitutes who are arrested, work on the street, although only 10-20% of all prostitutes are street walkers. While approximately only 40% of street prostitutes are coloured women, 55% of those arrested are coloured. The racism becomes even more apparent when you look at the figures on who gets jailed. 85% of prostitutes sentenced to do jail time are coloured women (Alexander, Priscilla; 1987; p.9).[1] Hence a prostitute who is a victim of exploitation is perceived and dealt with as a criminal by law.

Another outcome of the prohibitionist system is that the prostitute defined as a criminal, is often reluctant to turn in her pimp and until she does so prosecution of pimps is virtually impossible.

Also the prostitute with a criminal record is branded for life and has no place to turn to. The system reinforces her already tight dependence on pimps and virtually locks her into prostitution (Barry, Kathleen; 1979).[2]

The Prohibitionist system also leads to clandestine prostitution and brothel keeping.

Finally, the Prohibitionist system is an overt manifestation of the double standards of male sexual morality, because while it socially acknowledges the need for prostitution and the inevitability of it, it not only makes prostitution illegal, but also castigates and criminalizes the women in prostitution, while often allowing the clients and prostitution racketeers to go scot free.

2. Tolerationism

Toleration of prostitution is closely in accordance with the United Nations 1949 Convention decision and has been adopted in several countries.

The Tolerationist system does not seek to abolish prostitutes or prostitution *per se*. It is only targeted at trafficking in women and girls for prostitution, brothel keeping, pimping and procuring. Under this system prostitutes are not supposed to be criminalized by virtue of their work and have more or less the same rights as other citizens.

Though this system does not forbid the act of prostitution *per se,* surprisingly, each country espousing toleration has other laws or has clauses within the same law, to penalize soliciting or loitering by prostitutes. Prostitutes are thus criminals. They are controlled and harassed by law enforcing authorities (Barry, Kathleen; 1979).[2]

It must be mentioned that the client is not considered an offender under such laws. This betrays the double standards of male sexual morality.

3. Legalization of Prostitution (Regulationist System)

Many countries have adopted the system of legalized prostitution. Prostitution was a legal activity in 19th century England and India. Today, West Germany and the state of Nevada in the USA have legalized prostitution.

Legalization permits prostitution especially in "closed houses" or Eros centres. Under this system, prostitutes are required to register themselves with the local authorities and submit themselves for periodic health check-ups. On the basis of this, they are issued a health certificate and a VD clearance card, which must be presented at every periodic examination at the VD control clinic. It is only after this formality that a prostitute is issued a police clearance and a government licence, which permits her to ply her trade professionally.

This system thus blatantly sanctions the patriarchal institution of prostitution.

The Suppression of Immoral Traffic in Women and Girls Act (1956)

India embraces the tolerationist system of law, which is embodied in the Suppression of Immoral Traffic in Women and Girls Act, 1956 (SITA), a penal law, which governs prostitution in India. The SITA passed in 1956, and enforced in 1958, was not the outcome of an independent, sustained, consolidated mass movement in the country, but rather the result of India being a signatory to the United Nations International Convention for the "Suppression of Traffic in Persons and of the Exploitation of Others" passed in New York in 1950. This Act has now been amended by the Immoral Traffic in Persons Prevention Act, 1986, which has yet to come into force. The SITA as its name suggests, aims at abolishing traffic in women and girls for prostitution. It, therefore, penalizes brothel-keeping, pimping, procuring, detention of a woman or girl for prostitution and seduction of a woman in custody (See Annexure-I; D'Cunha, Jean; 1986).[6]

The SITA does not seek to abolish prostitutes or prostitution *per se* and hence the practice of prostitution individually, independently and voluntarily by a woman does not constitute an offence. However, sections 7(i) and 8(b), which respectively penalize the practice of prostitution in or near a public place [7(i)], and seduction or soliciting for prostitution [8(b)], thus in effect, allow for the treatment of the prostitute as an offender. Further, a magistrate can order a prostitute to be removed from any place and failure to obey this order can result in punishment for the woman. Hence, contrary to its declared objective, these sections of SITA criminalize the prostitute (D'Cunha, Jean; 1986).[6] The client is not an offender under the Act.

Bias in Scope and Formulation

A perusal of the aims, objectives, scope and formulation of the Act, reveals the underlying sexist assumptions of the Act and the gender bias against female prostitutes.

The patriarchal attitudes about prostitution that form the underlying assumptions of the Act are that man's aggressive and uncontainable sexuality and polygamous nature considered "natural and biological", have an outlet in prostitution which thus safeguards the family structure and prevents rampant rape.

As regards the gender bias against women, prostitution is defined as a purely female phenomenon and the SITA only incorporates criminal sanctions against female prostitutes, while male prostitutes escape penal provisions.

This is perhaps the product of structural and cultural factors which account for both gender role and trait stereotypes in society and in crime. Traditionally attitudes to women's crimes have been linked to assumptions about determinants of human behaviour, defined in terms of biology - 'the weaker sex'. The patriarchal division between 'madonnas' and 'whores' and good and evil in women become most conspicuous in discussions and explanations of crime, as here woman's so-called negative side is carried to extremes. According to Klein, the psychoanalyst, characteristics used to describe women are often sexual and this is reflected in criminology, where female crime is defined as the inability of certain women to adhere to cultural standards. As these standards are often sexual, deviation is seen as a sexual abnormality and crimes of women are consequently defined in such terms even if another more appropriate and accurate explanation exists. For instance, prostitution could be financially motivated and linked to economics and not sexual disturbance, but it is seldom viewed this way (Leonard, B. Eileen; 1982).[12]

Secondly, while prostitutes are penalized, there are no such penal provisions against the client, which clearly reveals the double standards of male sexual morality.

Another aspect of these double standards is that it is only street prostitution which is criminalized, while prostitution behind closed doors is left untouched.

Biases in implementation

Paradoxically, while tolerating the institution of prostitution, women providing the service are socially castigated. Street prostitutes are harassed to preserve a hypocritical veneer of morality and public decency, while prostitution behind closed doors is ignored.

Class and gender biases also operate in the implementation of the Act. Extensive data collected by this author clearly shows that not only was the Act tardily implemented but it operates decisively against the prostitute (victim, survivor, worker), while allowing the prostitution racketeers (entrepreneurs, landlords, brothel managers, pimps, procurers) to go scot free. This reflects a class based discrimination in enforcement.

It is also indicative of a gender-biased implementation in favour of the male. In a male-controlled institution like prostitution, the police, landlords of premises rented for prostitution, entrepreneurs, brothel managers, pimps, procurers, clients and the like, mainly men, exercise various forms of power over the prostitutes and are seldom brought to book, while the women who are exploited by them as sex commodities, so as to make the enterprise possible in the first place, are penalized.

Penal Sanctions Against Prostitution Rackteers, Prostitutes and Clients - A Discussion

While the provisions under the Act penalizing prostitution racketeers are steps in the right direction, criminal sanctions against female prostitutes are a cruel irony. They contradict and violate the declared spirit of the Act, namely, not to penalize the individual prostitute operating independently. The prostitute is not a criminal. She does not violate anybody or anything, but is herself violated. This is particularly true for the vast number of female prostitutes who are victims of the structurally induced forces of circumstance - both direct and indirect - victims of the system - struggling to cope with their experiences of exploitation. Thus the penal sanctions under the Act unjustly amount to victim punishment and must be deleted.

While the law does not penalize the client, the demand for penal provisions against him have been raised in several quarters - firstly because the client is perceived as an active and exploitative participant in the institution of prostitution and secondly because penal sanctions should have a deterrent effect. My thinking on this issue is tentatively to the contrary, because the idea of introducing penal sanctions against clients appears too simplistic. While it is true that clients benefit immensely from the institution of prostitution by way of pleasure and/or power, their demand for women in prostitution is a structurally created condition whose economic, political, social and cultural ramifications need to be understood in all its complexity and cannot be dealt with by penal sanctions alone. Secondly while in the short run, prostitution is bound to continue, penal sanctions against clients may work adversely against the prostitutes. The trade may suffer a recession, leaving the women in dire financial straits in the absence of job alternatives.

However, placing the client totally outside the scope of penal provisions is dangerous. It ignores the role played by the client within the institution of prostitution, fails to check, or rather may encourage, the further exercise of brutality against the prostitute. It is a known fact that there is a rising demand for child prostitutes, that clients indulge in violent, kinky or perverted sex with adult female prostitutes, that the latter are often raped on the job and often go unpaid by clients.

Thus, while the clients need not be made offenders for going to prostitutes, they must be penalized for such brutal and exploitative acts against the prostitutes (D'Cunha, Jean; 1988)[8].

Study of Implementation of the Act

A study of the implementation of the Act during the years 1980 - 1987 in Bombay (India), a major centre of urban prostitution, reveals these trends in the executive and procedural aspects, court hearings, penal measures and the rehabilitative aspects of the Act.

The executive and procedural aspects of the Act concern provisions relating to the suppression of trafficking in women and girls for prostitution, brothel-keeping, raids, rescue of minor girls and arrests.

Trafficking and brothel-keeping: Although the Act prohibits trafficking and brothel-keeping, brothels are mushrooming and trafficking continues unabated. Reliable sources maintain that the city of Bombay alone has over 50,000 brothels with over 1 lakh prostitutes, 20% of whom are minors (Gilada; 1984)[10].

Raids: A raid on a brothel can be conducted by the police on their own initiative, when they are informed by a lay source that the place is a brothel, that is, on the basis of an application made by a prostitute to the magistrate under Section 19 of the Act, asking to be rescued for protective custody.

Between the years 1981 and 1987 only 533 brothels were raided under the SITA in Bombay. Thus the annual average rate of brothel raids is only 76. By the above mentioned estimate of the existing number of brothels at 50,000, it would mean that each brothel would be raided once in 658 years. (See Table 1: Total number of brothel/hotel raids between 1981 and 1987 under the SITA).

TABLE 1

Total Number of Brothel Raids and Hotel Raids Conducted U/S 3,4,5,7(1) and 7(2) of the SITA in the years 1981 - '87

Year	Total number of brothel raids u/s 3,4,5,7(1) of the SITA Act.	Total number of hotel raids u/s 7(2) of the SIT Act.	Total
1981	73	11	84
1982	71	10	81
1983	72	13	85
1984	80	13	93
1985	113	15	128
1986	68	9	77
1987	58	5	63
Total	**533**	**56**	**611**

(Source: Vigilance Cell, Crime Branch, CID, Bombay)[14]

Applications for rescue/protective custody and rescue of minors. During the year 1984, for which a study was done, not a single application was made for rescue or protective custody by any prostitute in Bombay.

Again, if we consider the more accurate estimate of the total number of minor prostitutes as around 20,000, the percentage of girls rescued annually in Bombay during 1985-87 under section 16 and 19 of the SITA is much less than 1% (See Table 2:Total number of minors rescued by Vigilance Cell, Crime Branch, Bombay between 1985 and 1987).

TABLE 2
Total Number of Minors Rescued by the Vigilance Cell, Crime Branch, CID, Bombay between Jan 1 and Dec 31, 1985.

Year	Section	Act	Number
1985	16(1)	SITA	55
1985	19(1)	SITA	72
1985	78(B)	Bombay Children Act	2
		Total:	129

(Source: Vigilance Cell, Crime Branch, CID provided to me in 1986).[14]

Conclusion

The above information indicates that brothels are hardly ever raided and minor girls are rarely rescued by the police. Prostitutes are ignorant of their rights to apply for rescue.

In fact brothels are allowed by the police and the state to exist and proliferate without check, thus encouraging traffic in women and girls for prostitution.

Arrests

Arrests of offenders can be made under various sections of the SITA. In addition, section 110 B of a local law, the Bombay Police Act, (BPA), penalizes indecent behaviour and provides for arrests of prostitutes and pimps. (See Tables 3 to 7: Total No. of arrests of various categories of offenders under the SITA and Section 110 B of the Bombay Police Act for the years 1980-'87).

Table 3
Total Number of Brothel-keepers Arrested under Section 3,4 & 5 of SITA from 1980 to '87

Year	Total number arrested
1980	60
1981	73
1982	71
1983	72
1984	80
1985	113

1986	69
1987	68
Total	596

(Source: Vigilance Cell, Crime Branch, CID, Bombay provided to me in 1984 & 1988).[4]

Table 4
Total Number of Procurers, Pimps and Landlords arrested under the SITA between 1980 and 1984 (May-end)

Year	No. of procurers arrested Section 3(b)	No. of pimps arrested	No. of landlords arrested under
1980	60	nil	nil
1981	73	nil	nil
1982	71	nil	nil
1983	72	nil	nil
1984(May end)	28	nil	nil
Total	304	nil	nil

(Source: Vigilance Cell, Crime Branch, CID, Bombay, provided to me in 1984).[14]

TABLE 5
Total Number of Prostitutes Arrested under Sections 7(1) and 8(b) of SITA

Year	Total arrested u/s 7(1)	Total arrested u/s 8(b)
1980	358	NA
1981	395	810
1982	479	812
1983	508	830
1984	436	915
1985	520	772
1986	430	843
1987	438	694
Total:	3564	56766

(Source: Vigilance Cell, Crime Branch, Bombay, provided to me in 1984).[14]

TABLE 6
Total Number of Pimps arrested for Indecent Behaviour under Section 110 B of the Bombay Police Act

Year	Total arrested
1980	138
1981	183

1982	193
1983	188
1984	212
1985	202
1986	206
1987	73
Total	1395

(Source: Vigilance Cell, Crime Branch, CID, Bombay, provided to me in 1984, 1986 and 1988.)[14]

TABLE 7
Total Number of Prostitutes Arrested for Indecent Behaviour under Section 110 B of the Bombay Police Act from 1980 to 1987.

Year	Total arrested
1980	8596
1981	8731
1982	8748
1983	4883
1984	7480
1985	6225
1986	6241
1987	2962
Total	53866

(Source: Vigilance Cell, Crime Branch, CID, Bombay, provided to me in 1984, 1986 and 1988.)[14]

An examination of Table 1 relating to the total number of brothel raids and hotel raids with Tables 3 and 4 relating to the total number of brothel keepers and procurers arrested under SITA respectively, shows that the yearly figures for arrest of brothel keepers and procurers tally perfectly with each other for the years 1980-83, and with the yearly number of brothel raids for the years 1981-87.

This leads to two observations:

(a) The annual average rate of arrests of brothel-keepers and procurers for the years 1980-87 is about 74 per year (Tables 3 and 4). A brothel keeper or a procurer of a particular brothel would thus be arrested only once in 670 years, if the number of brothels is estimated at 50,000.

(b) Secondly, the figures seem constructed to tally. They presume the existence of a single brothel keeper and procurer for a particular brothel. This explains the numerical equality between the total number of raids per year and the total number of arrests of brothel-keepers and procurers per year. This would appear to be done to keep the record "straight", so to speak, to satisfy any questions raised by "higher ups".

However, brothels are often run by more than one person and several individuals procure and sell women and girls to brothels. Thus the presumption of a single brothel keeper and procurer for a particular brothel allows several other vital links in the chain of racketeers to go scot free.

Similar trends are evident in the data on hotel raids and hotel owners/managers arrested. Although statistical records of hotel raids are maintained, there appear to be no separate records of the number of hotel managers and owners arrested. This indicates that either no hotel owners or managers have been arrested or there exists the presumption of a single owner and manager for a hotel, thus leading to an inference of the total number of owners and managers arrested from the number of hotels raided.

Further, while only 596 brothel keepers and 304 procurers were arrested during 1980-87 and 1980-84 (May end) respectively, 9,240 prostitutes were arrested between 1980-87, that is, 3564 for the practice of prostitution in a public place [u/s.7(1)] and the rest for soliciting for prostitution [u/s. 8(b)] (See Tables 3.4, & 5).

Not a single pimp was arrested during the period 1980-84 (May end), nor has a single landlord been arrested since the enforcement of the Act in 1958 to date (See Table 4).

The same trend persists under the Bombay Police Act. Thus while only 1,395 pimps were arrested between 1980 and 1987 for indecent behaviour under this Act, 53,866 prostitutes were arrested in the same period (See Tables 6 & 7).

The data on arrests indicates that contrary to the objectives of SITA, sections 7(1) and 8(b) penalise the prostitutes.

Arrests are biased against the prostitutes, as is borne out by the larger number of prostitutes arrested compared to the prostitution racketeers, thus indicating, as mentioned earlier, a class and gender bias in implementation against the female prostitutes.

Also street prostitutes are subject to great harassment by way of arrests, than prostitutes in brothels, as is clear from the larger number of arrests under section 110 B of the Bombay Police Act, and 8(b) of SITA. This further indicates discriminatory enforcement on the basis of class, within the prostitute population itself.

Court Hearings and Penal Measures

Offences under SITA are bailable. Penal measures in the form of fines and prison sentences are supposed to be awarded for different categories of offenders. While acquittals and discharges are made after the trial, custodial provisions can be made during or after the trial.

The court proceedings, punitive measures and discharges are also biased in favour of prostitution racketeers and are necessarily detrimental to the interests of the prostitute. This is evident in the data relating to bails, fines, convictions, acquittals and discharges.

Bail:

A comparison of the data for arrests and releases on bail of brothel keepers (See Tables 3 and 8) and procurers (see Tables 4 and 9) for the years 1980-87 and 1980-84 (May end) respectively, reveal that all brothel keepers and procurers arrested were released on bail.

TABLE - 3		TABLE - 8	
Total Number of Brothel Keepers Arrested U/S 3,4,5 of the Sit Act from 1980 - 1987		**Total Number of Brothel Keepers Released on Bail from 1980 to 1987**	
Year	Total number of brothel keepers released on bail	Year	Total number of brothel keepers arrested
1980	60	1980	60
1981	73	1981	73
1982	71	1982	71
1983	72	1983	72
1984	80	1984	80
1985	113	1985	113
1986	69	1986	69
1987	58	1987	58
Total:	596	Total:	596

(Source: Vigilance Cell, Crime Branch, CID, Bombay provided to me in 1984, 1986 and 1988)

TABLE - 4
Total Number of Procurers, Pimps and Landlords arrested under the Sit Act between 1980 - 1984 (May end)

Year	Total number of pimps arrested under the SIT Act	Total number of procurers arrested under the SIT Act	Total number of landlords arrested u/s.3(b) of the SIT Act
1980	60	nil	nil
1981	73	nil	nil
1982	72	nil	nil
1983	71	nil	nil
1984(May end)	28	nil	nil
Total: 304		nil	nil

(Source: Vigilance Cell, Crime Branch, CID, Bombay provided to me in 1984)

TABLE - 9
Total Number of Procurers released on Bail from 1980 to 1984 (May end)

Year	Total number of procurers released
1980	60
1981	73
1982	72
1983	71
1984 (May end)	28
Total:	304

(Source: Vigilance Cell, Crime Branch, CID, Bombay, provided to me in 1984)

Reliable sources maintain that prostitutes may be released on bail, if arrested from brothels, as bail is offered by their brothel-keepers. However, a street prostitute arrested under section 8(b) of SITA or 110B of the Bombay Police Act, has neither the money nor the contacts for a release on bail and is consequently put in custody or fined (D'Cunha, Jean, 1986)[6].

Cases sent to Court:

Table 10 indicates that very few cases of brothel keepers,

brothel prostitutes and hotel owners are sent to court under
sections 3,4,5,7(1) and 7(2) of the Act.   Out of 453 persons
arrested under sections 3,4,5 and 7(1) in 1984, 215 were sent
to court and 238 were disposed of. Similarly, out of 624 persons
arrested under the same sections in 1985, 52 were sent to court
and 572 were disposed of, indicating that a large number of
persons were disposed of before being sent to court.

TABLE - 10
Number of cases filed in court U/S 3,4,5, 7(1) and 7(2) of the S.I.T. Act

Section Year	Total No. of raids	Total No. of persons arrested	Total No. of cases filed in	Total No. of persons sent to Court	Category of persons sent to Court		Total cases disposed
					Brothel keepers	Prosti- tutes	
3,4,5,7(1)1984	80	453	44	215	44	171	238
3,4,5,7(1)1985	113	624	11	52	11	14	572
7(2) 1984	13	49	3	11	NA	NA	38
7(2) 1985	15	NA	NA	NA	NA	NA	NA

(Source: Vigilance Cell, Crime Branch, Bombay provided to me in 1986)

Table 11 which shows the number of prostitutes cases filed in
court for soliciting and seducing for prostitution under section
8(b) of the SIT Act and for indecent behaviour uder section 110
B of the Bombay Police Act, presents a contrasting picture.

TABLE - 11
Number of cases filed in court U/S 8(b) of the Sit Act U/S 110 B of the Bombay Police Act

Section	Year	Cases Regis- tered	Cases filed in Court	Total No.of persons arrested cases	Total No. of convic- tions	Total No.of acquitted cases cases
S 8 (b)	1984	915	757	757	757	..
S 8 (b)	1985	772	373	373	373	..
S 110(B)	1984	7480	7480	7480	7480	..
S 110(B)	1985	6031	6031	6031	6031	..
S 110(B)	1984	212	212	212	212	..
S 110(B)	1985	198	198	198	198	..

S 110(B)	1984	212	212	212	212	..
S 110(B)	1985	198	198	198	198	..

(Source: Vigilance Cell, Crime Branch, CID, Bombay provided to me in 1986)

A comparison of tables 10 and 11 reveals the following:

(a) The number of street prostitutes arrested and sent to court under section 8(b) of SITA and 110B of the Bombay Police Act is larger than that of brothel-keepers, hotel owners and brothel-attached prostitutes sent to court under sections 3, 4, 5 7(1) and 7(2) respectively of SITA.

(b) The number of pimps arrested and sent to court under sections 110B of the Bombay Police Act is larger than that of brothel-keepers and hotel owners sent to court under sections 3, 4, 5 and 7(2) of SITA respectively.

Convictions

Of the 409 cases of brothel raids conducted under sections 3, 4 and 5 of SITA between the years 1981 - 1985, only 94 cases were heard in Court. Of these only 2 cases of brothel-keepers were convicted, 63 cases were acquitted and 29 cases remained pending in the dormant file (See Table 12).

TABLE - 12

Total number of cases heard in court under section 3,4 and of the Sit Act between the years 1981 - 1985: Verdict

Year	No. Of Raids	No. Of Cases Heard In Court	Verdicts Convictions	Acquittals	Dormant File
1981	73	26	-	20	6
1982	71	38	1	25	12
1983	72	18	-	13	5
1984	80	10	1	5	4
1985	113	2	-	-	2
TOTAL	409	94	2	63	29

(Source: Vigilance Cell, Crime Branch, CID, Bombay provided to me in 1986).

By contrast, all prostitutes sent to court under sections 8(b) of SITA and 110B of the Bombay Police Act (See Table 11) were convicted.

Discriminatory Penalties

Penalties imposed on prostitutes are far more severe than those on brothel-keepers or pimps. The average fine for a prostitute on brothel-keepers or pimps. The average fine for a prostitute in 1980 was Rs. 60 and the average number of days for imprisonment was 7. There were only two cases of convictions of brothel-keepers in the period 1981-1985, one in 1982, carrying a fine of Rs. 150 or one day's rigorous imprisonment. The other conviction in 1984 carried a fine of Rs. 10. According to reliable sources pimps too are fined a meagre sum of about Rs. 25 and for 3 or 4 days imprisonment (See Annexure II; Vigilance Cell Records, 1986).[14]

Advisory Board:

Section 13 of SITA stipulates that the state government should associate with the Special Police Officer (who conducts the raids) and a non-official advisory body consisting of not more than five social welfare workers of that area (who should be women wherever practicable) to advise him on questions of general importance under the Act.

No such body has been constituted even in a large metropolis like Bombay with well established traditions of social work and a large number of persons willing to offer their services (Barse, Sheela; 1984).[4]

Reasons for Tardy and Discriminatory Implementation

We must now explain the tardy and discriminatory implementation of the Act, with respect to the executive aspects, court hearings and penal measures.

Raids on brothels are conducted infrequently. The various circumstances that lead to raids are: Clash or hostility between brothel-keeper and the police; instigation or payment of a higher bribe to the police by a rival brothel-keeper; pressure from authorities to conduct raids due to a crime increase in the area; specific information and pressure from "higher ups" to act; and the need to maintain records and quotas (D'Cunha, Jean; 1986).[6]

One of the most important factors for the existence and proliferation of brothels, the negligible number of raids and the failure of such raids are the economic and political linkages between prostitution racketeers, the police and important local politicians. Lucrative earnings from brothel-keeping, high client demand, and the patriarchal society saying that prostitution is a necessary and inevitable social evil, make for the continued existence and operation of brothels.

Brothel Management - police nexus

It has been observed that police officials from the Vigilance Cell of the Crime Branch, CID, Bombay, collect Rs. 30-50 per month as bribes from each brothel, depending on the earnings of the brothel-keeper. Women constables collect around Rs. 20 on each visit to a brothel and the Juvenile Aid Police Staff around Rs. 50 (Barse, Sheela; 1983).[3]

Brothel-keepers pay the police around Rs.500 if the latter receive information that a new minor girl has been forced into prostitution. Tulasa, a new child prostitute, bears evidence to the following: When the police discovered her in a brothel raid, they demanded Rs. 700 as a bribe for her return to the brothel-keeper. The deal was settled at Rs. 500 (Gilada; 1984).[10]

Consequently, the monthly income of the Vigilance Cell, through bribes from brothel-keepers approximates to more than Rs. 100,000 (Barse, Sheela; 1983).[3]

Another reason for the poor success rate is the paucity of staff and meagre wages. There are only 243 staffers, including 5 inspectors at a major police division like Bandra, a Bombay suburb. The situation in the 10 other police stations in the area is more or less the same.

A sub-inspector attached to the Bandra Police Station who pleaded anonymity stated, "We are class III government servants; our basic salary is Rs. 445 and we get an increment of only Rs. 15 every year. If after eight years of service our total salary is not over Rs. 1500, why should we not take money from brothel- keepers and hoteliers?" Insiders claim that corrupt police officers can earn up to Rs. 10,000 by way of bribes from the prostitution business each month (Prabhu, Uma, 1987).[13]

Brothel-management - Political nexus

According to police sources, there is a close nexus between politicians and brothel managements. Brothels finance elections and are substantive vote banks. They also provide sex favours to local political bigwigs. Brothel-keepers and their thugs who are the opinion leaders of the area, are thus in league with the municipal corporation, with MLAs and MPs. They are permitted to run brothels and are granted sanitation, water and other facilities as special favours (Sawant, Prabhakar; 1984)[11].

A news report in the *Telegraph* dated August 24,1985 bears evidence of this. According to the news item, Shantabai, a big-time brothel-keeper, from Kamatipura, one of Bombay's largest red light areas, was launched into the limelight when she figured in a squabble between the Bharatiya Janata Party (BJP) and the Congress (I) in the then recent assembly session.

On June 11th, a BJP MLA alleged in the Maharashtra Legislative Assembly that the Congress (I) had got Shantabai's help to get a large number of votes from Asia's largest red light area which she controlled for seats for the Lok Sabha Assembly and Civic elections. Among the accusations hurled, was one that said that the then Bombay Regional Congress Committee Chief and South Bombay MP, was associated with Shantabai and his electoral victory was aided by her. Khetwadi, the Assembly Constituency which the BJP MLA represented, fell under the Congress Committee Chief's South Bombay Parliamentary Constituency and the City's famed red light area.

Riding roughshod over Shantabai's claim that she had left the profession, the BJP MLA, Mr. Prem Kumar Sharma charged that she was the biggest 'Madam' in the city, controlling most of the Nepalese girls, 30,000 of whom were in the flesh trade. He had pointed out to the election commission that the voting list included only the first names of a number of Nepalese girls, which was an irregular practice, surnames or second names were essential. After an enquiry in 1978, many of these entries were found to be out of order and they were deleted from the list. But they reappeared during the subsequent elections, specifically to help the Congress (I), as the girls were compelled to vote for the party under Shantabai's influence, the BJP MLA alleged.

Shantabai countered these charges at a press conference. And later, in an interview with *The Telegraph,* she detailed the political parties' quest for votes and her own emergence from a rustic girl to a power to be reckoned with in the area.

"The Congress (I), the Shiv Sena, the BJP members of all these parties come to me and ask me to influence the women in my locality to vote for them in the elections. But I work only for Indira Gandhi's Party. I tell the girls - they come to me with their problems, they respect me - to vote for Indira Gandhi as she is a martyr and has shed her blood for our country. Prem Kumar Sharma came to me for help in the elections. When I refused he started accusing me of being a big brothel conductor. After I had helped the Congress (I) candidate, Mr. Russy Mehta, in the corporation elections, Mr. Sharma distributed pamphlets in which he alleged that I ran a liquor, gambling and prostitution den. Why did he not make these accusations earlier? Why were they made only after the elections were over?

"Nana Rane, a local Congress (I) worker used to bring people he supported to me for help in elections. Mr. Prem Kumar Sharma also stays in this area. He came to me before the 1980 elections when Mr. Murli Deora was contesting this constituency. I refused to help him then as I do now. This time I told him that I could not leave the party of a woman who had given her life for the nation. Mr. Sharma threatened me with dire consequences if I refused to support him. I supported Dr. Quereshi, the Congress (I) candidate who lost to him.

Mr. Russy Mehta, the Congress (I) candidate for the civic elections, whom I supported, brought Mr. Murli Deora here before the elections. Nana Rane and some other Congress (I) members were also present at that particular campaign meeting. We talked for an hour. Later, during the election campaign, all of us got together and lit up the area with coloured lights and decorations. It was only after the elections were over that the rivalry began and I am suffering because of the rivalry between the two parties" (Dhar, Lekha, 1985)[9].

In a well-documented record of hotel raids in Bombay suburbs, the police issued show cause notices to several suburban hotels and in some cases cancelled licences. But appeals from the aggrieved hoteliers resulted in the redemptive intervention of the State Home Department. The licences were restored and the hotels were back in business (See Annexure III; Prabhu, Uma; 1987).[13]

Lucrative Trade

Brothel-keeping is a lucrative trade. A minor girl who is a virgin is sold for anything between Rs. 500 and Rs. 7000 in Kamatipura. The child prostitute Tulasa, kidnapped from

Nepal, was sold to a Nepali brothel-keeper Tulli at Kamatipura for Rs. 5000. Two months later, she was sold to Gauri, another brothel- keeper, for Rs. 7000 and later sold to a third brothel-keeper for Rs. 7500 (Gilada; 1984)[10]

The brothel-keeper confines the prostitute till she makes at least twice the amount she has had spent on her. Clients are usually charged anything between Rs. 20 to Rs. 50 per visit depending on their status and that of the girl. Arabs may pay between Rs. 150 - 500 or more per night (D'Cunha, Jean; 1986)[6].

Sexist Attitude of Law Enforcers

The sexist attitude that prostitution is a necessary and inevitable social evil prompts the police, courts and society at large to turn a blind eye to trafficking in women and girls for prostitution.

Mechanisms by Which Raids Fail

Often raids fail because

(a) information may be leaked for a consideration to an active spy or to a Police Officer who is in league with the brothel-keeper. The girls may then be sent elsewhere by the latter. Alternatively the brothel-keeper may live independently elsewhere, while the women operate under the informal supervision of the brothel-keeper's favourite girl from the brothel. The women in such cases themselves receive the money from the bogus customer. They subsequently maintain that they operate independently, but only live in the same premises for convenience. The premises thus technically cannot be defined as a brothel under the Act. The raid fails and arrests cannot be made.

(b) Some brothels prohibit the entry of unknown persons. Muscle men are used to prevent entry. Suspicion is particularly aroused if the person has been a bogus customer on more than one occasion.

(c) In the event of a raid some hotels produce 'loan- debt' agreements. They reserve a certain number of rooms separately in the names of the women that they supply for prostitution. If marked currency notes are recovered from the hotel manager in the raid, he may produce a false loan document, previously drawn up with the woman, stating that she was a paying guest in his hotel and that she had an outstanding loan to repay him, which she was repaying. He denies running a prostitution racket or having any other connection with her.

(d) Some brothel-keepers send girls out with clients to a hotel. In a previously worked out arrangement between the hotel manager and the brothel-keeper, the former is given a cut. Raids in such hotels may fail as no one can object to two individuals sleeping together in a hotel room per se. The existence of a brothel- keeper or evidence against the hotel management is hard to prove (D'Cunha, Jean).[6]

Reasons for Higher Number of Arrests of Prostitutes

The arrests of prostitutes far outnumber those of prostitution racketeers for a number of reasons:

Hypocritical morality: The police who are empowered to make arrests under the Act, wish to maintain a hypocritical veneer of morality and public order. They thus 'clean up' the streets of street prostitutes.

Quotas: Mass arrests of prostitutes help maintain 'arrest quotas'.

Police Power: Penal sanctions against prostitutes incorporated in the Act and empowering the police to enforce them, have invested the police with political power. Police arrest prostitutes and extort fines and bribes from them. So the police benefit economically. Arrests are often a form of harassment by the police to extort sex favours from prostitutes. Arrests of prostitutes by the police are thus a demonstration of male power over vulnerable women.

Harassment by brothel-keepers: Arrests of prostitutes are also made at the instigation of a brothel-keeper who does not like the prostitute.

Circumvention of arrest by racketeers through bribes, muscle power and legal loopholes: The racketeers avoid arrests through bribes, muscle power and loopholes in the law. Landlords can only be arrested if they 'knowingly' rent their premises for prostitution. To circumvent the law, the landlord and brothel-keeper enter into a predated lease agreement, prohibiting the lease of the premises for illicit purposes. Using this clause, the former asserts that he did not 'knowingly' and 'wilfully' hire out his premises for prostitution and goes scot free (D'Cunha, Jean; 1986).[6]

Lastly, there are no arrests of clients, as the client is not an offender under SITA. As mentioned earlier, this is consistent with the double standards of male sexual morality in a patriarchal society, that believes prostitution to be a universal and inevitable social evil, which satiates man's 'agressive sexuality and polygamous nature', while simultaneously condemning the woman in prostitution.

Reasons for Biases in Penal Sanctions

Prostitution racketeers often go scot-free while prostitutes are penalized. The reasons for this are: that offences are bailable and there is no political will to trace racketeers after their release on bail; the failure to record statements or to record them accurately thus rendering prosecution of offenders ineffective; problems related to production of evidence, payment of bribes to drop a case, submission of false age certificates in court leading to failure of cases against racketeers; and appearance of false parents in Court which results in callous discharges of prostitutes to their care.

Bail: Offences under the Act are bailable. Racketeers obtain a bail release and avoid the police dragnet. There is also a lack of political will on the part of the police to trace them or produce them in Court (D'Cunha, Jean; 1986).[6]

Record of Statements: There is a failure to record a prostitute's statement. Recording of wrong statements or obvious untruths without a further probe; the following cases bear evidence of this:

(1) In the case of a 17-year-old Nepalese girl who had been rescued by a client, the V.P. Road Police Station, Bombay wrongly recorded that she had been found loitering in a red light area. Such a record makes it virtually impossible to bring the prostitution racketeers to book as it could well be shown that the woman practised prostitution independently. Had her authentic statement of her being rescued by the client from a brothel been recorded, charges could have been brought against the racketeers and she could have been put in protective custody because she was a minor (Barse, Sheela; 1983).[3]

(2) In another case, police records of the Vigilance Cell, Crime Branch, Bombay dated June 12, 1984, recording the statements of 17 prostitutes and a brothel-keeper seem obviously untrue. The brothel, Bunglow no. 711, Falkland Road, Bombay was raided and 17 prostitutes and a brothel-keeper were arrested under sections 3,4,5 and 7 (1) of the SITA. The brothel-keeper in her statement admitted that the 17 girls lived on her premises, but stated that each operated as an independent prostitute and only paid for her board and lodging. Her statement was supported by the 17 prostitutes, who each maintained that they had come to Bombay from different

villages in search of jobs. Finding neither job nor shelter, each said they had taken refuge with this woman who provided them with board and lodging. They stated that they practised prostitution independently, had no grievance against her and did not wish to return to their native places. So the brothel-keeper went scot free, as the practice of prostitution independently is not an offence. (D'Cunha, Jean; 1986).[6]

Problems in Producing Evidence: There are numerous problems in producing evidence. For lack of women *panchas* (witnesses) and 'respectable' people as 'decoy' witnesses, sleazy persons and persons with no fixed residence are often picked on as bogus customers and *panchas*. They are either untraceable when later needed in court or do not turn up in court as this is a time, money and energy consuming process. They often also turn hostile and un-cooperative in court under pressure from prostitution racketeers.

At such times, they usually maintain that they were coerced by the police into signing documents that they could not read or understand and that they had never accompanied the police on raids. They pretend not to know or recognize the prostitution racketeers. The court does not take a serious view of prostitution racketeers. According to the Rules of Evidence, police evidence is not considered binding, as the police are considered interested parties in the prosecution. Besides, if their evidence is not corroborated by the evidence of bogus customers and panchas, the racketeer's are given the benefit of doubt (D'Cunha, Jean; 1986).[6]

In the eyes of the law the prostitute can give evidence against the racketeers. She is also an accused. This puts her in a Catch-22 situation. Coercion from, fear of and dependence on the brothel-management render her hesitant to turn against the racketeers. A prostitute can deny that the raid occurred, pretend not to know the brothel-keeper, or plead that the police are forcing her to give evidence against the brothel-keeper. She may even falsely depose that she operates as an independent prostitute or state that she is 21 years old, in which case she is let off and no measures can be instituted against the brothel-management (D'Cunha, Jean; 1986).[6]

Submission of False age Certificates: Submission of false age certificates in Court leads to the failure of cases against racketeers. The following cases are clear evidence of it.

(a) On March 28, 1983, Meena Viren Mody was rescued by Sub-Inspector T.V. Bhambre from Khodada Building, Kennedy Bridge. She was brought to the police hospital on March 13 and 15. She was certified as 21 years old, although no X-rays for age determination were taken (one means of age determination is the observation of gaps between the bones, perceived on X-ray pictures). Although the police said her parents were in Shivdi and she could be handed over to them, she was put in the 'bail' category for release after the determination of age (Barse, Sheela; 1983).[3]

(b) In another case, Jyothi Krishnaya and 18 others were rescued from Room No. 20, Crescent Building, Paowala Street, Lamington Road area. On October 13, 1983, she was certified as being 21 years old and subsequently released on bail. However, subsequent examinations of her X-ray by the police surgeon revealed that she was 15-16 years old (Barse, Sheela; 1983).[3]

False Parentage: Also, prostitution racketeers often pose as parents on the basis of an affidavit or bond before the magistrate, and the girl is often handed over to them without any probe into her antecedents, although the law provides for such a probe. It has been observed that if on verification 'the parent applicant' is found to have committed a breach of the bond, the only penalty is the payment of a fine, which the applicant readily pays and then goes scot-free (D'Cunha, Jean; 1986).[6]

So, the court, in effect, orders girls back to the brothel. There are obviously no estimates as to the number of individuals who have thus returned to the brothel.

It is therefore obvious that not only is the Act tardily implemented but is discriminatorily enforced on the basis of class and gender, in favour of prostitution racketeers and against female prostitutes.

Sexist attitudes of Magistrates: Lastly, magistrates themselves believe prostitution is a necessary and inevitable evil. There are known cases of magistrates asking lawyers defending prostitutes in court, to send the latter to them. It is therefore obvious that not only has the Act been tardily implemented but is discriminatorily enforced on the basis of class and gender in favour of prostitution racketeers and against the female prostitute.

Trends in Rehabilitation

The rehabilitation of girls or women rescued or arrested under SITA 1956 is the responsibility of the protective homes or corrective institutions set up under the Act. Minor girls rescued or picked up under section 40 of the Bombay Children Act (for safe custody and shelter as they are destitute and have no fixed abode) and under section 78 of the same act (for being exposed to moral danger or being in prostitution) and minor girls and women rescued and produced under various sections of the Indian Penal Code relating to rape, kidnapping, and abduction for illicit sexual intercourse, wrongful confinement or procurement for prostitution and the like, are sent to rescue and rehabilitative homes for females, which are not the same places as those set up under SITA.

As access was denied to the protective home set up under the SITA, only preliminary observations and comments from interviews with two of the protective home staff have been noted. However, some description and assessment has been made of another home, Asha Sadan, which is not a protective home set up under SITA, but a rescue home for children and girls. This institution also receives cases of and rehabilitates prostitutes rescued from brothels or street walkers under section 40 and 78 of the Bombay Children Act.

Protective Home, Chembur, Bombay

The protective home set up under SITA for the rehabilitating of women and girls in prostitution, is located at Chembur in Bombay. It is the only one of its kind in Bombay and is one of the three protective homes for the entire state of Maharashtra, but at the end of 1983, according to the superintendent of the home, the total number of inmates was 16 while the home could actually accommodate 100 people.

The gross underutilisation of capacity was said to be the result of a paucity of raids, transfers to other institutions and repatriations to other states. The underutilised capacity also shows the negligible degree of rehabilitation available for prostitutes. Considering the extent of prostitution, the existence of only three protective homes under SITA is woefully inadequate.

The superintendent of the protective home was also the superintendent of the beggars' home, Chembur. Her workload was, therefore, enormous and she lacked the time to run the protective home effectively.

There was no psychiatrist, psychologist or counsellor for the inmates, although many of the inmates suffered from hysteria, insomnia, depression and the like. The medical officer visited the institution every alternate day. There was no separate private room for medical examinations. The inmates queued up and were examined behind a curtain. An adequate stock of penicillin was not available for the treatment of VD.

The Board of Visitors for the protective home, which ought to have existed as per the rules of the protective homes under the SITA, was defunct.

The inmates came from various parts of India, particularly Karnataka, Andhra Pradesh and Nepal. They were from the lower socio-economic strata and most of them were victims of forced prostitution. They were in awe and fear of the staff, especially when they first arrived, and often withheld or distorted information relating to their background when initially interviewed.

Communication was also difficult to build up because of language barriers between the staff and inmates and between the inmates themselves. Coupled with the quick turnover of girls, this inhibited the building up of a rapport between the staff and inmates and among the inmates themselves. The inmates also suffered from hysteria and emotional outbursts and resorted to thefts and the like.

Asha Sadan, the other institution, was set up under the aegis of the Maharashtra State Women's Council. It provides shelter and rehabilitiation to children up to 6 years and girls between the ages of 14 and 20.

The number of staff was woefully small and therefore inadequate. The yearly average number of girls between 1982 and 1985 was 80 and the average number of admissions per year for the same period was 170. It was hard for a single superintendent to assume overall supervision of the institution. The superintendent did not reside in the home, though it was a residential post. There was a sanctioned post for an assistant superintendent but this had not been filled. It was also taxing for the single social worker to handle both rehabilitative and some administrative functions. The social worker had to deal both with inmates and new admissions, making her workload gigantic.

The inmates were in acute need of medical and psychological care because of their traumatic experiences. But the psychologist was appointed on a part-time basis and spent only 72 hours a month with them. Likewise the honorary psychiatrist spent 12 hours a month with the inmates. Even if we assume that they devoted all their time to the regular inmates (psychologist thrice a week from 11 a.m. to 5 p.m. and psychiatrist once a week), this gave each inmate about 54 minutes per month of the psychologist's time and nine minutes per month of the psychiatrist's time. This by any standard is grossly inadequate.

The educational qualifications of the superintendent (SSC) and the in-house supervisor (4th standard) left much to be desired. Ad-hoc appointments and promotional appointments were made in the case of the psychologist, supervisor and superintendent rather than appointments on the basis of educational qualifications, age, experience, commitment, orientation and understanding of the structural aspects of social problems and women's oppression.

Salaries of both the professional and non-professional staff were extremely low. The matron, for instance, who had worked for 13 years received a salary of Rs. 365. Except for the DA, the professional staff were not entitled to other monetary allowances and benefits. Also, their salaries were insecure, because a major portion of the salaries was paid through donations rather than through fixed government grants.

The grants provided by the state government and the Bombay Municipal Corporation were too meagre. The allotted expenditure on the inmates of Rs. 100 per capita per month from these funds was paltry. The Home authorities asserted that at least Rs. 300 to 400 was required per female inmate per month. The funds were thus grossly inadequate. The grant of Rs. 5,000 for the child guidance clinic was also too meagre to provide adequately for the medical staff salaries.

The following observations were made for 29 inmates between the years 1983 and 1984: 23 of the 29 individuals were 19 years old or below. The majority came from Nepal, Andhra Pradesh, Karnataka and Tamil Nadu. But, accurate estimates were difficult to establish as the rescue home records did not distinguish between native place, place of procurement and residential address. 22 individuals had given incomplete addresses or only the state from which they came, making tracing of antecedents difficult.

The mother tongues of the majority were Telugu and Nepali. But others spoke Kannada, Bengali, Urdu, Marathi and Tamil. As a result, there were problems of communication between staff and girls and amongst the girls. 17 individuals were unmarried, 6 were married and 6 were unable to inform the authorities of their marital status. 19 individuals had not had education.

The inmates came from the lower socio-economic strata, with families involved in farming as agricultural labourers, *coolie* workers and factory workers. Other work was woodselling, rice selling, domestic work and the like.

Of the 29 individuals 25 had been forced into prostitution. The reasons were poverty and the lack of education and job skills making some girls susceptible to procurers who promised them good city jobs. Kidnapping, abduction, drugging and rape were other means by which some of these individuals had been forced into prostitution. Family problems and tensions like alcoholic fathers, broken homes, cruelty to the girls, a feeling of neglect and rejection had led some to run away from home. Being alone and vulnerable, they were trapped into prostitution by procurers.

The majority, that is, 11 individuals, wanted to give up prostitution, go home to their parents and find some work. Some who wished to leave the profession wanted to stay on at Asha Sadan or work in that district rather than return to their families. Five individuals wanted to remain in the profession as they feared that because of the social stigma attached to it their families would not accept them and the girls lacked the wherewithal to find alternate jobs, accommodation and so on.

Of 12 individuals in the institution under section 40 of the Bombay Children Act (BCA),[6] had been rescued from brothels. The others who had come because of section 40 were either picked up at railway stations or had no records showing why they were there. 17 individuals were there under section 78 of the Bombay Children Act. Of these, 11 girls were rescued by the police after having escaped from brothels, 2 were rescued by the police just before they were sold into prostitution and the remaining had no records to show how they were rescued under this section. Rescuing girls under section 40 rather than 78 of the Bombay Children Act or the relevant section of SITA is a convenient means to avoid bringing racketeers to book.

The conditions forcing women into prostitution and the desire of most to leave the profession point to the urgent need for serious and committed efforts for rehabilitation. The process of rehabilitation should begin from the time an individual enters the institution and continue till the time she leaves and is absorbed into the mainstream of social life. So institutions must aim at the total integration of the individual.

On admission, the girl is interviewed by the social worker who prepares the intake sheet, giving the girl's antecedents and background. The girl is then subject to an age determination test at the police hospital and a medical check-up. She is also given an IQ test by the psychologist to assess her mental ability.

The files of the 29 cases reviewed in 1983-84 revealed that the information on the intake sheets was inadequate, incomplete or absent. There were no records of court proceedings in any of the cases, and detailed progress work records maintained in only 3 out of the 29 cases.

C.M. Bhatia's battery of performance test and Standard Performance test were used to assess the IQ level of the girls - the components of Bhatia's tests being tests for goal directed ability and anticipatory planning, analytic and synthetic ability, memory and form perception. 3 of the 29 cases were declared as moderately mentally retarded (IQ 45 - 55), 6 had below average intelligence (IQ 65 - 90). Others were found to have average intelligence. There were no records of results for the rest.

The concepts, images, symbols, ideas and vocabulary used in these tests are biased in favour of the middle class literate persons with some intellectual exposure, general knowledge, experience of drawing, and playing games like puzzles. The illiteracy of the inmates, their alienation from the idea of such tests and the concepts and imagery used in them, the inmates emotional battering and diffidence due to their traumatic experiences, poor socio-economic backgrounds, fear of the staff and surroundings, inability to visualise bright futures and poor self-images were not considered as factors that could influence the tests.

Because of their traumatic experiences, most of the inmates suffered from hysteria, neurosis, insomnia, restlessness, depresion and the like. Typical behavioural responses were lying, stealing food, provisions and belongings from the institutions or from other inmates, picking locks, jealousy, lesbianism, physical fights, defying the staff, resisting rules, sulking, shirking work, missing classes, hiding notes in sarees and sanitary pads and passing them on to outsiders and so on.

The following is an example:

Lakshmi, aged 14 years, had periods of deep depression. She had a pathological need to establish her innocence and often talked in a rambling manner and sleepwalked. This was the result of an unresolved conflict with her mother who had deserted her lame father. It was also the product of her hostility towards her mother's paramour, her resentment against her elder brother who often beat her up, her traumatic brothel experiences, the feeling of rejection and poor self-image internalised as a result of these experiences. Her medical report from Nair hospital in 1983 showed mental retardation and temporal lobe epilepsy. She was advised to have treatment for five years subject to improvement. Her medical records in Asha Sadan dated March 30, 1983 showed personality changes due to epilepsy and abnormal involuntary movements of both the shoulders.

Lakshmi was prescribed Gardinal (30 mg-1-1) and Eptain (100 mg-1- 1). She was also under shock treatment at Nair Hospital. It is pertinent to note that the case records of Lakshmi reveal that Nair hospital authorities had certified her as mentally retarded and though the social worker at Asha Sadan had also certified her as mentally deficient, this same social worker had recorded that Lakshmi asked intelligent questions.

The staff and society perceived these inmates as delinquents, offenders, immoral and irresponsible persons. This was evident from the following facts:

(a) Memos from the police and the metropolitan magistrate of the Juvenile Court to the superintendent refer to the girls as 'girl juveniles'.

(b) A girl called Faimida was told by the social worker that she was kept in Asha Sadan because of her 'irresponsible' behaviour. She felt a deep sense of rejection from her parents because they had kept her there.

(c) The attitude of the psychologist towards prostitution was that it was 'the immoral profession'. She counselled the girls to give up prostitution because it was bad.

(d) If there were quarrels, the in-house servants in particular raked up the girls' pasts and abused them as prostitutes. The same occurred in quarrels between the inmates.

(e) Counselling was also resorted to in order to remedy abhorrent behaviour. Beating and physical punishment were also very common. The law permitted five canings. The first offence might be punished by a light caning and the whole event was to be recorded in writing. Other punishments like salt-free food and barring the girl from watching TV were also resorted to by the Home authorities. The hardened girls were isolated. A room was maintained without bulbs, fans and long pieces of cloth to avoid the occurrence of suicide.

As mentioned earlier, the more serious cases of psychological maladjustment were immediately treated with shock treatment and some medication.

Literacy classes were held for the inmates. Training in sewing, embroidery, textile block printing, cardfolding and paper pad making were also imparted. Lack of interest, orientation, aptitude and concentration were some of the key problems that the staff faced from the inmates during these classes. It was also particularly difficult for the girls who were illiterate to cope.

Constant orders were not received for the crafts learnt due to the quick turnover of girls. The crafts and skills imparted were not based on assessments of the market value of the jobs.

Between the years 1982 and 1985 the largest number of cases (all inmates, included) were discharged after reconciliation with parents, husbands and guardians. This is difficult to believe as 22 out of the 29 cases of prostitutes·studied in 1983-84 had incomplete addresses or only the name of the state from which they came making tracing of antecedents difficult.

Of the four girls whose file records showed they had been handed over to parents, two were forced to go back against their wishes. One of these two girls was pressurised into returning to her alcoholic father against her wishes. She was counselled that she should contribute to her family as the state would not pay for her. Another inmate did not wish to leave the institution, but being perceived as a danger to other inmates she was ordered by the metropolitan magistrate of the juvenile court to be sent back to her parents. Although her complete address in Karnataka was recorded in the file, there was no record stating whether her parents had been contacted or traced. Her records merely stated that she had been sent to the mental hospital in Bangalore against her wishes.

It should be noted that it is pointless to send a girl home if the home environment is not at all conducive to rehabilitation or if the girl resists going home. (D'Cunha, Jean; 1986).[6]

From the foregoing discussion, it is obvious that the SITA operates against the prostitute woman while the racketeers are seldom penalized.

Implementation of the Act Nation-wide

As mentioned earlier, data on the details of the implementation of SITA has been restricted to the city of Bombay. Data for the Act's implementation at the national level is very difficult to compile as the implementation of the law depends on the respective police departments, who work under the respective state governments. However, at the central level, a statistical compilation of the level of implementation of various laws is done by the Bureau of Police Research and Development, New Delhi, an institution under the Ministry of Home Affairs, Government of India. In their annual publication 5 *Crime in India* under its section on local and special laws, the data regarding the implementation of the SITA (one of the special laws) is collected and published. Extracts from this data are reproduced here which give interesting indications about the trends in implementation at the national level.

This data is presented in 5 tables as follows:

Table 13: Cases reported all over India for the years 1974 - 1982.

Table 14 & 15: Cases reported and persons arrested in various states and union territories for the years 1980 - 1982.

Table 16 & 17: Cases reported and persons arrested in various major cities during the years 1980 - 1982.

Certain trends are clearly visible as follows:

1) It is a well established fact that there exists widespread trafficking in women and that prostitution exists all over the country. The fact that from 14,000 - 16,000 cases and more are filed every year under the SITA only corroborates its existence. This however does not indicate its real magnitude and spread. Even conservative estimates indicate that there are at least 3 - 4 times as many brothel prostitutes forced into the trade in the city of Bombay alone (D'Cunha, Jean; 1986).[6]

Secondly, though the report records the variations between the years, there appears to be no significant shift whatsoever in the extent of cases filed over the years. This should not be interpreted to mean that significant control over forced prostitution has been achieved nor that the level has been kept in check. In fact, it probably means that the extent of prostitution has to be assessed independently of the figures, and that the inability of these figures to increase reflects a failure on the part of the enforcement agencies to take more stringent action against the problem.

Another aspect of these figures conceals more than it reveals. The statistics in these tables record cases filed, and persons arrested. This would lead us to believe that it is the prostitution racketeers at various levels who are being acted against. It is well known from certain city level studies (D'Cunha, Jean; 1986)[6] that this is not the case, and that of the total number of persons arrested, it is the prostitutes who form the largest percentage. This trend can also be seen to continue in later reports as an examination of Tables 3-5 of this chapter reveal. It shows that over 90% of the total number of arrests made in Bombay during the years 1980 — 1987 were prostitutes. Thus it is suspected here as well that a large number of the 'persons' arrested are prostitutes (victims) rather than the racketeers!

2) Tables 14 & 15 indicate the regional spread of the cases filed and persons arrested. Interpreting the data, the report states,

"the main contributors for the year 1980 are Tamil Nadu (8438), Andhra Pradesh (1926), Karnataka (1587), U.P. (1201) and Maharashtra (899) who accounted for 98.2% of the total offences registered in India under the Act". Similarly the reports for 1981 and 1982 record that "these five states account for 98.6% and 98.5% respectively". Also, the report says, "no cases were registered in Himachal Pradesh, Jammu & Kashmir, Meghalaya, Nagaland, Sikkim, Tripura, Haryana and all the Union Territories except for Delhi, Goa and Pondicherry. This gives the impression that there is significant regional variation in the incidence of prostitution itself and there exist some areas where it is absent. Rather than ponder over the sociological reasons of why prostitution is limited to only 5 states in India, we should realise that the statistics are faulty. Prostitution is widespread, relatively evenly distributed and on a much higher scale than these figures would indicate (Rosario, Rita - 1988[15] and D'Cunha, Jvan 1986).[6]

These figures should be interpreted to indicate how well the investigating agencies are doing their job of implementing the SITA. This leads us to the conclusion that the quality of enforcement needs to be improved.

3) Tables 16 & 17 indicate the number of cases reported in 8 major cities in India. Here again the variation can only be explained by variations in the quality of enforcement rather than any variation in the extent of prostitution in the cities for the reasons already cited above.

Another aspect that must be highlighted is the urban bias of the implementation. Comparison of the arrests made in these 8 cities with the arrests made in the corresponding states (Table 18) reveal that the share of cases filed in these cities alone are 4.2 to 94.8% of the total number of cases in the state. This only indicates that there is stricter enforcement in mofussil areas compared to the metropolitan cities.

In conclusion, it may be said that the Act has made little difference to the magnitude of trafficking in women and the existence of forced prostitution in the country.

TABLE - 13:
Cases reported all over India under the SITA during the years 1974 - 1982

1974	:	14,825
1975	:	14,708
1976	:	16,150
1977	:	13,924
1978	:	75,448
1979	:	14,196
1980	:	14,308
1981	:	15,658
1982	:	15,890

Source: Table No. 9: Cases reported under local and special laws during 1974 - 1982; "Crime in India"[5] - Bureau of Public Research and Development, Ministry of Home Affairs.

Table - 14
Cases reported under the SITA in the states and union territories for the years 1980 - 1982

States	1980	1981	1982
1. Andhra Pradesh	1926	2127	2177
2. Assam	13	1	2
3. Bihar	14	7	17
4. Gujarat	11	4	12
5. Haryana	-	-	1
6. Himachal Pradesh	-	-	-
7. Jammu & Kashmir	-	-	-
8. Karnataka	1587	2145	2753
9. Kerala	19	15	22
10. Madhya Pradesh	2	1	2
11. Maharashtra	899	908	924
12. Manipur	5	10	4
13. Meghalaya	-	-	-
14. Nagaland	-	-	-

15.	Orissa	9	5	5
16.	Punjab	1	1	3
17.	Rajasthan	3	5	8
18.	Sikkim	-	-	-
19.	Tamil Nadu	8438	9665	8919
20.	Tripura	-	-	-
21.	Uttar Pradesh	1201	595	880
22.	West Bengal	51	51	55
	Total (States)	14,179	15,540	15,784
23.	A. & N. Islands	-	-	-
24.	Arunachal Pradesh	-	-	-
25.	Chandigarh	-	-	-
26.	Dadra & Nagar Haveli	-	-	-
27.	Delhi	115	86	85
28.	Goa, Daman & Diu	14	10	9
29.	Lakshadweep	-	-	-
30.	Mizoram	-	-	-
31.	Pondicherry	-	22	12
	Total (UTs)	129	118	106
	TOTAL	14,308	15,658	15,890

Source: Table No. 10, Cases reported under special and local laws in 1980, 1981 and 1982, "Crime in India"; Bureau of Police Research and Development.[5]

TABLE - 15
Persons arrested under SITA in States and Union Territories for the years 1980 - 1982

	States	1980	1981	1982
1.	Andhra Pradesh	1842	2095	2209
2.	Assam	25	3	3
3.	Bihar	11	44	8
4.	Gujarat	47	15	94
5.	Haryana	-	2	5
6.	Himachal Pradesh	-	-	-

7.	Jammu & Kashmir	-	-	-
8.	Karnataka	2,466	2621	3327
9.	Kerala	39	49	74
10.	Madhya Pradesh	3	2	2
11.	Maharashtra	1358	1419	4736
12.	Manipur	3	26	16
13.	Meghalaya	-	-	-
14.	Nagaland	-	-	-
15.	Orissa	12	19	-
16.	Punjab	4	3	6
17.	Rajasthan	6	12	19
18.	Sikkim	-	-	-
19.	Tamil Nadu	8443	9670	8915
20.	Tripura	-	-	-
21.	Uttar Pradesh	1482	943	1173
22.	West Bengal	36	64	61
	Total (States)	15,797	16,987	20,648
23.	A. & N. Islands	-	-	-
24.	Arunachal Pradesh	-	-	-
25.	Chandigarh	-	-	-
26.	Dadra & Nagar Haveli	-	-	-
27.	Delhi	167	141	240
28.	Goa, Daman & Diu	52	54	31
29.	Lakshadweep	-	-	-
30.	Mizoram	-	-	-
31.	Pondicherry	-	38	18
	Total:	16,016	17,220	20,937

Source: Table 24: Persons arrested under local and special laws in states and union territories; "Crime in India"; Bureau of Police Research and Development, Ministry of Home Affairs.[5]

TABLE - 16
Cases reported under the SITA for the years 1980 - 1982 from major cities in India.

City	1980	1981	1982
Ahmedabad	7	3	10
Bangalore	293	228	205
Bombay	863	890	893
Calcutta	49	48	55
Delhi	115	86	85
Hyderabad	144	66	25
Kanpur	91	91	95
Madras	1174	1362	1314
	2736	2775	2682
Jaipur	NA	2	3
Lucknow	NA	NA	501
Nagpur	NA	NA	-
Pune	NA	7	11

Source: Table No. 10: Cases reported in cities under local and special laws during 1980 - 1982; "Crime in India"; Bureau of Police Research and Development, Ministry of Home Affairs.[5]

Table - 17
Persons arrested under SITA for the years 1980 - 1982 from major cities in India.

City	1980	1981	1982
Ahmedabad	29	12	4
Bangalore	479	450	588
Bombay	1206	1365	4548
Calcutta	53	61	58
Delhi	167	141	240
Hyderabad	163	99	-

Kanpur	91	91	95
Madras	1174	1362	1310
	3362	3581	6843
Pune	NA	7	145
Jaipur	NA	7	7
Lucknow	NA	NA	501
Nagpur	NA	-	-

Source: Table No. 24: Persons arrested under the local and special laws in years 1980 - 82; "Crime in India"; Bureau of Police Research and Development, Ministry of Home Affairs.[5]

Table - 18

State	Total arrests in the state during years 1980 - 1982	City	Total arrests in the city during years 1980 - 82	Percentage of arrests in City compared to entire State
1. Gujarat	156	Ahmedabad	45	28.8
2. Karnataka	8,414	Bangalore	1,537	18.3
3. Maharashtra	7,513	Bombay	7,119	94.8
4. West Bengal	161	Calcutta	152	94.4
5. Andhra Pradesh	6,146	Hyderabad	262	4.2
6. Uttar Pradesh	3,598	Kanpur	277	7.7
7. Tamil Nadu	27,028	Madras	3,846	14.2

(Ref: Based on Table 15 and 17)5

Annexure - I

Important Penal Sanction under SITA

1. Brothel-keeping:

Keeping a brothel or allowing a premise to be used as one (Section 3).

2. Pimping

Living on the earnings of a prostitute (Section 4).

3. Procuring:

Procuring, inducing or taking a woman or girl for prostitution (Section 5).

4. Detention of a woman or girl:

Detaining such a person in a brothel or in a premise where prostitution was carried on (Section 6).

5. Prostitution:

In or in the vicinity of a public place (Section 7 (i)). Seducing or soliciting in a public place for the purpose of prostitution (Section 8(b).

6. Seduction of a woman or a girl in custody (Section 9).

7. Failure by a previously convicted offender under the Act to notify his/her address to the concerned Magistrate (Section 11(4).

8. Establishing or maintaining a protective home without a licence (Section 21).

(D'Cunha, Jean; 1986)[6]

Annexure - II

Penal Measures For 14 Cases Of Prostitutes Under Section 8(b) Of The SITA

S. No.	Name	Section	Charge	Date of arrest	Time of arrest	Date of conviction	Penal measures
1.	Rekha Dilbahadur	8(b)	Soliciting	1st Jan 1980	5.30	12th March	15 days imprisonment and fine of Rs. 100 by Metro-Court, Mazagon, Bombay.
2.	Thulsi	"	"	"	"	"	
3.	Saila	"	"	"	"	"	
4.	Maya Kanch	"	"	4th Jan 1980	NA	14th April 1980	5 days imprisonment and Fine of Rs. 50 by Girgaum Court.
5.	Kamala Maila	"	"			"	
6.	Rajeswari	"	"	"	"	"	
7.	Lala Kancha	"	"	"	"	"	
8.	F. Mohidri	"	"	"	"	6th May 1980	4 days imprisonment and fine of Rs. 40 by Mazagaon Court.
9.	Pinki Kalu	"	"	5th Jan 1980	5.30 p.m.		
10.	Rita Maila	"	"	"	"	6th Aug 1980	

81

11. Padma Ramday	"	"	NA		7 days rigorous imprisonment and fine of Rs. 50 by Girgaum Court.
12. Mira Kasinath	"	7th	NA	7th	5 days imprisonment and fine of Rs. 50 by Girgaum Court.
13. Maili Maila	"	"	Jan 1980	Sept 1980	
14. Gita Maila	"	"			

(Source: Vigilance Cell, Crime Branch, CID, Bombay records provided to me in 1986).[14]

ANNEXURE - III

LIBERAL LET-OFFS

Following a sapte of raids, the police issued show-cause notices to several suburban hotels, and in some cases, cancelled licences. But an appeal from the aggrieved hoteliers, and the State Home Department waved its magic wand: the licences were restored and it was back to 'business' as usual.

HOTEL	OFFENCE	POLICE ACTION	FOLLOW-UP
PAGODA S. Mithila Shopping Centre, Juhu-Parle (W) Owner: Rafiq Habib Khan	Following a raid conducted by Juhu police on July 2, 1986, seven women dancing in the nude were nabbed.	The Licensee and the conductor of the orchestra were arrested and a case filed under Sections 294-292-114 of the IPC vide CR No. 346/86. Police Commissioner cancelled the police licence (No. 73/Juhu dated November 9, '83).	Following an appeal to the Home Dept., the cancellation orders have been revoked.

Hotel	Action	Appeal
HOTEL SNOWWAYS 33 Gazdar Park Road, Santa Cruz (W); Owners: Prakash Karamchandani.	Following raids on August 31,'86, and September 1, '86, 19 prostitutes and their customers were arrested. Nine were minors. Cash worth Rs.6,266, including marked currency notes, was seized. Manager Harish Keshwani and Asst. Manager Naresh Tilani were charged under Sections 7 (i), (ii) and 8 (B) of the SITA. Police Licence No.83/Santa Cruz dated November 28, '83 cancelled.	Appealed to Home Department.
PICNIC PARADISE Near Vihar Lake; Owner: Kishore k Badiani	Following a raid conducted on Jan 1, '86, by the DCP Zone V, 12 prostitutes along with their customers were found in all the 12 rooms of the hotel. Cash worth of Rs. 2,532 including marked currency notes, was seized. Three girls along with manager-cum-receptionist of the hotel were charged under SITA. Police licence cancelled.	Appealed to the Home Dept.
HOTEL GLAMOUR INN Plot. No. 684, TPS III Mahim.	Raids on August 6 and 7, '84 under SITA. Police Licence cancelled.	Licence restored on appeal to the Home Dept.
HOTEL NEEL KANTH 354, Shanti Bhavan Linking Road, Khar.	Raided on July 2 and 3, '81 under SITA. Police Action deferred till decision of the case.	--
ARAM HOTEL 341/254, Government Colony, Bandra (E) Owner: P.M. Barot	Raided on Feb.4, '83 under SITA. Police Licence cancelled.	Appeal admitted, vide Home Dept. Order no 0182/5834/SPL-5 Police licence re-issued.

Establishment	Details	Action	Appeal / Remarks
JEWEL PALACE Plot No. 57, Khar Owner: Motiram Chawle	Raided under SITA on Sep.9, '83.	Police Licence cancelled	Appeal admitted vide Home Dept. letter no. PPE-0184/2393/S PI-5 dated 30.11.84 Police Licence re-issued.
COMMANDO 531, Dr, Ambedkar Road, Khar; Owners: Radhakrisha Rohra and others.	Raided under SITA in August '81.	Police Licence cancelled.	Appeal admitted vide Home Dept. letter no.PPE-0184/1150 -SPI-5 dated 12.10.18. Police Licence re-issued
HOTEL MAYURA 352, Linking Rd. Owner: Dattaram Koli and others	Raided on March 28, '86, by ACP Minoo Irani of Vigilance Branch. Two prostitutes with customers nabbed. On Dec.22, 49 prostitutes were nabbed on the premises.	Show-cause notice issued. Case vide CR No.340/341 of '86 is pending in 9th Court, Bandra.	Mayura claims it hasn't received the show-cause notice.
HORIZON 37, Juhu Beach; Owners: Indrajit Sharma and others.	Organised mujrah dances and other musical performances without prior permission of the licensing authority.	Show cause notice issued to the General Manager Viswanath and others Bosco D'souza, working in the hotel, was charged under Sec.33(wa) for conducting mujrah dances without licence. On May 17, '86 Ghazal singers Sanjeev Dakya Bhai Shingodia & Shabir Moterwala were also prosected.	
WELCO 128, Station Rd. Santa Cruz; Owners	Four prostitues hauled at the premises following raids on Nov. 30 & Dec. 1, '86	Show cause notice issued	

Chapter - 4: The Immoral Traffic in Persons Prevention Act 1986 - A Critical Review

The Immoral Traffic in Persons Prevention Act 1986 (ITPPA) was passed in the winter session of Parliament 1986. This Act is an amendment to the Suppression of Immoral Traffic in Women and Girls Act 1956 (SITA), and was passed primarily in the context of the latter's failure to suppress traffic in women and girls for prostitution.

As an amendment Act, the basic aims, objectives, logic and premises of the ITPPA remain similar to the SITA. While the ITPPA introduces several positive amendments, it still retains the clauses in the SITA used to penalize the prostitute. Similarly, it leaves much to be desired in its provisions for rehabilitation and general implementation.

The following are the major amendments in the Act.

Change in Title and Scope

The title of the Act has been changed from "Suppression of Immoral Traffic in Women and Girls for Prostitution, 1956" to "Immoral Traffic in Persons Prevention Act, 1986".

This includes two important aspects which widen the scope of the Act. Firstly, the drive to 'suppress' traffic has been replaced by a need to 'prevent' it. Secondly the words, 'Women and Girls' have been replaced by the term 'Persons'. This indicates recognition of the fact that it is not just females, but also males who engage in prostitution, and that consequently individuals of both sexes, including eunuchs are trafficked in for prostitution.

Definitional Changes

Changes have been introduced in the definitions of prostitution, protective home and the like. The Act also makes definitional distinctions between an adult, minor and child.

Prostitution

The definition of prostitution has been changed from, 'the act of a female offering her body for promiscuous sexual intercourse for hire, whether in money or kind', to 'the sexual exploitation or abuse of persons for commercial purposes'. The expression 'prostitute' is to be construed accordingly.[2]

The new definition of prostitution (and prostitute) has therefore been widened to include: (a) both male and female prostitutes and (b) any form of sexual exploitation or abuse for commercial purposes, instead of narrowly restricting prostitution to 'promiscuous sexual intercourse'.

This is welcome because of the often perverted and kinky sexual demands made of prostitutes, apart from routine sex.

Brothel

The definition of a brothel is likewise widened to include any place used for the purpose of sexual exploitation or abuse. This broader definition of a brothel would make it easier to prosecute brothel keepers under section 3 of the Act for all kinds of sexual abuse and exploitation which may not strictly amount to sexual intercourse alone (The Lawyer, 1986).[3]

Protective home

Under the SITA, a protective home refers to an institution where women and girls rescued from prostitution are kept in protective custody.

The ITPPA incorporates an additional clause stating that such a home must have appropriate technically qualified persons, equipment and facilities.

Distinction between major, minor and child

The SITA makes a distinction between a woman and girl, defining the former as one who is 21 years of age or older and the latter as below 21 years of age. This distinction is made in view of the nature of rehabilitation to be provided for a woman and a girl, and is based on the assumption that a woman has the right to decide whether or not she should stay in prostitution, while a girl cannot. Consequently, while a woman is tried in court, if she is booked for prostituting in a public place or soliciting, and then convicted, acquitted or referred to a protective home or corrective institution, a girl rescued from a brothel is immediately referred for rehabilitation. There is no difference in the amount of punishment for exploiters of either the woman or girl.

The ITPPA on the other hand distinguishes between a major, minor and child. It defines a major as a person who is 18 years old, a minor 16 years but not 18 years and a child who is under 16 years old. In contrast to the SITA, the ITPPA has introduced additional categories and decreased the age limits for each.

This distinction and the inclusion of the definition of a child in the new Act, is firstly a recognition of the existence of child prostitution and traffic in children for prostitution.

Secondly, the need for these definitions is explained in the context of penal measures under the Act, to be meted out to those using persons for prostitution. The younger the person who is sexually exploited and abused for commercial purposes, the more stringent is the punishment for the exploiters. This new clause is also based on the presumption of the innocence of children. In contrast to the SITA, the ITPPA seems to take a more serious view of child prostitution.

Penal Measures

Penal measures for an owner, lessor, landlord of a brothel (or agent of such): Under the SITA, an owner, lessor, landlord (or agent of such person) of a premises being used as a brothel cannot be prosecuted unless he 'knowingly' or 'wilfully' allows the premises to be used for prostitution. Under cover of 'lack of knowledge', landlords avert prosecution.

The ITPPA seeks to plug this loophole. It states that it will be presumed, until the contrary is proved, that a landlord knowingly allows or has knowledge that his premises are being used as a brothel under two circumstances. Firstly, if a report published in a newspaper circulating in his residential area states that his premises were found to be used for prostitution, as a result of a search made, and secondly if a copy of the *panchanama* made during the search is handed over to the landlord.[2]

The ITPPA thus places the onus of proof on the landlord conditionally. This is farcical, firstly because raids are seldom conducted, far less reported. Secondly, the landlord, often manages the brothel himself or is hand in glove with the brothel manager and thus usually knows that the premises are being used for prostitution. Providing a conditionality for onus of proof is a sure loophole that landlords will use to circumvent prosecution.

Once a brothel is raided, it should be presumed that the landlord, unless proved to the contrary, knowingly let his premises for prostitution or knew it was being used for prostitution. The burden of proof must thus be placed on him at any cost.

*Increase in penal measures for offences under the Act:*The ITPPA introduces more stringent penal measures for several categories of offences, with the intention that such stringency will act as a deterrent to the offender.

Procuring, inducing or taking a person for prostitution, detaining a person for prostitution, seduction of a person in custody: Under the SITA offences like procuring or detaining a person for prostitution or seduction of a person in custody, on average, incurred a rigorous imprisonment on first conviction for a term of between one or two years plus a fine of up to Rs. 2000. A second conviction brought with it, on average. an imprisonment lasting between two and four years, together with a maximum fine of up to Rs. 2000.

The same offences under the ITPPA are penalized, on average, with a minimum of seven years imprisonment which may extend to life or for a period of 14 years together with a fine.

The new Act also grants discretionary powers to the court to reduce the term of imprisonment to below the seven-year minimum for offences such as detaining a person for prostitution or seduction of a person in custody.

While an increase in penal measures under the new Act is

welcome, provision or discretionary powers to the judge to reduce the term of imprisonment below the stipulated minimum of seven years for certain offences defeats the deterrent effect of an increase in penalties. It must therefore be binding on courts trying offences under the Act, to give the minimum punishment laid down, if not more.

Suspension of hotel licenses: The ITPPA like the SITA penalizes practice of prostitution in or in the vicinity of a public place. The former incorporates a new clause stating that if the public place happens to be a hotel in which prostitution of majors is carried out, the license of the hotel can be suspended for a period of not less than three months and can extend to a year.

This is welcome, given the magnitude of hotel prostitution.

Seducing or soliciting for prostitution: Under the SITA, punishment for seducing or soliciting for prostitution incurs an imprisonment extending to a year as the case may be.

The new Act penalizes such an offence by a man with imprisonment for a period of not less than seven days extendable to three months.

Both the SITA and the ITPPA do not, in their declared objectives, intend penalizing prostitution *per se*. However, the aforesaid clauses punishing prostitution in a public place and soliciting or seducing for prostitution are ambiguously formulated. They do not specifically state who is to be penalized, nor do they clearly specify non-usage against the prostitute. There is every reason to believe that these sections present in the SITA and retained in the ITPPA will be used against the prostitute, in the course of implementation, as is the case under the SITA. This only amounts to punishing the much exploited prostitute.

If the newly incorporated penal measures against soliciting by males is applied to male prostitutes, it is a sure discrimination against female prostitutes for whom penal measures for the same offence are higher. If this clause is used against male pimps and touts, it undoubtedly mitigates the offence committed by them.

Yet another anti-prostitute bias is that while the prostitute can be penalized under the Act, there are no penal measures for clients. This indicates the double standards of sexual morality in general and the double standards of male sexual morality in the case of female prostitutes. Considering the magnitude of forced prostitution, the Act must explictly state who can be booked for practice of prostitution in a public place or soliciting for prostitution in order to eliminate the discrimination between buyers and providers of sex. All clauses penalizing the prostitute must be deleted.

Penal Measures For Prostitution Of Minors And Children

Taking a graver view of prostitution of minors and children, the ITPPA has introduced more severe penal measures for those indulging in sexual exploitation of minors and children for prostitution.

Living off the earnings of child prostitution: The SITA has no provisions for punishing those who live off the earnings of child prostitution. The ITPPA, on the other hand, incorporates an additional clause which makes such an offence in relation to a minor or child, punishable with imprisonment for not less than seven years and not more than ten years.

Procuring, inducing or taking a minor child for prostitution: *Prostitution of a minor or child in or in the vicinity of a public place:* The ITPPA introduces special measures to penalize procuring a minor or child from prostitution and for prostitution of a minor or child in a public place. The former offence carries rigorous imprisonment of between seven and fourteen years with respect to a minor a seven years to life when a child is procured.

The latter offence carries either an imprisonment for not less than seven years but extendable to life or for a period up to ten years together with a fine. The same punishment exists with respect to both minors and children. The court has discretionary powers in this offence to reduce the prison term to below the seven year minimum, provided it mentions its reasons for doing so in the judgement.

However, such discretionary powers as mentioned earlier defeat the purpose. The ITPPA must make it binding on the judge to prescribe the seven year minimum punishment at the very least.

Cancellation of hotel licence: If a minor or child is used for prostitution in a hotel, the ITPPA provides for cancellation of the hotel license.

Detaining a minor or child in premises where prostitution is carried on: The ITPPA introduces another clause, stating that if a person is found with a child in a brothel it will be presumed, unless proved to the contrary, that he/she has detained the child for prostitution.

Similarly, if a minor or child found in a brothel is on medical examination detected to have been sexually abused it will be presumed, unless the contrary is proved, that they have been detained for prostitution or sexually exploited for commercial purposes.

Closure of brothels and eviction of offenders from the premises: The SITA empowers a magistrate to order the closure of brothels and eviction of offenders therein if it is situated within 200 metres of a public place. The brothel owner must get the approval of the magistrate for one year after the closure order, if he/she wishes to release the premises.

Making a small change to the above, the ITPPA increases the one- year period to three years, if a child is found on the premises.

The Changes at a Glance

Comparison of offences and penal measures under the SITA and ITPPA

SECTION AND OFFENCE (1) S 3(1)	PUNISHMENT UNDER SITA (2)	PUNISHMENT UNDER ITPPA (3)
1) Brothel Keeping	First conviction Rigorous imprisonment (RI) between 1 - 3 years and fine upto Rs. 2000/-	Unchanged
	Second conviction Rigorous imprisonment between 2 - 5 years and fine upto Rs. 2000/-.	Unchanged

2)	S 3(2) Abetment to brothel keeping	First conviction Imprisonment up to 2 years and fine upto Rs. 2000/-	Unchanged
		Second conviction: RI up to 5 years and fine.	Unchanged
3)	S 4 Living on the earnings of prostitution	Imprisonment up to 2 years or fine up to Rs. 1000/- or both	Imprisonment not loss than 7 years and not more than 10 years where offence is committed against a child or minor.
4)	S 5 P r o c.u r i n g , inducing or taking for prostitution	First conviction RI between 1-2 years and fine up to Rs. 2000/-	On conviction RI between 3 years and 7 years and fine up to Rs. 2000/-
		Second conviction RI of 2 - 5 years and fine up to Rs. 2000/-	I m p r i s o n m e n t between 7 and 14 years when committed against the will of any person.
5)	S 6	First conviction: RI between 1 - 2 years and fine up to Rs. 2000/-	On conviction with simple or RI between 7 years and life or up to 10 years with or without fine.
		Second conviction: RI between 2 - 5 years and fine up to Rs. 2000/-	D i s c r e t i o n a r y powers of the court to provide imprisonment for less than 7 years.
6)	S 7(1) Prostitution in a public place	Conviction up to 3 months.	Simple or RI of not less than .7 years in case where the offences are committed against children. Lesser punishment at the discretion of the judge.

7)	S 7(2) Abetment of prostitution in a public place	First conviction: Imprisonment up to three months or fine up to Rs. 200/- or both.	
		Second conviction: Imprisonment up to 6 months and fine up to Rs. 200/-	Under section 7(2) suspension of hotel licenses between 3 months and 1 year if used as brothels. Cancellattion of hotel licenses if minors or childen are found therein for prostitution.
8)	S 8(a) Soliciting or seduction for prosititution	First Conviction: Imprisonment up to 6 months or fine up to Rs. 500 or both	Unchanged If the offence is committed by a man, imprisonment between 7 days and 3 months.
		Second conviction: Imprisonment up to 1 year or fine up to Rs. 500/- or both.	
9)	S 8(b) Soliciting by nuisance	- do -	
10)	S 9 Seduction in custody for prostitution	First conviction: RI between 2 - 5 years and fine up to Rs. 1000/-	On conviction with s i m p l e imprisonment or RI between 7 years and life or up to 10 year's with or without fine.
		Second conviction: Imprisonment up to 5 years and fine up to Rs. 1000/-	

Other Measures

No release on probation: The new Act deletes section 10 of the SITA which provides for release of offenders on probation of good conduct or after due admonition. This deletion has two negative effects. Firstly, it is detrimental to the interests of the prostitute because she is denied probation. Secondly, pimps, touts and other traffickers cannot be released under section 10.

Section 10 could have been amended so as to provide probation to prostitutes and to specifically exclude traffickers from its purview.

No security for good behaviour: Section 12 of the SITA empowers the court when passing a sentence for an offence, to obtain a security for good behaviour from habitual offenders. This section has been deleted under the ITPPA as penal provisions for offences under it have been enhanced.

Provisions For Implementation

Executive and Procedural Aspects: Trafficking Police Officers.

In view of the magnitude of interstate traffic in persons for prostitution, the Act empowers the Central Government to appoint police officers called Trafficking Police Officers, to crack down on interstate traffic.

Their powers and functions extend to the whole of India, thus widening the authority of Trafficking Police Officers over Special Police Officers (under SITA & ITPPA), who have territorial restrictions placed on them.

Powers to search without a warrant: The SITA empowers a Special Police Officer to search any premises without a warrant.

The ITPPA extends this power to the trafficking police officers who together with the former can enter such premises and remove all persons found therein.

The new Act inserts a new clause which mandates a medical examination of these persons to determine age or to detect injuries caused by sexual abuse.

Women Police Officers: Another clause has been inserted into the ITPPA prohibiting male police officers (empowered under the Act) from making a search without a warrant, unless accompanied by at least two women police officers. The interrogation of women or girls so removed must be carried out by women police officers, failing which the prostitutes can be questioned only in the presence of a female member of a recognised social welfare institution or organisation.

Such a clause is welcome in view of the harassment, sexual and otherwise that women and girls rescued from the brothels or other places face from male police officers. This clause can help curb such harassment to some extent.

Court Procedures

Power of the Magistrate: Section 16 of the SITA empowers a magistrate to direct a Special Police Officer to rescue any person who is living, carrying on or being made to carry on prostitution in a brothel.

To ensure the safe custody of minors and children, the new Act confers discretionary powers on the magistrate for interim placement of children and minors so rescued, in any recognised children's institution set up under any Children Act.

So as to prevent persons from falling back into the clutches of prostitution (eg., racketeers who pose as lawful guardians) the ITPPA empowers the magistrate to verify the bona fides of such guardians by ensuring that an investigation is conducted by a recognised welfare institution or organization.

Special Courts: The new Act also empowers the Central Government to establish special courts for speedy trial of offences under this Act including those committed in more than one state.

Rehabilitation: The ITPPA incorporates a new section which requires that persons in charge of protective homes or corrective institutions produce relevant records and documents before the court, as and when needed by it.

This provision will ensure accurate maintenance of records - a function much neglected by protective institutions. Such information could help in the prosecution of offenders.

Further, the ITPPA, like the SITA, retains a reformative and corrective orientation towards rehabilitation. Such an orientation must be changed to an interaction with individuals with dignity, who have been exploited and are survivors struggling to cope with their experiences of exploitation.

By way of conclusion, it may be said that although the intention

to prevent rather than suppress traffic in person
prostitution is laudable, the Act itself has few provision
prevention. Firstly, it makes no explicit provisions
crackdowns on places where there is buying and sellin
persons for prostitution. Such provisions must be categoric
laid down. Secondly, prevention has little meaning in ti.
absence of society's aggressive efforts towards (a) improving the
quality of material life of its members in general and women
in particular or (b) questioning and changing consumerist and
sexist attitudes.

Further, though an increase in penal measures is commendable,
the impact of this would be negligible, in view of the enormous
powers invested by the Act in the police and courts and the
known connivance between these implementing authorities and
prostitution racketeers.

The involvement of social workers and the public in general is
optional and marginal under the Act. The Act must therefore
statutorily and mandatorily provide for the constitution of
citizens' committees, not only to harness public participation
and responsibility but also to effectuate vigilance.

Lastly, implementation is left solely to the state governments.
There is no machinery to oversee and coordinate at a central
level.

References

1. Association for Social Health in India (1987); - Paper on "The
Immoral Traffic Prevention Act 'A Resume'."

2. Bill No. XXXF of 1986, The Suppression of Immoral Traffic in
Women and Girls Amendment Bill 1986" (as passed by the Houses of
Parliament): An Act.

3. Dutta, Nilima(1986); "Trafficking in Women"; *The Lawyer;*
September.

Part - IV

Chapter - 5: Legalization of Prostitution: Review of Issues Raised in India

Introduction

While the Indian Government continues to follow the tolerationist system of law articulated in the Immoral Traffic in Persons Prevention Act 1986 (the amendment to the SITA), which has yet to be enforced, the issue of legalizing prostitution continues to be discussed and proposed by state governments like Maharashtra and Karnataka and certain medical bodies.

In the wake of the AIDS scare, proponents advocate legalization so as to curb AIDS. They perceive prostitutes as the primary risk group - the source of STDs and AIDS. They claim that legalization would involve registration and licensing of prostitutes for their identification. Health measures to curb STDs and AIDS could then be given to prostitutes, thus helping to preserve public health.

Apart from this, they also maintain that legalization is a viable alternative because of the SIT Act's failure. Legalization is also advocated by this group as it believes prostitution to be a necessary and inevitable social evil which will continue to exist in society because of man's aggressive and uncontainable sexual drive. Legalization will help prevent the breakdown of the family structure and prevent rape.

It is necessary to probe each of these arguments advanced in favour of legalization to ascertain its desirability and feasability.

Prostitution as a Universal Necessity and Inevitable Social Evil

Proponents of legalization claim that man's sexual drive is naturally and biologically aggressive. Such an irrepressible sexuality requires prostitution as a safety valve against rampant rape and the breakdown of the family structure. Prostitution is therefore considered a universal, inevitable and necessary social evil.

This is a historical untruth. Although prostitution has existed in all class-based patriarchal societies where power is vested in the hands of men, and women are dominated and maintained in conditions of slavery, prostitution was and is still unknown in many so-called primitive societies. (Barry, Kathleen; 1979).[2] The Warli tribe of Dahanu provides an example of the absence of prostitution. though prostitution has started now that the tribe is being absorbed into the mainstream capitalist system. (Interview with Shiraz Bulsara, Activist, Kashtakari Sangatna; Dahanu, Thana District.)[8]

In recognizing the systemic causes of prostitution, the onus of responsibility is shifted from the women in prostitution to the social system and the controllers of prostitution, so much so that, in the words of Kathleen Barry, author of Female Sexual Slavery, "Pimping becomes the oldest profession" - not prostitution (Barry, Kathleen; 1979).[2]

To perceive prostitution as an inevitable and necessary social evil, is to deny the exploitative socio-economic and ideological roots of prostitution and to perceive society and its institutions as immutable. This further implies a condemnation of prostitutes . It perceives men as incapable of ever having any human sexual expression.

Reality disproves the assumption of inevitability and assumes that the profession will exist for perpetuity.

Kathleen Gough in her article on prostitution in Vietnam states that at the conclusion of the war in Vietnam, there was a total of nearly half a million prostitutes. This number plummetted to 50,000 in 1976, 30,000 in 1981 and to a couple of hundred in 1982. Post-war measures like equal re-distribution of income, development of more human sexual values, strict implementation of laws against prostitution racketeers, provision of rehabilitation facilities for prostitutes and provision of equal opportunities for women in society have helped this process (Gough, Kathleen; 1984).[6]

Further, prostitution has been drastically, if not completely, reduced in China and Cuba (Barry, Kathleen; 1979),[2] throwing serious doubts on the assumption that prostitution is a necessity and inevitable social evil.

Man's uncontainable sexual appetite and sexual aggressiveness is natural and biological.

Patriarchal society equates sex drive with male sexuality which is erroneously assumed to be naturally active and aggressive. Women, on the other hand, are attributed with sexual feelings of a diffuse and passive nature (Barry, Kathleen; 1979).[2]

Male researchers aver that male aggressiveness and sexual virility are dictated by hormones possessed chiefly or solely by males. They maintain that the male drive is overwhelmingly uncontrollable and demands a fitting object for release, in which terms the female role is defined (Narayan, Uma).[11]

However, there is much evidence from animal and human life that disproves "natural' male sexual aggressiveness and passive female sexuality (Narayan, Uma).[11]

A castrated male animal is supposed to be more docile, but so is a splayed female animal. There is a widespread belief that injecting testerone into a female makes her more aggressive. We are seldom told that an injection of oestrogen causes the same behaviour in males and females. Very large doses of testerone injected into either sex makes them so passive that they don't eat or fight (Davis, D.E.; 1971).[4]

Kinsey was one of the first sexologists to perceive that the sex-drive was learned behaviour, not an uncontrollable instinct - a conclusion supported by Masters and Johnson in their research on males in clinical settings (Barry, Kathleen; 1979).[2]

Kinsey's study of American adolescents revealed that boys learnt two things from cultural myths - that the sex drive must be fulfilled because it cannot be contained and that they have the implicit right to use girls and women to fulfil that drive. Sexual power is gained via sexual experience (Barry, Kathleen; 1979).[2]

Cultural elements like the media and pornography reinforce these patriarchal myths.

It has also been found that the so-called uncontrollability of an erection can be controled by the time the boys are adults. There are males who are questioning the performance criteria that they have been taught to live under and demand of their partners. They aver that male sexual satisfaction need not depend on an erection, but on more diffuse sensations (Barry, Kathleen; 1979).[2]

The findings of a survey of 4,066 men on male sexuality reported in "Beyond the Male Myth', revealed that 981 of the men surveyed felt that it was important for a woman to have an orgasm. Over half of them were self critical if their partner did not respond fully and 4 out of 5 men were making conscious efforts to delay their orgasms as long as possible (Reynaud, Emmanuel; 1981).[14]

So the sex drive is not just a physiological response of the sex organ dictated by hormones. It is learned behaviour conditioned by patriarchal societies.

For a long time a woman's sex organ was considered by scientists to be 'nothing in itself', the vulva being only the entrance to the vagina. It was considered to be a mere recipient for the male organ. It was only in the 20th century that it was recognized in western scientific circles that not only did a woman have a sex organ, but that it functioned similarly to a man's.

Warning us against the myth of passive female sexuality, Montaigne in his *Essays* says, "Women are incomparably more capable and ardent than we men in their act of love". Later on, in his book, *The Sensuous man*, he says, "Sexually speaking we are mistaken if we think we are the stronger sex. Women are capable of having orgasms ten times as intense as ours". Even more recently, Pascal Bruckher and Alain Tinkietkraut in *le Nouveau de Sordre Amoureux* observe that in comparison with the sad simplicity of man's pleasure, "a woman's orgasm is like a small-scale production of the creation of the universe".

It has further been observed that women's so-called sexual passivity is the result of female socialization. They have learned to be passive and docile. Emotional or psychological blocks with respect to males, sex and sexuality, or the fear of violence and pain in a physical relationship may result in a lukewarm female sexdual response.

Prostitution as a safeguard against rampant rape of women

While rape and prostitution both have sexual connotations, they are not per se sexual phenomena. While men may consider both as substitutes for sex, neither gives sexual gratification to the women. Rape is tantamount to assault and prostitution is nothing but an economic transaction. The extent of sexual gratification for both the rapist and client is questionable. Recent studies suggest that rape occurs not for lack of sexual alternatives, but because of power dissatisfaction. The motive of the client in prostitution is also partly the exercise of consumer power. The act of buying gives a sense of power and control. The act of buying sexual intimacy with women represents the logical marriage between sexism and consumerism (Macmillan, Jackie; 1976).[9]

In a culture in which virginity is highly valued and a rape victim is considered to have lost her honour, the woman may even enter prostitution after being sexually abused or raped. She has internalized the society's perception of her as a fallen woman. Rape is used to break a woman's resistance in a brothel and initiate her into prostitution as she feels she is now worthless (D'Cunha, Jean; 1984).[5]

The sexually non-exclusive nature of a prostitute's job casts her into the stereotype of a 'bad' woman, who is fair game for rapists and must be denied protection available to 'good' women. While prostitutes are not responsible for rape, they are one of the most vulnerable sections of women in society subject to the possibility of rape, theft and murder by males - pimps, police and clients. Both rape and prostitution are a manifestation of women's powerlessness in society (Macmillan, Jackie, 1976).[9]

Individual and mass rapes, assertions of class and male power, occur every day despite the existence of prostitution, and will continue to occur in a class divided, patriarchal society. The prevalence and sanction of rape in class struggles and war is evidence of this.

Rape as a military strategy and personal outlet is inseparable from prostitution, when one considers that large numbers of women and girls from war-torn countries like Paraguay, Laos and Vietnam, for whom prostitution would have been unknown had the demands of the military not brought these women to the cities (Barry, Kathleen; 1979).[2]

In Japan the colonization of women's bodies which began with rape during the Second World War led to the Japanese Government presenting Japanese women as comfort girls to the U.S. occupation force in post-Second World War Japan (Barry, Kathleen; 1979).[2]

Lastly, there is no reason to believe that the abolition of licensed brothels would lead to an increase in rape of women. The report of the League of Nations Committee on Traffic in Women and Children in 1934, in countries like U.S.A.and Nicaragua and continents like Africa and Asia stated that the abolition of licensed brothels in these places did not give rise to an increase in sex offences. Rape continues to occur in countries that have legalized prostitution. Connections have been posted between organized crime, rape and prostitution by a District Attorney in Lincoln county, the nearest place to Las Vegas that has legalized prostitution (Barry, Kathleen; 1979).[2] Also, there is no reason to believe that more men would patronize prostitutes with the repeal of legal sanctions against prostitution, as sanctions either do not exist or are not currently enforced against men. Men are usually free to frequent prostitutes without legal threat.

Prostitution maintains the family structure

To advocate legalization of prostitution because it is supposed to protect the family structure is very reactionary. It is the standard functionalist explanation which serves to conserve a patriarchal and exploitative status quo. It shies away from attacking the sexist and exploitative basis of the institution of prostitution i.e. "Male sexuality is naturally uncontainable and must find an outlet through the purchase of sex". It also shies away from challenging the oppressive basis of the patriarchal family in contemporary society, which gives males the moral and legal right to a woman's body in marriage in exchange for financial support; which endorses dual standards of morality for men and women, in order to accurately determine paternity and safeguard the purity of race and property concerns of the ruling elite and ensure a steady legitimate supply of workforce. These economic functions of the patriarchal monogamous family unit, lead to the contracting of marriage arrangements on the basis of economic status, caste, and religion. The genuine basis for a marital compatability is rejected. The proliferation of such depersonalized relationships in society coupled with double standards of morality provide the justification for males to seek pleasure outside the institution of marriage in prostitution.

LEGALIZATION TO PREVENT THE SPREAD OF STD AND AIDS

In a male-dominated cultural setting where a woman's nature and being are defined in terms of her sexuality and her reproductive organs and functions, a woman's health problems are also so defined. It is no wonder that a prostitute whose work is to provide sex services for a price is defined in terms of a sex commodity. So too, are her health and problems defined and linked to sexuality.

Prostitutes have thus been historically blamed for being the source of sexually transmitted diseases (STDs) and the authorities have, over the years, justified the social and legal control of prostitutes as a public health measure. It is not surprising therefore, that certain state governments in India like the Maharashtra and Karnataka governments, together with certain medical bodies, have been discussing legalization and licensing of prostitution in the context of a programme to prevent the spread of STDs and AIDS, in the interest of public health.

Public health in this context implies male health, which must be maintained for the production of capital. Although the government is very concerned to preserve 'public health', it shows blithe unconcern for all the other health problems of prostitutes such as tuberculosis, anaemia, gynaecological ailments and the like.

STDs and Prostitution

The assumption that prostitutes are more responsible for the transmission of STD's than other groups and that state control of prostitutes will prevent such transmission is contradicted by research findings. For instance, the U.S. Department of Public Health has consistently reported that only 5% of V.D. in the U.S.A. is related to prostitution, compared with 30-35% among teenagers (Alexander, Priscilla; 1987).[1] Further, in Third World countries like India, where forced and child prostitution is rampant, the woman or child enters the trade disease-free and contracts STD's in the course of work. Blaming the prostitute and directing policy measures at her, while forgetting the role of the client as a carrier, is an example of the sexist bias which leads to controlling and punishing the woman who is often a victim too.

An attack directed at the prostitute who is seen as the sole source of STDs, without any preventive or adequate curative health measures being prescribed for the client and the rest of the population, reflects a male bias and can hardly effect a curb on STDs.

A prostitute woman who remains in the trade could be reinfected at any time between two medical examinations. So, measures to reduce and control STDs through the legalization and control of prostitutes are useless.

The experience of countries legalizing prostitution has revealed that compulsory registration of prostitutes to facilitate health checks doesn't work because prostitutes shy away from registration which identifies and labels them, making them vulnerable than ever to blackmail and impeding their social mobility (Barry, Kathleen; 1979).[2]

AIDS and Prostitution

AIDS (Acquired Immuno Defficiency Syndrome) is invariably fatal. AIDS which is associated with the HIV virus, has caused much furore worldwide. For the purpose of this discussion it suffices to say that there is presently no adequate or active surveillance for detection of cases of AIDS in India (Cases of AIDS in India: A Future Scenario projected by CARE; 1988),[3] nor are there systematic and comprehensive epidemiological studies conducted. This makes it difficult to conclusively establish the magnitude of the problem for India.

However, prostitutes are made to bear the blame for transmitting AIDS to the heterosexual community. This began when researchers and physicians the world over first recognized that the disease was transmitted sexually.It must, however, be pointed out that this is not the only mode of the virus transmission.

Other modes of AIDS Transmission: AIDS can also be transmitted through infected blood and blood products, or through contaminated needles and syringes. Haemophiliacs and others who receive blood transfusions or blood products containing the virus are very likely to become infected because the virus is injected directly into the blood stream. The other high risk group is intravenous drug users who share unsterilized syringes.

Another mode of transmission is prenatal transmission, that is from an infected mother to the offspring during her pregnancy or at the time of birth (Parvi, Khorshed; 1988).[12]

While sexual transmission is one of the modes of transmission, researchers at first believed that the number of sexual partners was the deciding factor in such transmission. More recent studies have, however, suggested that general sexual activity and unprotected sexual contact may be more important (Alexander, Priscilla; 1987).[1]

While anal intercourse appears to be the most risky activity for the receptive partner, fellatio does not appear to be a high risk activity. Very little virus is found in the saliva and it is believed that the enzymes in the saliva and acids in the digestive tract kill the virus contained in the ejaculation. Vaginal intercourse is not thought to be as risky for either partner, because the vaginal walls are quite thick. Although researchers in San Francisco and Boston have been able to culture the virus from the vaginal secretions of some women with AIDS, it is difficult to do and the quantity of the virus appears to be small, in marked contrast to the amount of virus to be found in blood or semen. However, it may be that during menstruation the risk is greater because the blood vessels are closer to the surface at that time. Cunnilingus is also thought to be a relatively low risk activity. Research in U.S.A. reveals that male-to-female transmission appears to be more efficient than female-to-male transmission (Alexander, Priscilla; 1987)[1]

*Predisposing Factors For Contracting AIDS:*It is strongly suspected that the AIDS virus which replicates itself in the T4 cells (the mastermind for the immune system), is greatly helped if these cells are 'activated' by other infectious agents. This emphasizes the importance of environmental factors which facilitate the spread of the AIDS virus. An unhygienic environment and malnutrition seem to play an important part in aiding the AIDS virus, particularly among populations of poor 'developing' countries in Africa (Pavri, Khorshed; 1988).[12]

Studies reveal that the overall prevalence of AIDS in economically developed countries is dependent on sexual behaviour, except among the poor ethnic groups. In contrast, among the economically developing countries, AIDS appears to be more of an environmental problem, except perhaps among their richer populations (Pavri, Khorshed; 1988).[12]

*Are Prostitutes the Primary Source of AIDS Transmission in India?:*In the absence of adequate data, it is difficult to conclusively assert that prostitutes are the primary high risk group for transmission of the AIDS virus in India. It must however be pointed out that Indian prostitutes generally visit private doctors including STD specialists and generally do not donate blood. By contrast promiscuous males frequent STD clinics and outdoor departments of public hospitals. Several of these men may be paid blood donors. They are more likely to spread HIV infections sexually, through blood transfusions and injections (Pavri, Khorshed; 1988).[13]

Studies on Prostitution and AIDS in the U.S.A: Several studies have been undertaken in the U.S.A. on prostitution and AIDS and are being cited to suggest that prostitutes are largely responsible for AIDS transmission to heterosexual males. But researchers have pointed out methodological problems with such studies.

The first studies reporting the incidence of infection among prostitutes, were from New York and Miami, cities with a high incidence of AIDS and AIDS Related Complex (ARC). The first New York study was an informal one done by a clinician Joyce Wallace, M.D., who had little epidemiological experience or research credentials. She tested the blood of several prostitutes and found some of them to be infected. She did not systematically determine the source of their infection nor did she protect their anonymity or even their confidentiality. Virtually all of her test subjects were street prostitutes, a skewed population, since only about 10-20% of United States prostitutes work on the streets (National Task Force on Prostitution, 1986).[10]

A second early study in Miami, Florida was done either in an AIDS screening clinic, a V.D. clinic or a drug treatment programm (the press reports were conflicting). In this case, 10 of 25 subjects i.e. 40% were found to be antibody positive. Again, this was a skewed sample (National Task Force on Prostitution; 1986).[10]

Both these studies have been repeatedly cited to show that

prostitutes are infected and that they are transmitting the virus to the heterosexual population even though the students have serious methodological flaws.

A third study was done in Seattle, under the direction of Hunter Hansfield, M.D., Director of Public Health in that city. He tested all women arrested for prostitution for a period of time. Out of 92 women tested, 5 (or 5.5%) were found to be positive using the ELISA test. This study has also been cited repeatedly all over the U.S.A., to support the conclusion that prostitutes were a source of contagion. What has not been reported is that when the samples were re-tested by the Western Blot test, not one was found to be antibody positive. Although Mansfield has been under some pressure, from Debra Boyer, Ph.D., and other members of Seattle's AIDS Advisory Task Force to publish the later results exonerating the prostitutes, he has refused (National Task Force on Prostitution; 1986).[10]

By contrast Project AWARE, a study in San Francisco, under the direction of Constance Wofsy, M.D. and Judith Cohen, Ph.D. has taken a different approach. They are testing women who fit into one of the two criteria: they have either had five or more male sex partners in the previous three years or one male sex partner in a high risk group. Their subjects have included prostitutes and non-prostitutes. They have found that 4% of each group were antibody positive (the non prostitute group included one anti- body positive woman who had had only one male sex partner in her entire life). Their conclusion is that, it is not the number of partners that is significant but rather the specific sexual behaviour. Most of the antibody positive women have had a history of IV use themselves, while others have been in a regular ongoing sexual relationships with an IV drug user or a bisexual male. The primary difference between the prostitutes and non- prostitutes was that prostitutes were much more likely to use condoms for all sexual contact with their clients (National Task Force on Prostitution; 1986).[10]

While prostitutes continued to be blamed for transmitting AIDS to heterosexual men in the U.S.A., studies by the Centre for Disease Control in the States during the period 1981-1986 show that in terms of percentages, the percentage of men who got AIDS through heterosexual contact has remained constant, while the percentage of women who got AIDS through sex with men is much more. This suggests that the risk for heterosexual women is increasing at a faster rate, than it is for heterosexual men(Alexander, Priscilla; 1987).[1]

If prostitutes were effectively transmitting the AIDS virus to their customers, there would be far more cases of white heterosexual males diagnosed with AIDS, than is reflected in current statistics (Alexander, Priscilla, 1987).[1]

High risk groups for AIDS in the U.S.A. are homosexuals, IV drug users and IV drug user prostitutes. It has been difficult to estimate the number of homosexuals and IV drug users in India, far less to what extent they constitute a risk group for AIDS.

Prostitutes and AIDS Transmission in Developing Countries:

In Central Africa there have been a number of studies of prostitutes and their clients in several countries in Central Africa, where AIDS is almost exclusivery a disease of heterosexuals and prostitutes have been found to be a high risk group(Alexander, Priscilla; 1987).[1]

Different patterns in the high risk groups in the U.S.A. and the countries of Central Africa may be attributed to the way prostitutes work and the health systems in the two places. To begin with, while the use of condoms is widely prevalent in the U.S.A. particularly since the AIDS scare, they are not much used in Central Africa partly due to their cost, partly due to cultural reasons, including the influence of Catholicism (Alexander, Priscilla; 1987).[1]

While in the U.S.A., most prostitutes who have been diagnosed for AIDS or whose AIDS antibodies were positive have a recent history of IV drug use, such IV drug use is reported to be rare among prostitutes in Central Africa. However, many clinics in Rwanda and other Central African countries are not able to sterilize needles after each patient because of the prohibitive cost, and some researchers think that the virus may be transmitted via unsterilized needles in clinics, particularly in urban clinics as well as through heterosexual contacts (Alexander, Priscilla) 1987).[1] The same may also be true of India.

Finally, female genital circumcision and infibulation appear to be more common in Central Africa, than it was previously thought, and that as a result, women often bleed during sexual intercourse, which would greatly increase their infection rate, which could account for both the high seropositivity rate among women and the high incidence of actual AIDS (Alexander, Priscilla; 1987).[1]

The fact that in Central Africa, studies show that a lower percentage of male customers (9-28), than female prostitutes (54- 90%) are seropositive, suggests that female to male transmission is not as efficient as the reverse although it does occur. The figures suggest that male clients are infecting female prostitutes, although there has been no concern expressed, except in the American feminist press, about risk to prostitutes (Alexander, Priscilla, 1987).[1]

Some researchers have begun to speculate, that since the virus is relatively difficult to culture from vaginal secretions, in contrast to blood or semen, men may be infecting each other through prostitutes. So it is possible that men who do not use condoms may be infecting both women and each other(Alexander, Priscilla) 1987).[1]

Measures to Control the Spread of STDs and AIDS

From the above one can see it is erroneous to blame prostitutes for AIDS transmission:

Secondly, apart from ideological disagreements with perceiving prostitutes as the source of AIDS and consequently legalizing prostitution to control the spread, legalization appears to be unpractical. The stigma attached to AIDS victims, to prostitutes and prostitution would deter prostitutes from registering themselves, as has already been shown by countries legalizing prostitution to control the spread of STDs.

Rather than legalize prostitution as a measure to control the spread of STDs and AIDS, the following measures need to be undertaken:

a) epidemiological studies: studies of risk factors exposing individuals and groups to infectious agents and diseases; monitoring of health and environmental factors; health surveillance programmes and investigation of seropositivity in prostitutes to get an accurate picture of seropositivity.

b) preventive educational programmes and motivation to high risk groups and the general populace to adopt safe sex practices. It is now widely accepted that the careful use of condoms reduces the risk of contracting the AIDS virus and other STDs.

c) use available infrastructure with additional inputs to strengthen research and training in family welfare planning, blood banking and safe hospital practices and lastly,

d) enforce screening of donors and good manufacturing practices for commercial concerns manufacturing blood products and blood- based diagnostic agents.

LEGALIZATION AND LICENSING TO PROVIDE FOR UNIONIZATION OF PROSTITUTES

The demand for legalization and licensing of prostitution has been raised, so as to allow for unionization of prostitutes against police harassment and for provision of welfare measures for prostitute women and their children. It is necessary to critically examine existing prostitutes' organizations and their demands, so as to determine the real interests that these organizations represent.

The Bharatiya Patita Udhar Sabha

The Bharatiya Patita Udhar Sabha, a Delhi-based Prostitutes' Rights Organization was founded in May 1984 by Khairati Lal Bhola, who claimed to be a social worker. The president of the organization in 1985 was reported to be Nimmibai, a big time brothel-keeper from G.B. Road, Delhi's main red-light area. She has been arrested for brothel-keeping several times and has several charges against her, under the Suppression of Immoral Traffic in Women and Girls Act 1956. (Subharwal Jyothi, 1985).[15] In March 1985, she was arrested for allegedly abducting a minor girl and forcing her into prostitution (Telegraph, 1985).[18] The General Secretary of the organization, Amina Bai, is also a brothel-keeper, with several charges pending against her (Sabharwal, Jyothi, 1985).I[15]

Protesting against police harassment, leaders of the organization claim that enormous amounts are paid to the police for each new girl inducted into the trade. The police also take hefty monthly 'haftas' and extort money from the pimps. The spokespeople of the Organization have therefore written to the Lok Sabha Speaker, Home Minister, Lieutenant Governor and Police Commissioner to curb police harassment of prostitutes.

Believing that prostitution is a necessary and inevitable social evil and is here to stay, the Organization demands legalization and licensing of prostitutes, a measure by which they also wish to monitor the health of prostitutes. "If the Government gives women licences and taxes them, then the eduction of their children (another demand), should be taken care of. We have already begun this opinion-building campaign', said Bhola. (Incidently, the organization secured a Supreme Court Judgement ruling that children of prostitutes be admitted into schools on the basis of the mother's name) (Sabharwal, Jyothi, 1985)[15]

The Asahaya Tirskrut Nari Sangh

The Asahaya Tirskrut Nari Sangh, another prostitutes rights organization was established four years ago in Kamathipura, Bombay's largest red-light area. At the time of its inception, it had 300 members, all of whom were brothel-keepers. The Sangh was floated primarily by the Indian Health Organization (IHO), a Bombay-based group of predominantly male doctors, whose president is Rukminibai Bansode, a formidable 'Madam' in Kamathipura. Bansode who owns at least three large brothels, is a known Congress-I supporter (Sadasivam, Bharathi; 1987).[16]

According to Dr. I.H. Gilada, General Secretary of the I.H.O. and spokesman for the Sangh, prostitution is a necessary and inevitable evil, necessary for the preservation of the family structure and the prevention of rape of women. Within this context, the Sangh has been demanding licensing of prostitution, registration of prostitutes, monitoring of prostitutes' health to curb the incidence of STDs and AIDS, for whose spread prostitutes are considered responsible, abolition of forced and child prostitution, curbs on police harassment of prostitutes, provision of creches and boarding schools for children of prostitutes. The Sangh also formed a Cooperative Credit Society to free prostitutes from the clutches of money lenders.

However, none of the Sangh's demands have been realized. The clinic for the treatment of STDs, through which the IHO made its first foray, was demolished in a Municipal Corporation drive. The Sangh's proposed construction of a new clinic is dependent on a grant from the Union Health Ministry. There is a sum of reportedly Rs. 1 lakh with the ministry (Sadasivam, Bharathi; 1987).[16]

Although the Co-operative Credit Society has been registered, its rules have not been framed and Rukminibai Bansode is totally ignorant of how to proceed further. She says an 'advisor' will tell them what to do (Sadasivam, Bharathi, 1987).[16]

The Sangh's pious plan to abolish forced and child prostitution has been a farce. The area is full of minor girls. The 14th lane in Kamathipura, where Bansode and other brothel-keepers own houses is no exception. After all, there is a high client demand for children in prostitution (Sadasivam, Bharathi) 1987).[16]

Social workers in the area maintain that organizations such as Asahaya Tirskrut Nari Sangh make it very difficult for them to function because they cut off their access to the women. According to Pratima Joshi, a city journalist and voluntary worker in the area, most women are too scared to say anything about Rukminibai, who has very close Congress-I connections. She maintains that the main difficulty of voluntary social work groups such as hers, is overcoming the political links of organizations of brothel owners like Rukminibai's, as voluntary groups have no backing of this sort (Sadasivam, Bharathi; 1987).[16]

Social workers also maintain that the IHO spokesman Gilada is well connected politically and with the press, and is using the issue of licensing and welfare of prostitutes for long term political gains. According to Joshi, Kamathipura has consistently voted Congress-I, the party to which all elected representatives from the area belong, and which has cultivated a few brothel-keepers to preserve the area as a "vote bank".

Prostitutes are cynical about the organization. They say that the few meetings have been mainly attended by brothel owners, while the common prostitute woman is ignorant of what is happening. Bansode refuses to let any of the Sangh members be interviewed by outsiders. Prostitutes say that the Organization has been formed to glorify the leaders and that Dr. Gilada is now desperately searching for cases of AIDS at Kamathipura (Sadasivam, Bharathi; 1987).[16]

The Pune Devadasi Sangatna

The Pune Devadasi Sangatna was established in 1981 in Budhwarpeth, Pune. The Organization is the brainchild of a well known trust in the area and an allegedly big time pimp.

It was initially formed with 11 members - 9 "gharwallis", 1 eunuch and 1 prostitute. It has an advisory committee which includes a member of the trust, the alleged pimp and a local cloth store owner. The spokeswoman for the Organization is Shalinitai Kurade, a brothel-keeper who owns four buildings and who says that she once attempted standing for corporation elections but withdrew because of threats from the opposition.

Asserting prostitution is a social necessity, the Organization demands that prostitution be given social and legal recognition and prostitutes be given licences to practice. It also demands curbs on police harassment, free health care to licensed prostitutes and bank loans to old prostitutes to set up small businesses.

The Sangatna has formed a co-operative credit society with funds from the Government and a local trust. An automobile dealer disburses low interest loans to prostitutes thereby curbing the exploitative practices of local moneylenders. The Chairman of the Society's Board of Directors, which consists of brothel owners, a eunuch and a prostitute, is Shalinitai Kurade. But an alleged pimp enjoys veto powers even over unanimous decisions of the Board. When asked how the co-operative survices, if it provides loans to poor prostitutes, Shalinitai admits that loans are only granted to those who have repaying capacity.

Analysis of Organizations

The profiles of these organizations provide analytical insights into the ideology, social base, leadership and demands raised, so as to determine who benefits from the organizations.

Ideology

The profiles quite clearly indicate the patriarchal base of the Organizations, believing as they do in the inevitability and necessity of the institution of prostitution and that prostitutes are the source of STDs and AIDS.

Social Base and Leadership

The Organizations have been formed on the initiative of external agents who are males and not common prostitutes. Though formal leadership is vested in female brothel keepers who constitute the predominant membership and are the exploitative core of the hierarchically structured sex industry, control and decision- making is done by the male initiators of the Organization.

The brothel-owners in the leadership reportedly have close links with political persons or parties. The latter view the prostitute population as an important vote bank, ensured by the iron-hand of the brothel-keeper. The brothel-owner receives his/her trade-offs in return. According to social workers in some of these areas, the press publicity glorifying the philanthropic work of the leadership, and the political connections of some of these individuals show their political interests in forming prostitute Organizations. Actually there is an absence of the work the leadership claim to be doing in the areas.

Demands

While demands like creche facilities and education for children of prostitutes are in the interests of the women and children, the other demands betray the interests of the common prostitute. The demand for legalization and licensing of prostitution is unacceptable at an ideological level, as it sanctions the patriarchal and exploitative basis of the institution of prostitution and gives brothel-keepers full freedom to induct more women and girls into the trade. The experience of countries that have legalized prostitution, (see later chapters) reveals that instead of benefitting prostitutes, this system of law has only served to regulate, control and discriminate against prostitutes. Brothel-owners by contrast seem to benefit from such a legal system.

The demand to abolish forced and child prostitution is a farce. The brothel-keeper leadership of these organizations is itself currently guilty of forcing women and children into prostitution and will continue to do so for profits.

While curbing police harassment of women in prostitution is beneficial to prostitute women, it also works in the interests of brothel-owners and pimps who pay large bribes to prevent punishment for trafficking in women and girls for prostitution, brothel-keeping and living off the earnings of prostitution.

The formation of co-operative credit societies to protect prostitutes from money lenders is also rubbish. Most women in prostitution take loans from the 'gharwalli' and not the money lenders, and are in constant debt to her, repaying both the principal amount and the interest. Secondly, the cooperative credit societies appear to be the brothel-owners' strategy of obtaining low interest loans, when needed, as admitted by one of them. Loans are only given to women with repaying capacity. This includes 'gharwallis' and a few women who have managed to save - but not most of the common prostitutes.

Separate hostel accommodation for children of prostitutes also works to the advantage of brothel-keepers who would rather not have children in the way during business hours. It also serves to ghettoise and reinforce the already existing stigma attached to these children.

Prostitute women must be decriminalized and enlisted to the same rights and benefits that any other citizen is entitled to; special welfare measures for prostitute women and children only reinforce segregation and stigmatization.

Conspicuous by their absence are demands that would adversely affect the profit and control exercised by brothel-keepers over women 'owned' by them. There is no hint of a fairwage-rate for prostitute women or the percentage of their earnings that brothel-keepers could keep, as the latter currently appropriate anything between half to all of a prostitutes' earnings. Similarly, there is no mention of hours of work for the women or limits on the number of clients that the women must entertain in these sex factories. Nor is there any code of ethics for brothel-owners and pimps. These organizations clearly represent vested interests in the name of the common prostitute and must be condemned.

Legalization in order to Segregate Prostitutes into Isolated areas to avoid Public Nuisance:

Such a step assumes that prostitution is a necessary and inevitable evil. It exposes the double standards of male morality which promotes and protects prostitution, sexual violence and the exploitation which would then occur behind closed doors.

Segregation of prostitutes would isolate, identify and label them and would force them to accept the status of 'public' woman. This would destroy their private identities. The prostitutes would be less able to escape.

Also, the social and geographical isolation of prostitutes would lead to greater exploitation of the women and there would be no law to help them.

Legalization because the sita has failed to suppress prostitution

To advocate legalization because the SIT Act has not accomplished its objective of suppressing immoral traffic in women and children, is horrendous. It fights shy of investigating the causes for the failure of the SIT Act and abdicates responsibility for bringing the brothel-hierarchy, corrupt police, and political patrons to book. It thus gives free reign to prostitution racketeers at a local and international level to replenish their brothels with new inmates. This will lead to a massive increase in the number of women and children exploited for the purposes of prostitution. There would not even be the minimum of law to fight prostitution racketeers if the occasion arose.

India thus sanctions the exploitation of women and children, legitimizes sexual violence and enslavement and actively participates in exploiting by supporting a patriarchal and dehumanizing institution like prostitution.

This is a blatant constitutional violation of human and fundamental rights.

References

1. Alexander, Priscilla (1987); "Prostitutes are being scapegoated for Heterosexual AIDS",Paper for the National Task Force on Prostitution; San Francisco, U.S.A., February.

2. Barry, Kathleen (1979) *Female Sexual Slavery*; Prentice Hall, Inc., Englewood Cliffs, New Jersey.

3. "Cases of AIDS in India: A Future Scenario"; (1988); Projected by Centre for AIDS Research and Control (CARC); *Bulletin of the Centre for AIDS Research and Control*; No. 3, September - October.

4. Davis, D.E.; (1971); *Physiological Factors in Aggressive Behaviour in Animal Aggression*; ed. Southwick Van Nostrand Runhold; New York.

5. D'Cunha, Jean (1984); "Voices in the Dark'; *Eve's Weekly;* 19th - 24th May.

6. Gough, Kathleen; (1984); "The War Against Women : Prostitution in Vietnam"; *Manushi*; Vol.4, March-April:

7. Interview with Shalinitai Kurade of : .. Devadasi Sangatana, Pune; 1987.

8. Interview with Shiraz Bulsara, Activist Kashtakari Sangatna (1986) Dahanu Taluka, Thane District.

9. Macmillan, Jackie (1976); "Rape and Prostitution"; *Victimology International Journal*; Vol.I; No. 3.

10. National Task Force on Prostitution (1986); Paper on "Health Issues for Prostitutes"; San Francisco, U.S.A.

11. Narayan, Uma (1981); "Feminism and Psychoanalysis"; Term Paper; Ph.D. Course Work, Department of Philosophy; I.I.T., Bombay.

12. Khorshed, Pavri; (1988);"Epidemiological Features of AIDS - A Global Public Health Problem"; *CARC CALLING* : Bulletin

of the Centre for AIDS Research; and Control; Vol I; May-June.

13. Khorshed, Parvi; (1988); "AIDS and You, An Indian Point of View"; *CARC CALLING*; Bulletin of the Centre for AIDS Research and Control; Vol.I; May-June.

14. Reynaud, Emmanuel; *Holy Virility: The Social Construction of Masculinity*; Pluto Press.

15. Sabharwal, Jyothi; (1985); "The Girls of G.B. Road"; *Sunday Observer*; 20th October.

16. Sadasivam Bharathi; (1987); "False Beacons in Kamathipura"; *Indian Post*; 22nd December.

18. *Telegraph*; (1985); "Prostitutes' Union Chief Arrested"; 21st March.

Chapter - 6: Demand for Legitimizing of Prostitution in the West: A Critique

Introduction

A comprehensive understanding of the debate on legalization of prostitution necessitates an examination of issues raised by western protagonists of decriminalization of prostitution. Distinguishing between legalization and decriminalization of prostitution, sections of western civil libertarians together with certain prostitutes' rights groups are raising the demand for the latter. According to them, while legalization permits the existence of prostitution in society, it institutionalizes state control over prostitutes in the form of compulsory health check-ups, zoning laws and the like, the breach of which carries with it penal measures against prostitutes. There is no regulation and control of brothel managements under this system.

The groups mentioned above define 'decriminalization of prostitution' as the complete removal of any sanctions against prostitutes. They recommend that (a) third party managers (that is, brothel owners/managers, pimps) be recognized as legitimate business men/women (b) their businesses be regulated only by business and labour law and not criminal law (c) third party managers must provide safe, healthy and non-exploitative conditions of work for prostitutes and (d) that pimping laws be repealed. The establishment of any regulations developed for third party management of prostitution business should be carried out by prostitution boards or commissions, the majority of whose members should be prostitutes (National Task Force on Prostitution (NTFP); NTFP Policies; U.S.A.; 1984-1986, pgs. 3 and 6).[13]

While the western rationale in defence of decriminalization of prostitution appears different from the demand for legalization raised in India, both positions support patriarchy and serve the interests of capital accumulation.

The western position of "decriminalizing of prostitution and regulating third parties according to standard business codes" is best exemplified in the Draft Statement on Prostitution and Feminism formulated by the International Committee for Prostitutes' Rights (I.C.P.R.), at the second International Congress on Prostitution, Human Rights and Feminism, held in Brussels in 1986.

The I.C.P.R. consists of prostitute and non-prostitute women, primarily from Europe and the U.S.A., working to uphold the 'rights of prostitutes'. In its Draft Statement, the I.C.P.R. states that, "until recently, the women's movement in most countries has not, or has only marginally, included prostitutes as spokeswomen and theorists. Historically, women's movements (for example socialist and communist movements) have opposed the institution of prostitution, while claiming to support prostitute women. However, prostitutes reject support that requires them to leave prostitution; they object to being treated as symbols of oppression and demand recognition as workers. Due to feminist hesitation or refusal to accept prostitution as legitimate work and to accept prostitutes as working women, the majority of prostitutes have not been identified as feminists; Nonetheless many prostitutes identify with feminist values such as independence, financial autonomy, sexual self-determination, personal strength and female bonding".

"During the last decade, some feminists began to reevaluate, the traditional anti-prostitution stance of their movement in the light of the actual experiences, opinions and needs of prostitute women. The ICPR can be considered a feminist organization in that it is committed to giving respect to all women, including the most invisible, isolate, degraded and/or idealized. The development of prostitution analyses strategies within women's movements which link the conditions of women in general and which do justice to the integrity of prostitute women are therefore important goals of the committee". (*Draft Statement on Prostitution and Feminism*; International Committee on Prostitutes' Rights; 1986; Pg. 1).[10]

It is ironical that while the ICPR begins by criticizing feminists and feminism, it uses the feminist idiom to indicate that it considers itself feminist. To lend credence to the above, it claims that prostitutes identify with feminist values like financial autonomy, sexual self-determination, independence and so on. Significant by its absence in this list of values is the feminist struggle against sexual objectification and commodification of sex and women's bodies. Or is this being used as part of 'sexual self-determination'? The ICPR by its legitimation of the institution of prostitution explicitly endorses the sexual objectification and commodification of women - the exploitative core of the institution of prostitution.

Secondly, while legitimizing prostitution as a valid form of work, partly because of its overwhelming desire to give a voice to the most isolated and degraded of women (by society), groups like the ICPR are consciously or unconsciously committing a serious error. They are succumbing to the traditional patriarchal idea of the individual in prostitution and the institution. By ending distinctions between the individual and the institution, the latter's so-called inevitability, assumptions and existence remain unchallenged. Wittingly or unwittingly, they thus accept the institution of prostitution, which is based on patriarchal assumptions namely,. (a) sex is a male right (b) sex and women's bodies are commodities to be bought and sold in prostitution (Ed. by Barry, Kathleen; Bunch, Charlotte; Castley, Shirley; 1983; p. 26).[4]

Further, the line of distinction that organizations like the ICPR draw between legalization and decriminalization of prostitution is very thin. Both systems of law unequivocally endorse the institution of prostitution and third party management of prostitution - a postition that is blatantly reflective of 'patriarchal' and 'capital accumulation' interests.

The concerned groups could well have made out a case for completely decriminalizing the prostitute and demanding state provision of health facilities (not compulsory health checks), child-care and other welfare facilities for her, while still retaining penal provisions for brothel managers and pimps. Citizens Committees which include prostitutes or ex-prostitutes could act as overseeing and regulating bodies. Failure to demand these indicates that 'decriminalization of prostitution' is a demand that largely reflects "vested and exploitative interests" in the hierarchically structured sex industry.

Lastly, a brothel business bases itself on profit and its accumulation through the exploitation and commodification of women's bodies. Commodification of sex and women's bodies is itself an exploitative condition, rendering it farcical to state that brothels should provide non-exploitative conditions of work. It is also naive to believe that brothel managements will lower their profits to provide welfare facilities for prostitutes.

Moreover, it is far-fetched to believe that forced prostitution will stop, while brothels are allowed to flourish legally. This is especially so for those countries where forced prostitution has reached staggering proportions and the increasing market demand for children and minors for prostitution give brothel managements colossal profits.

Finally, while considering the representation of prostitutes on Citizens Committees that are supposed to regulate third party management one must identify which category of women in the hierarchically stratified sex industry finds representation on these boards. It will usually be the articulate and politically active initiators of the demand for decriminalization of prostitution that find places on these boards. The women are largely brothel keepers and elite call girls masquerading under the label of prostitute. With the possible inclusion of brothel-attached or street prostitutes on such committees, one can well imagine the manner in which third party managements are regulated, as their interests will, in the main, coincide with those of the prostitute members of the committees.

Against this backdrop, it is therefore necessary to examine each of the explicit reasons in favour of 'decriminalization of prostitution', advanced by western groups similar in thinking to the ICPR., in order to assess the desirability and feasibility of each measure.

The following are their reasons for validating the institution of prostitution:

(a) Prostitution is often a woman's occupational choice.

(b) It affords a woman freedom, financial autonomy and sexual- self determination.

(c) If a woman can sell her mental and manual skills, which are exploited, there is nothing wrong in commercializing her sexual skills in prostitution, which is only another form of woman's work.

(d) Prostitution is related to the exploitation of all women, looked upon as sex objects. A prostitute at least sells her sex and does not give it away for free as married women do.

(e) Decriminalizing prostitution would allow for unionization of prostitutes against brothel managers, pimps and the police. It would also enable prostitutes to press for welfare measures like health care, child care and educational facilities for their children, social security for themselves and the like.

(f) Decriminalization of prostitution would wipe out the stigma of immorality and criminality attached to prostitutes and prostitution.

Let us examine each of these arguments.

OCCUPATIONAL CHOICE

According to ICPR, "The lack of educational and employment opportunities for women throughout the world has been well documented. Occupational choice for men and women oppressed by class and race prejudice, is usually a choice between different subordinate positions. Once employed, women are often stigmatized and harassed. Furthermore, they are commonly paid according to their gender, rather than their worth. Female accessibility to jobs traditionally reserved for women is a necessary condition for true occupational choice. Those conditions entail an elimination of the sexual division of labour. Prostitution is a traditionally female occupation. Some prostitutes report job satisfaction, others job repulsion; some consciously choose prostitution as the best alternative open to them; others are compelled to go into prostitution through male force or deceit. Many prostitutes abhor the conditions of work and the social stigma attached to their work, but not the work itself. The ICPR therefore affirms the right of women to the full range of education and employment alternatives and due respect and compensation in every occupation, including prostitution." (Draft Statement on Prostitution and Feminism; International Committee for Prostitutes' Rights; 1986; Pg. 2).[10]

Prostitution as an occupational choice implied free choice. But the magnitude of forced prostitution is particularly high in developing countries. About 70%-80% of the women who work as prostitutes in India are forced into the life because of massive poverty and paucity of occupations open to women (Alexander,

Priscilla; 1987; Pg.11).[1a]

Trafficking in Women and Girls for Prostitution in India

Interstate Traffic in women and girls for prostitution in India continues unabated. Organized trafficking networks procures women and girls from the States of Andhra Pradesh, Karnataka, Kerala, Tamil Nadu, West Bengal, Uttar Pradesh, Goa and Nepal and the Union territory of Delhi for sale in the Bombay flesh market. Similarly, the primary procurement centres for the Delhi flesh market are Andhra Pradesh, Bihar, Karnataka, Madhya Pradesh, Maharashtra, Rajasthan, Tamil Nadu, Uttar Pradesh and Nepal. Women and girls procured from West Bengal, Assam and Sikkism are also auctioned at Biskoner, Domarigang, Pachparva and Itva Bazaar of Basti for supply to metropolitan flesh markets in Delhi, Agra, Kanpur, Varanasi and Lucknow (Sr. Rozario, Rita; 1988).[21]

In Uttar Pradesh over 10,000 children below 16 years of age are kidnapped or lured from rural areas to meet market demand. Uttar Pradesh has emerged as a major centre for export of children to other parts of the country, giving each exporter anything from Rs. 1,000 to 2,000 a child. The entire traffic is coordinated from Kanpur and the girls are sold in states like Rajasthan, Andhra Pradesh, Maharashtra and Punjab. (News items; *The Hindu*;1988).[15]

*Methods of Forcible Recruitment:*The principal methods of procurement for and recruitment into prostitution in these markets are abduction, kidnapping, deception, the false promise of good jobs, rape and sale into prostitution, fake marriage contracts and sale by parents due to poverty (Sr. Rozario, Rita; 1988).[21]

Forced Prostitution in Other South East Asian Countries

Similar situations prevail in other south east Asian countries where wars and economic crises, which have rsulted from their development strategies, have driven many women into prostitution. South of Manila in the Philippines, some 30,000 poor women went into the prostitution industry serving American bases at Subic Bay.

Thailand is another south east Asian country where the modern instutionalization of prostitution originating in U.S. bases and army 'rest and recreation' trips has grown rapidly into a sex tourism industry centred in Bangkok. Thailand now has a population of some 7,00,000 prostitutes, 20% of whom are below 14 years of age. In depressed economic conditions, many Thai rural parents are said to have been tempted with offers of 250 to 500 for their virginal daughters. Peasants and aboriginal families from northern Thai districts, now routinely send their daughters, some as young as 9 or 10 years, to work as prostitutes or child labourers in Bangkok establishments (Dr.Ong.A;1984).[17]

Traffic in Women and Girls from South East Asia to Europe

The poverty of Third World countries makes them rich hunting grounds for international traffic in poor black and south east Asian women for prostitution. Fake marriage contracts, mail order brides, and promise of lucrative jobs are means of procuring and trafficking in south east Asian women for prostitution. It is documented that agents deliver Thai girls for prostitution to German, Dutch or Danish clients for around 2,000 Dutch guilders. This has led to the establishment of a slave market in Frankfurt where an "employer" can hire a Thai woman for prostitution for a monthly fee of 5,000 German marks plus a 3,000 mark deposit. Earnings reach approximately 50,000 marks per quarter. If a Thai woman turns out to be unsatisfactory, she can be replaced with another.

According to the Thai embassy in Bonn, 2,000 Thai women are imported into the Federal Republic of Germany every year. In addition to renting them, there is the possibility of buying them outright for 20,000 marks per woman. (Sex Tourism in Thailand: the article appeared in Dutch in *Onze Wereld* in March 1979; available from Novib, Netherlands, translated by ISIS).[22]

This indicates that the bulk of prostitution in the developing countries is forced prostitution.

Forced Prostitution in the West

The above is not meant to absolve the west from the phenomenon of forced prostitution. In technologically developed western countries where most women are at least functionally literate and there is a significant number of occupational choices, about 10% of women who work as prostitutes are coerced into prostitution by third parties through a combination of trickery and violence. This figure appears to be relatively constant in the U.S., as reflected in studies done at the turn of the century and the current estimates of COYOTE (Prostitutes rights group) and some other prostitutes' rights organizations (Rosen, Ruth; 1982).[20] To gloss over this reality and overplay free choice, even in the west there is a distortion of the western reality with respect to prostitution.

Given the structural roots of prostitution, the so-called 'free' occupational choice dictated by a complex of prior exploitative and discriminatory circumstances, is no choice at all. In fact several Asian prostitutes demand the choice of not having to work as prostitutes at all. (Private conversations with Asian Prostitutes at the Brussels Congress on Prostitution and Feminism; Oct. 1-4; 1986).[19]

*Ideological problems with prostitution as an Occupational Choice:*Further, the ICPR's stance on occupational choice is glaringly contradictory. While admitting the exploitation of women in employment and making pious claims for genuine occupational choice not dictated by class, gender or race prejudices and oppression, they affirm the right to choose prostitution as an occupation. This only amounts to legitimizing prostitution as a traditional female occupation and the exploitation and sexual commodification that goes with it - an easy solution; a position that nullifies their claims for elimination of sexual division of labour and a dogged struggle for increase in employment opportunities for women in general.

Ironically, though the ICPR makes a mention of forced prostitution and repulsion that some prostitutes feel towards their profession, it almost seems to rationalize this by stating that many prostitutes abhor the conditions and social stigma attached to the work but not the work itself. Not only is this hairsplitting, but an exhibition of callous disregard for the specific oppression and alienation that women experience in prostitution.

PROSTITUTION ALLOWS A WOMAN FREEDOM, FINANCIAL AUTONOMY AND THE RIGHT TO SEXUAL SELF-DETERMINATION

Freedom

This is a myth. The experience of women in prostitution reveals it to be one of the most alienated forms of labour.

From the instant a woman is procured for prostitution, she is seasoned. Practices like changing the victim's name, factors like distance and separation from home, language barriers, denial of money to a woman for travel or otherwise, as well as more brutal methods like verbal abuse, isolation in a room, starvation, drugging, beatings, burns with cigarette or beedi butts, knifing, rape and sodomy are used to break the woman's will and ego; separate her from her previous life and create a new environment with new values, morals, attitudes and relationships to replace the old. Seasoning creates perfect subservience to the brothel management and pimps and serves as an effective method of putting and bonding a woman in prostitution (Barry, Kathleen; 1979).[3]

Women have been driven to suicide or have been murdered for refusing to trade their bodies (Sr. Rozario, Rita, 1988).[21]

For those women who have been forced into prostitution, the victim is first confronted by the immediate terror of kidnap, deceit and abuse. 'She tries to make sense of what is happening and figure out a means of escape but the external points of reference for maintaining her identity are cut off'. She finds she cannot escape (Barry, Kathleen;1979).[3] She is physically confined and concealed, a strict vigil is maintained over her interactions and physical movements. She is threatened with physical and mental torture or even death if she tries to escape (D'Cunha, Jean; 1984).[6]

The following experiences bear evidence of this; 13 year old Tulasa was kidnapped by one Kancha from her village in Thankut in the Bagmati district near the Nepalese capital, Kathmandu. Kancha brought her to Bombay and kept her under lock and key in a house for 2 days, before he sold her to a Nepalese brothel keeper in Grant Road, Bombay. Tulasa was subsequently resold to two other brothel keepers. The girl complained that though the older prostitutes were allowed by the brothel keeper to go out and see films, she was confined to the brothel premises. This was because the 'gharwalli' was afraid she would escape or be detected by the police. On the occasions when Tulasa was sent out with clients to hotels, an older prostitute always escorted her (*Probe India*; 1983).[25]

Confinement is a regular practice especially for minors or

women freshly induced into the profession. A 'gharwalli' only allows the women out on their own when they are seasoned, are much older, their earning potential has decreased or she has recovered the initial amount spent to purchase the woman or girl.

In another case, Champa, a prostitute from Kamatipura, Bombay, escaped with a client and married him. She was hunted down and discovered one and a half years later by her brothel keepers at her residence in Dombivili, Bombay. Champa was brutally murdered by them, bundled into a sack and thrown outside the City Light Market, Mahim (Slide Show and discussion with Forensic expert Pritam Phatnani).[24]

Control by Pimps

Another well-entrenched phenomenon in prostitution is pimping (poncing). According to a study of British prostitutes by Eileen Mcleod, the majority of British prostitutes have ponces; they are either heavy ponces who employ violence and intimidation and appropriate virtually all a woman's money or men who simply live off what the woman earns (Mcleod, Eileen; 1982).[12]

Heavy poncing is shockingly brutal and exploitative. It seems to be so widespread and well established that it has become an integral part of contemporary prostitution. The ponce characteristically moves from sweet talk to violence while bringing the woman under his control. This is evidenced in the following experience.

"At first sight, its kind of mental. They make you feel inadequate - that you can't do anything, that you can't help them in any sort of way. If they didn't have you, they'd have money or they'd be better off. You sort of want to do something to help them. They're only with you because they feel sorry for you. You'll find most ponces work around the same sort of theme. Then when you start hustling and making the money, they start beating you. It's not logical but that's the way it happens. You think that if I make so much tonight that'll please him. Then the money tends to go up. You start with $10 a night and then after six months you're still getting beaten and you're still trying to make more money. Most of them take all the money except for a fiver for Durex and food. Most ponces don't live with a girl."

Violence is used to discipline the women, when they hand over to pimps less than what they regard as their due. 'This may concern his cut of the earnings from prostitution but it could well be for showing insufficient respect to him by being cheeky at a party or daring to go out with another man'. Such a situation is compounded by women accepting their position as victims of violence.

Ironically, despite all this, women often relate to their ponces as boy friends, cohabitees or husbands, simply 'sharing the proceeds of prostitution on egalitarian basis'. Some women also take pride in their ponces and regard their attractive physical appearances and material possessions as a tribute to their earning power (Mcleod, Eileen; 1982).[12]

Such a complex relationship can be explained by several factors. The initial attraction of a ponce appears to lie in the fact that a prostitute woman like any other traditional woman tends to feel incomplete without a man, as the pivot of her emotitonal life (Mcleod, Eileen; 1982).[12] Also, because prostitutes can be penalized by law, they are especially vulnerable to being attracted to ponces. 'Prostitution is demanding because of the legal harassment and the risks involved. Support from 'straight' men is difficult to obtain or felt to be so, because such men are unlikely to accept prostitutes because of the stigma attached to prostitutes and prostitution. Alternatively, if the man has been 'straight' before, he may become attracted to living off a woman's earnings once he discovers she is a prostitute.

"In a situation where prostitutes are turning to men for emotional security, and because poncing exists on such an all pervasive scale, it is very likely that prostitutes will be sucked in" (Mcleod, Eileen; 1982).[12]

Once the prostitute and pimp are established, it is difficult to escape. There are practical problems of alternáte accommodation. The authorities in the form of the police may be more interested in intervening where violence is coming from a pimp because of securing a conviction for living off immoral earnings.

However, it requires a lot of courage after perhaps years of intimidation to approach the police. There is the further anxiety of the repercussions, when the man emerges from prison. And friends could make life unpleasant for someone who has turned in one of their lot to the police. Love for the pimp also seems to place prostitutes in a difficult position. Because they love the man, they forgive him or don't want to leave him or want to return to him, despite his physical and psychological brutality (Mcleod, Eileen; 1982).[12]

The above-mentioned torture or threats of it, coupled with female socialization of acceptance and submission, compel women to succumb.

The forced identification with the brothel management and the subjection to the control of ponces are two of the worst forms of depersonalization, as it means a total loss of freedom. The woman begins to live only for the present realising she has no control over her economic, emotional, physical and sexual life (Barry, Kathleen; 1979).[3]

Other curbs on freedom:

There are other curbs on the freedom and violation of human rights of prostitute women. Women known to be prostitutes or 'sex workers' are regularly denied custody of their children in many countries. The assumption that prostitute women are less responsible, loving or deserving than other women is a denial of human rights and human dignity. The laws and attitudes which punish sexually stigmatized women function to punish their children as well by stigmatizing them and by denying them their mothers. (Draft Statement on Prostitution and Feminism; International Committee for Prostitutes Rights; 1986).[10]

Restrictions on the business hours and activity spaces of prostitutes, stamping their passports to indicate prostitution districts in which they operate, registering, photographing and finger printing prostitute women are means used to identify a prostitute publicly. These measures are misused by authorities to harass prostitutes and result in impeding their social mobility. (Private discussions with prostitutes at the Brussels Congress; 1986).[19]

Financial Autonomy

The ICPR Draft Statement states that, "financial autonomy is basic to female survival, self-determination, self-respect and self-development. Unlike men, women are often scorned and/or pitied for making life choices primarily in the interest of earning money. True financial independece includes the means to earn money and the freedom to spend it as·one needs or desires. Such means are rarely available to women, even with compromise and struggle. The majority of women are financially dependent on men because of class, culture, race, education, etc. Females compromise and struggle are traditionally considered reflections of immorality and/or misfortune rather than of responsibility, intelligence and courage. The financial initiative of prositutes is stigmatized and/or criminalized as a warning to women in general against such sexually explicit strategies for financial independence. Nonetheless, 'being sexually attractive', and 'catching a good man', are traditional female strategies for survival, stragegies which may provide financial sustenance but rarely financial independence. All women, including prostitutes, are entitled to the same commercial rights as other citizens in any given society. The ICPR affirms the right of women to "financial initiative and financial gain, including the right to commercialize sexual service or sexual illusion, such as erotic media, and to save and spend their earnings according to their needs and priorities". (Draft Statement on Prostitution and Feminism; International Committee for Prostitutes Rights; 1986).[10]

Factors determining earnings: Economically, however, the trade is unpredictable and fluctuating. Earnings depend on (a) demand (b) competition in the supply of women (c) age, physical appearance and health status of a prostitute and (d) relationship with the brothel-keeper and the rest of the hierarchy.

Dependence on client's purchasing power (male purchasing power): Economically, prostitutes are under the control of men which has various restrictive and negative consequences. Ironically women may equalise their spending power with men's by becoming prostitutes but they are dependent on male clients, in order to be so. Clients' spending power is in turn related to general market forces. The decisive influence of these factors on the prostitution trade is demonstrated by the way in which recession and regional, seasonal and daily variations are reflected in the volume of business prostitutes do. Localized activities can also depress trade - notably police purges, or influx of young girls into a particular area, often undercutting as they go. Regional price variations also reflect the state of customer purshasing power' (Mcleod; 1982).[12] It is also a common practice for women to move their work from one place to another, often to evade police attention. But the supply of clients sill have to make it a worthwhile proposition (Mcleod, Eileen; 1982).[12]

The volume of business also depends on client availability in a certain place at a certain time. Work, leisure and family life patterns largely determine this. The slackest time of the year in Britan is during summer when men are away on holiday with their wives and children. During the day there are also peak and quiet times (Mcleod; 1982).[12]

Most prostitutes have certain exceptional customers - "the regulars", with whom friendly relations may develop. The degree of friendship that may be involved can blur the commercial nature of the contract to a certain extent. However, descriptions of what happens reveals the degree to which prostitutes are as reliant on these clients' ability to pay - if not more so - as on the spending power of the more fleeting trade.

For example, Betty said, "I've had a couple of regulars for the last two years, a travelling salesman who'd come and sit and play with the baby and have tea and I never asked for anything. One way of keeping a regular client is if you don't push him for anything unless you're really desperate. He used to come and take me and the kids out to zoos and for days out" (Mcleod; 1982).[12]

Independent streetwalkers are often in an even more precarious and dependent situation, with clients often refusing to pay them.

Lack of control over earnings and expenditure: The above apart, a prostitute rarely has control over the money she earns and the manner in which she would like to spend it. Nearly half to three-fourths of the earnings of brothel-attached prostitutes in Bombay City are appropriated by the brothel- keeper, leaving the women penniless and in a perpetual state of debt(D'Cunha,Jean; 1984).[6] The same is true of individual prostitutes and street walkers who have pimps. Although it is the women who earn the money and the pimps who are financially dependent on them, ponces take away virtually all the women's money and simply live off what she earns. Such control of prostitutes by pimps is not just the result of the individual weakness of the women but the product of the subordinate position of women in general - exacerbated by their criminal status.

To sum up, therefore, not only is a prostitute dependent for her earnings on males, but control over her earnings also rests with brothel managers or male pimps. A prostitute thus rarely enjoys financial autonomy.

Ideological Contradictions: Apart from this, it is a strange contradiction that while the ICPR advocates elimination of sexual division of labour in society and sex stereotypes, it affirms the right of prostitutes to use traditional female strategies like 'being sexually attractive' and 'catching a good man' for financial initiative and gain, including the right to commercialize sex services in prostitution.

Sexual Self-Determination

According to the ICPR Draft Statement, "the right to sexual self- determination includes women's right to set the terms of their own sexuality, including the choice of partners, behaviour and outcomes such as pregnancy, pleasure or financial gain. Sexual self determination includes the right to refuse and initiate sex, as well as the right to use birth control (including abortion), the right to have lesbian sex, sex across lines of colour or class, sadomasochistic sex and the right to offer sex for money. Those possibly self-determining acts have been stigmatized or punished by custom or law. No one has to act out a sexual desire that includes another party unless that party agrees under conditions of total free will. The feminist task is to nurture self-determination both by increasing women's sexual consciousness and courage and also by demanding conditions of safety and choice. The ICPR affirms the right of all women to determine their own sexual behaviour, including commercial exchange, without stigmatization or punishment" (Draft Statement on Prostitution and Feminism; International Committee for Prostitutes' Rights; 1986).[10]

The truth of the matter, however, is that gender subordination in the sex industry is at its very worst. In the case of prostitutes, both their labour and sexuality is controlled. Their labour is considered a human resource and their sexuality a natural resource from which men of all classes can appropriate sexual pleasure (Werlhof, Claudia; 1980).[28]

This is particularly true and more crassly obvious for prostitutes attached to brothels, bars, sex clubs and the like and is evident in their lack of control over their choice of clients, pace of work, price fixation, form of sexual activity, sex practices and the like.

Control over choice of clients and pace of work

Once in the trade, these women rarely have control over the choice of clients or the pace of work. The prostitute becomes the shared property of any male who can pay a price for sex and her body.

Asha who is attached to a brothel in Budhwarpeth, a red light area in Pune City, (India) says, "The clients either state their preference for a woman or are directed by the 'gharwalli' to those among us who are free. I have to entertain any client at any time of the day, regardless of whether he is ugly, stinking, diseased or drunk". Failure to do so, incurs verbal or physical abuse from the brothel-keeper (D'Cunha, Jean; 1984).[6]

In one of the lowest grade massage parlours in one of Bangkok's business streets, the women sit in dimly lit glass cages, while clients pick the women by numbers pinned on their blouses and pay the appropriate fee at the counter (Phongpaichit; 1981).[18]

According to a German prostitute working in a sex club in Hamburg, it is the client who selects the women from behind a glass door. Refusing a client would mean being fired by the Club Manager (Private discussions with Prostitutes at the Brussels Congress; 1986).[19]

Also, brothels often turn out to be sex factories with the women having no control over the number of clients they must entertain. In the Maisons D'Abbattage (cage brothels in the Northern African Quarter of Paris), 6 to 7 girls entertain 80 to 120 clients every night and up to 150 clients on holidays (Barry, Kathleen; 1979).[3]

Interviews with cage brothel prostitutes in Pune reveal that they entertain every day at the will of the brothel keeper. The physical or mental state of these women is of no consequence. They are often forced to take clients even during menstruation or pregnancy. Those among them who have contracted STDs or Pelvic Inflammatory Diseases (PIDS) find their work very painful (D'Cunha, Jean; 1985).[7]

Failure to succumb to the dictates of the brothel-keeper meets with verbal and physical abuse and mental torture, as borne out by the following incident. The Colaba (Bombay) police recovered the body of a 28-year-old prostitute, Laxmibai, who was done to death and was being disposed of with the help of six coolies at Chandanwadi Crematorium, Marine Lines (Bombay). According to the police, the brothel-keeper Vijay Shankar and his lover Sulochana assaulted Laxmibai with a wooden plank and wire the whole night for showing negligence to her "professional duties". The woman vomitted blood and collapsed. Failure to obtain a natural death certificate from a medical practitioner led them to hire coolies to dispose of the body (News Item; *Daily*; India; 1983).[14]

Price fixation

Likewise, prostitutes often have no control over price setting. In Bombay brothels, rates are fixed by the brothel-keeper on the basis of age, physical appearance and health status of the prostitute, client status, form of sexual activity and market forces (D'Cunha, Jean; 1984).[6]

Further, as mentioned earlier, brothel keepers forcibly appropriate nearly half to three-fourths of a prostitutes' earnings. According to the V.P. Road Police Station, a 25-year-old prostitute,Ratna Jagtap of Falkland Road was kicked in the abdomen and kidneys for not parting with Rs. 400, which the brothel keeper Sulochana Nair extorted weekly from her. The woman collapsed and died on the spot (News Item; *Indian Express*;India; 1985).[16]

Women in low class massage parlours in Bangkok, such as the one mentioned earlier, are divided into the pretty - who cost $ 3 an hour and the plain - who earn $ 2 an hour. The women receive between one quarter and one half of this fee, depending on their status. The lower rate goes to the bonded women, brought to the place by a recruiting agent, who has usually advanced money to their parents and requires them to work off the debt (Phongpaichit, Pasuk; 1981).[18]

Price fixation by street prostitutes

The situation is not too different for a street prostitute. Conditions of economic depravity, fierce competition and lack of protection, especially in the case of independent street prostitutes may result in a total loss of sexual self determination. Janabai Avade, an independent street walker who operates in Pune City, has no choice over whom and how many clients to accept. Her only concern is her next meal. There are days on which she has earned only 50 paise and days on which she has earned nothing. She has been gang-raped by clients who have refused to pay her (D'Cunha,Jean; 1984).[6] Gauri, an independent street prostitute in the Kolhapur districtr, Maharashtra, was kidnapped by four men while she was soliciting. They drove off with her in a car to a bungalow outside the town where they sexually assaulted her for 3 days. Then, they knifed her and threw her into a *nullah*. The water revived her and she slowly walked back to Junapur (Barse, Sheela; 1982).[5]

Price fixing is carried out among street prostitutes working the same area, by means of informal discussion and arrangements. The women are able to quote the standard rates for various forms of sexual intercourse in their work setting or local area. But given the individual nature of work, it is impossible for women to be absolutely certain of what other women actually are charging, but when undercutting comes to light, the deviants are warned off or chased off (Mcleod; 1982).[12]

Lack of control over kind of sexual activity demanded

Further, the service provided in prostitution is not traditional sex, but kinky, perverted, violent sex which men cannot or choose not to fulfill with a wife or girlfriend. Some forms of perverted sexual activity demanded by clients are: the client dressing in women's or children's clothes, domination i.e., the prostitute exerting various forms of psychological or physical control over the client, including lashing him and drawing out blood, the client dominating the prostitute, anal or oral sex, involving another woman in intercourse, being urinated or defecated upon (Mcleod, Eileen; 1982).[12]

Two extensive American studies of prostitutes' clients undertaken by C. Winnick and M.L. Stein in 1962 and 1974 respectively, document the desire for being dominated by the prostitute and the obsession with dressing up in female attire, as two of the most important demands by clients. The studies concluded that these demands were an expression of the need to escape from the socially prescribed stereotype of male aggressiveness and display of male sexual prowess (Mcleod, Eileen; 1982)[12]

Non-compliance with these forms of sexual activity may lead to violent physical abuse by clients or brothel keepers. The well documented case of a 36-year old Bombay-based call girl Marilyn Montgomery bears evidence of this. Montgomery, who refused to comply with her Yugoslavian client's demand for anal sex was flung down by him, from the sixth floor of the Yugoslavian Embassy building in Colaba, Bombay City. She died instantaneously (Slides and discussion with forensic expert Pritam Phatnani).[24]

Also, high demand for particular forms of sexual activity may leave a prostitute little option but to succumb to client demand. German prostitutes complain that the degree of sex consumerism in Germany has reached such a perverted pitch, that German males demand newer forms of sex and frequently new women - 'exotic' black or Asian women to satiate their demands. Most of these women being bonded submit to the increasing local male demand for sadomasochism, (SM), which is now replacing 'straight' sex. Several German prostitutes have to submit to SM, in the face of such changes in market conditions (Private conversations with German prostitutes at the Brussels Congress; 1986).[19]

Criminalization of Prostitutes

Sexual violence and other forms of abuse by pimps, clients and the police: A prostitute is denied the right to set the terms of encounter in the U.S.A., as the law states that the contract is illegal. Consequently in 1983, there were 1,22,000 prostitution arrests in the States, 71% of whom were prostitute women. Clients on the other hand are hardly ever arrested. Prostitutes have between 1 to 15 clients a day, with more clients on the streets, where 85- 90% of prostitute arrests occur. Also, while prostitutes in the U.S. work on an average of 4 years, the client may continue going to a prostitute throughout his life. In spite of this, courts uphold a discriminatory enforcement of laws on the ground that the prostitute is a habitual criminal (Alexander, Priscilla; 1986).[1]

The situation in India is no different for prostitute women. As discussed in Chapter III, prostitution per se is not illegal in India, but the Indian law has clauses penalizing a prostitute for practice of prostitution in a public place and soliciting for prostitution. By contrast there are no penal provisions for the client under the Act. Implementation of the Act for the years

1980-1986 in the city of Bombay reveals that arrests and convictions of prostitutes far outweigh those of prostitution racketeers - brothel keepers, pimps, procurers, landlords renting premises for prostitution (D'Cunha, Jean; 1986).[8]

The criminal status of prostitutes and their powerlessness, the sex-linked nature of their activities and the stigmatization and lack of public support to them all contribute to the vulnerability of prostitute women. The danger to prostitutes in the form of violent sexual and other forms of abuse comes not only from pimps but clients and the police as well.

Rape of Prostitutes and Acquittal of Rapists: According to a study on Street Prostitutes and Sexual Assault by Mimi Silbert of Delancey Street Foundation in San Francisco, 70% of the women interviewed are raped on the job or forced to go beyond the terms of the contract with the client. According to Silbert, those who had been raped, had been victimized on an average of 8-10 times a year. Only 7% had sought any kind of help and only 4% had reported any of the rapes to the police (Silbert, Mimi; 1981).[21]

The prevailing sexist belief that because of the nature of their work, prostitutes cannot be raped; that if a woman or prostitute woman has agreed to one sex act, she has no right to refuse any other) and so long as women trading sex services are arrested and jailed they have no right to set the terms for sex encounters. This makes prostitutes vulnerable to men who assume they can act out their misogyny with impunity.

'The woman is a prostitute', has thus become a standard defence for rape, as borne out by the following incidents. In 1986, a Judge in Pasadena, California, dismissed a rape charge because the survivor was a prostitute. He said, "A whore is a whore is a whore", and that he was not going to "enforce an illegal contract". The rapist in this case was an employee of the South Gate Police Department who had coerced sex from a woman in jail. He had brutally raped and sodomized a prostitute woman because he was 'dissatisfied with the oral sex he had contracted for' (Alexander, Priscilla; 1986).[1]

In the same yar a district attorney in Fresno, California, dropped all but three of thirty-two charges of forcible sex crimes against a man, alleged with raping 6 women, because at least four of the women he raped were prostitutes (Alexander,

Priscilla; 1987)[1a]

Prostitute women are thus denied the right to say 'yes' to prostitution when they are arrested; they are denied the right to say 'no' when they are blamed for being raped.

So long as men can rape and kill with little fear of retribution, all women, let alone prostitute women, are unsafe.

Murder of Prostitutes: Murder is another serious problem for prostitutes, particularly since serial murders are rarely investigated thoroughly by the police until at least ten or more women have been killed or the killer emboldened by his "success", begins to kill "square" or "innocent" women.

In New York city alone, in 1975, police statistics documented, 71 prostitution homicides, 54 of which were committed by pimps and clients. This figure, however, is extremely conservative.

In late 1977-78, a Los Angeles strangler carried out brutal rape-murders. Most of his victims were prostitutes. In the same period many street-walkers in Northern England were victims of a ripper's mutilation and murder (Barry, Kathleen; 1979)[3]

In Marin County, California, Leslie Arthur Byrd, a resident Vice- President of a Bank, was convicted of second degree murder of a prostitute woman Cynthia Engstrom. Byrd had hired the woman for $ 500 to allow him to bind her before sex. He then drowned her in a bath tub and dumped her body in a driveway. When arrested he claimed it was an accident. The police at first believed him and said they were not pressing charges, but with the help of COYOTE, a prostitutes' rights group, they were able to interrogate several prostitutes who knew both the killer and the victim. These women testified that many of them had also been similarly hired by the same man for binding before sex and that he verbalized his fantasy of killing prostitute women during sex.

The Jury in this case believed the women, and convicted Byrd of second degree murder. Byrd could have become a serial murderer (Alexander, Priscilla; 1986).[1]

In Seattle, Washington, the Green River killer killed between 40 - 80 women, most of whom were prostitutes (Alexander, Priscilla; 1986).[1]

Police Harassment of Prostitutes: The 'custodians of law' are no less guilty of abuse of prostitute women. The police are largely negligent when it comes to people who are perceived as powerless, and that includes prostitutes. As prostitutes are ostracized by society, the police feel free to rough up prostitutes they arrest with physical abuse ranging from tightly handcuffed hands, sex demands before or during arrest, to beatings and kickings. Verbal abuse ranges from specific insults about the prostitute's body, taunts about how the police officer could get a free 'blow job' with no one the wiser, to suggestions that the prostitute give the 'higher ups' a blow job to get out of jail. Few prostitutes file complaints, unfortunately, feeling they have no choice but to accept this abuse as part of the job and so the few accounts that surface must be seen to be symptoms of a much larger problem (Alexander, Priscilla; 1987).[1a]

*Use of Prophylactics and the Right to Decide Pregnancy and Abortion:*While prostitutes in the West, the U.S. in particular, now insist on condom usage to protect their own health and that of their clients, the situation is different in other countries. Indian clients do not use condoms, nor do brothel keepers insist that they do (D'Cunha, Jean; 1985).[7] The situation is similar in Central Africa, in part because of the cost, in part for cultural reasons not the least of which is the impact of the Catholic Church (Priscilla, Alexander; 1987).[2]

In Germany males prefer not to use condoms. Any insistence by prostitutes on condom usage leads to a drop in prices. German prostitutes are thus often unable to insist on males using condoms (Private discussions with German prostitutes at the Brussels Congress; 1986).[19]

Interviews with prostitutes in Kamatipura, a red-light area in Bombay, revealed that 'gharwallis' often decide whether or not a prostitute should continue with her pregnancy. If the 'gharwalli' herself has no children; if she feels that the prostitute can bear the expenses for the child or that the pregnancy will not significantly alter the prostitute's earning power and hence the brothel keepers profits; if she perceives the children as a source of cheap labour or has designs to induce them into the trade, she does not mind the women bearing children. There have been instances of women who got pregnant soon after their induction into the profession, the news of which was not well received by the 'gharwalli', who saw the pregnancy as a decrease in earning capacity of the women and a subsequent cut in her profits. One particular prostitute who decided to have the child despite the 'gharwalli's' opposition, was forced to bring in her regular income by taking on clients up to her ninth month of pregnancy. She had to plead with clients to come to her, as there is a severe lack of client demand for pregnant women. The woman delivered her baby 4 hours after entertaining a client (D'Cunha, Jean; 1987).[9]

Health Problems: The long hours of work, lack of rest, inadequate food, poor sanitation, and the sadism and violence in the life of a prostitute make her vulnerable to numerous physical and psychological problems. Physically, the Indian prostitute, often suffers from tuberculosis, anaemia, hepatitis-B, STDS and gynaecological ailments like vaginal infections, PIDS, leucorrhoea and the like and physical injuries. In the case of prostitute children, cases of rectal fissures, lesions, poor sphincter control, lacerated vaginas, foreign bodies in the anus or vagina, perforated anal and vaginal walls, death by asphyxiation, chronic choking from gonorrheal tonsillitis are almost always related to adult sexual contacts with children (Ed. Barry, Kathleen; Bunch, Charlotte; Castley, Shirley; 1983).[4]

In India, for instance, either through child marriage or the use of young girls in prostitution, hospitals have revealed haemorrhaging, ruptured vaginas and uteruses, lacerated and mutilated bodies, peritonitis, V.D. and even death resulting from sexual relations between these children and much older men. Such a child cannot either sustain pregnancy or child-birth; sometimes she labours upto 6 days and unable to stand the process, her body is torn apart and she dies (Mayo, Katherine, 1927).[11]

The psychological trauma that manifests itself in severe depression, hysteria, nightmares, insomnia, psychosis, fear and revulsion to men and the sex act, distrust and suspicion of people and lastly even suicide are even more serious consequences (D'Cunha, Jean; 1985).[7]

Sexual Alienation

It is important to note a prostitute's response to perverted sexual demands. Disgust, contempt, pity, indifference to clients, feigning responses and jeering clients who fall a prey to her pretences are common reactions of the prostitute. Interviews with prostitutes reveal that they are often cold and frigid when professionally at work and this may be a revolt against male arrogance, as well as a defence against fusing their love life with their profession. The trade is only perceived as a source of income and the control of emotionality and sexuality is a safeguard against male exploitation and monopoly(D'Cunha, Jean; 1984).[6] Sexual pleasure and control over one's body and sexuality is rarely present in prostitution.

'Such a separation of sexual experience involving the most personal and erotic parts of one's physical and psychic being from the total person is indicative of the objectification and depersonalization of a prostitute. A prostitute is thus alienated from this 'intimacy' (Barry, Kathleen; 1979).[3]

In the final analysis, sexuality in prostitution ultimately means a male sexual experience, the power of conquest and ego gratification of the male and the male desire to believe that he is the subjective choice of the woman. Even in sadomasochistic acts he is all-powerful, because in the pain and suffering that he commands to be inflicted on himself he demonstrates a martyrdom which he has chosen. Any guilt he may have had is wiped away. This indicates the socially created emotional and sexual poverty in men (Barry, Kathleen; 1979).[3]

Also certain types of sexual activity demanded by men such as the demand to be dominated indicates the desire to withdraw from the pressures of conforming to socially prescribed 'aggressive' male stereotypes, which males may find oppressive.

Self Perceptions of Prostitute Women

Female sexuality exploitation in prostitution is an invisible and hidden reality. Female socialization compels prostitutes to docilely accept pain and suffering and consider themselves as the second sex. This, coupled with the social perception of prostitutes as scum, immoral women, nymphomaniacs and criminals, is internalized by prostitutes. Prostitute women are unable to perceive themselves as human beings, as victims of an exploitative system and surviving subjects. They are unable to define their experiences of exploitation in prostitution in these terms. They therefore live with a negative identity and poor self image. The estrangement from intimacy and love, and the social ostracism that prostitutes face, inhibit them from

...to a love relationship for fear of being deserted or pasts being raked up in such a relationship. A prostitute is thus alienated from society at large and deemed to live the life of social condemnation.

The hardened prostitute who tries to prove that she enjoys the trade and is the toughest prostitute in the street is no less a victim of a similar alienation. Her above mentioned reactions are the defence and survival mechanisms she has built up to cope with life. ·

A prostitute is thus alienated from her total self, her sexual being , erotic life, earnings, her freedom to live without physical and mental violence. She is boycotted by society at large. She has no control over her body, sexuality and freedom.

If a woman can sell her mental and manual skills, which are exploited, there is nothing wrong with commercialising her sexual skills in prostitution which is only another form of women's work.

Traditionally a woman's nature and entire being have been defined in terms of her sexuality, her reproductive organs and functions. The traditional sex-trait stereotypes have always projected a woman as a docile, weak, chaste, hysterical and non-intellectual being, while sex role stereotypes have reiterated her status as wife, mother or vamp. While upper class women have always been protected, restricted and controlled within the confines of their homes, the working class woman's labour outside the home has always been ignored in terms of its contribution to larger socio- economic life. Likewise all women's contributions to domestic work has been considered unproductive. Hence, although exploited, the use or sale of a woman's mental or manual skills represents a break with traditional trait and role stereotypes of women.

But to view prostitution as a legitimate form of women's work is to accept and reinforce, the already prevalent patriarchal notion that sex and women's bodies are commodities over which a male acquires a right for a consideration. Prostitute women are thus the shared property of several males. This sexist idea which is at the core of sexual violence and oppression in a male dominated society gets reinforced in prostitution and only serves to reduce and maintain women at the lowest and most debasing level in such a society.

Legtitimizing prostitution as a valid form of women's work refrains from putting pressure on the government for providing occupational skills and education for women, increasing their absolute and relative numbers in employment and paying them living wages commensurate with their skills. There would hence be a lack of economic rehabilitation facilities for those wishing to leave prostitution. Decreased or lack of employment opportunities for women would go a long way in preparing the ground for more prostitution.

Lastly, licensing prostitution as a legitimate form of work is discriminatory and humiliating as most other forms of male or female labour does not require a license.

(a) Prostitution is related to the exploitation of all women looked upon as sex objects.

(b) A prostitute at least sells her sex and does not give it away free as married women do.

(c) It is sexual objectification of women that must be eliminated and not just prostitution as a profession.

It is true that sexual objectification, violence and oppression are common experiences of all women, be it the prostitute or the wife; there is however a difference of degree. But to use the above cited reason to justify prostitution as a valid form of work for women, is to accept and legitimize sex and women's bodies as market commodities. The prostitute thus becomes the shared property of several males.

It also amounts to romanticizing the institution of prostitution and negating the 'specific' experience and alienation - economic, physical, sexual, emotional and social - of a prostitute who is today one of the most exploited and oppressed among women.

It is also paradoxical that while certain sections of feminists have criticized the institution of marriage as being oppressive to women and are experimenting with new man-woman relationships as an alternative to the institution of marriage they have failed to address themselves to the exploitative, oppressive and patriarchal institution of prostitution and have gone even further to advocate its decriminalization.

Decriminalization of Prostitution so as to Facilitate Unionization of Prostitutes for Welfare Facilities and

Better Conditions of Work.

The International Committee for Prostitutes' Rights has drawn up a World Charter for Prostitutes' Rights, stating its position in prostitution laws, human rights and working conditions of prostitutes, health and social services for prostitute women, taxation of prostitutes, social attitudes to prostitution and organization of prostitutes.

Laws

They wish to decentralise all aspects of adult prostitution resulting from individual decision.

- Decriminalize prostitution and regulate third parties according to standard business codes.

- Enforce criminal laws against fraud, coercion, violence, child sexual abuse, child labour, rape and racism across national boundaries, whether or not in the context of prostitution.

- Eradicate laws that can be interpreted to deny freedom of association or freedom of travel, to prostitutes within and between countries.

Human Rights

- Guarantee prostitutes all human rights and civil liberties, including the freedom of speech, travel, immigration, work, marriage and motherhood and the right to unemployment insurance, health insurance and housing.

- Grant asylum to anyone denied human rights on the basis of a "crime of status", be it prostitution or sexuality.

Working Conditions

- There should be no zoning laws for prostitution.

- There should be a committee consisting of prostitutes and other professionals to ensure the protection of the rights of prostitutes and to whom prostitutes can address their complaints.

- There should be no law discriminating against prostitutes associating and working collectively in order to acquire a degree of personal security.

Health

- All women and men should be educated to have periodical health screening for sexually transmitted diseases.

- Mandatory checks for prostitutes are unacceptable unless they are mandatory for all sexually active people.

Services

- Employment, counselling legal and housing services for runaway children should be funded in order to prevent child prostitution and promote child well-being.

- Prostitutes must have the same social benefits as all other citizens according to different regulations and different countries.

- Shelters and services for working prostitutes and re-training programmes for prostitutes wishing to leave the life should be funded.

Taxes

- No special taxes should be levied on prostitutes or prostitute business.

- Prostitutes should pay regular taxes as other independent contractors and employees, and should receive the same benefits.

Public Opinion

- Support educational programmes to change social attitudes' which stigmatize and discriminate against prostitutes or ex- prostitutes.

- Develop education programmes which help the public understand the crucial role the client plays in the prostitution phenomenon, this role being generally ignored.

- The customer like the prostitute should not be criminalized or condemned on a moral basis.

Organization

- Organization of prostitutes and ex-prostitutes should be supported to further implementation of the above charter.

- *(World Charter of Prostitutes; International Committee for Prostitutes' Rights; 1985)*[29]

COMMENTS

Prostitutes must be treated with dignity as human beings. They must not be stigmatized or discriminated against *vis a vis* any other citizen.

It is, therefore, necessary to delete all penal provisions against the individual prostitute and provide her with welfare facilities and other benefits made available to other citizens.

So a distinction has to be made between the individual prostitute and decriminalizing the individual prostitute and the institution of prostitution and the decriminalizing of the institution of prostitution. While the former is acceptable, the latter is not.

The ICPR is however demanding the latter. Partly, in an overwhelming desire to protect the individual prostitute, it has removed the distinction between the two, leaving the patriarchal and exploitative assumptions of the institution unchallenged.

Secondly, as mentioned earlier, decriminalization of prostitution includes decriminalization of third party managements. This reflects the profit-oriented interests.

It is contradictory to demand the repeal of laws against pandering and pimping, while simultaneously making pious wishes for the abolition of force, coercion and violence against prostitute women. This is because third party managements inclusive of pimps are a well established phenomenon within the institution of prostitution which is rooted in and thrives on the exploitation, physical and psychological oppression of prostitute women.

It is also naive to believe that in a patriarchal class-based society, third party managements will be effectively regulated in the interests of prostitute women.

It is, therefore, necessary that third party managements be penalized. Also, while the ICPR almost appears to exonerate the client, such double standards of male sexual morality must be unequivocally questioned.

While prostitutes must assert their rights as human beings and must demand welfare and other benefits like any other citizens, any union of prostitutes must be carefully examined in terms of the nature of its social base, leadership, demands, ideology and structure of organization. This is because, as mentioned before, these organizations could well be controlled and financed by brothel keepers and pimps in their own interests, rather than in the interests of prostitutes.

The following example bears testimony to the above. In 1975, prostitutes took over a church in Lyon in France and began a strike against the increase in fines against prostitutes which the police were appropriating for themselves. Although many of the women involved in the strike did not have pimps, it was later learnt that one of the main organisers worked for a big time pimp, who encouraged the strike to protest the way his income was being affected by the fines (Barry, Kathleen; 1979).[3]

Legalization Would Wipe Out the Stigma of Immorality and Criminality

Law plays an ideological role in a class-based patriarchal society. It reflects and reinforces the status quo. Within these limits, it plays a progressive role whenever it is used as an instrument to mete out justice to the oppressed and bring exploiters to book. By itself, law cannot bring about radical changes in society.

Far from erasing the stigma attached to prostitution, legalization is a blatant expression of the double standards of male sexual morality. It reinforces the sexist myth that prostitution is an inevitable social service. It simultaneously segregates prostitutes from the rest of the community with a view to preserving public morals, thus reinforcing the 'madonna-whore' norms.

Such deeply internalized sexist values and practices can only be combated by determined struggles against an exploitative social order that breeds prostitution, the re-definition of the relationship between men and women, and practice of values of gender equality.

Unfortunately from this discussion on the demand for decriminalization of prostitution in the west, it is obvious that such a demand is unacceptable and undesirable from the ideological point of view.

References

1) Alexander, Priscilla; (1986); "Customer Violence against Prostitutes"; Paper for the National Task Force on Prostitution; San Francisco, U.S.A.; June.

1a) Alexander, Priscilla; (1987); "On Prostitution"; Paper prepared for the National Task Force on Prostitution; San Francisco, U.S.A., February.

2) Alexander, Priscilla; (1987); "Prostitutes are being Scapegoated for Heterosexual AIDS"; Paper prepared for the National Task Force on Prostitution; San Francisco; U.S.A.

3) Barry Kathleen; (1979); *Female Sexual Slavery;* Prentice Hall Inc.; Englewood Cliffs, New Jersey.

4) ed. Barry, Kathleen; Bunch, Charlotte; Castley, Shirley; 1983); "International Feminism; Networking against Female Sexual Slavery"; Report of the Global Feminist Workshop to organize against Traffic in Women; Rotterdam; The Netherlands; 6th to 15th April.

5) Barse, Sheela; (1982); "The Right to a Profession"; *Indian Express:* 21st November.

6) D'Cunha, Jean; (1984); "Voices in the Dark"; *Eve's Weekly;* 19th - 22nd May.

7) D'Cunha, Jean; (1985); "No, this can never be a profession like any other"; Femina Controversy; *Femina.*

8) D'Cunha, Jean; (1985) "The Suppression of Immoral Traffic in Women and Girls Act - 1985. A Critical Review"; Research project for Research Unit on Women's Studies, SNDT Women's University, Bombay, India.

9) D'Cunha, Jean; (1987) "Children of the Night"; *Indian Express;* 19th April.

10) Draft Statement on Prostitution and Feminism; (1986) International Committee for Prostitutes' Right; European Parliament; Brussels; 1st-4th October.

11) Mayo, Katherine; (1927) *Mother India*, New York.

12) Mcleod, Eileen; (1982); *Working Women Prostitutes Now.*

13) National Task Force on Prostitution (NTFP) Policies; (1984-1986); San Francisco, U.S.A.

14) News Item; (1983); "Prostitute bashed to death"; *Daily;* 11th Jan.

15) News Item; (1988); "Delhi a Major Transit Point for Trafficking in Women", *The Hindu;* 3rd February.

16) News Item; (1983); "Prostitute done to death"; *Indian Express;* 29th September.

17) Ong, Aihawa Dr. (1984); "Industrialization and Prostitution in South East Asia"; Paper for U.N. N.G.L.S. Invitational consultation on "Female sexual Slavery and Economic Exploitation".

18) Phongpaichit, Pasuk; (1981); "Bangkok's Masseuses; Holding up the Family sky"; *South East Asian Chronicle;* Issue No. 78.

19) Private Discussions with Prostitutes at the Brussels Congress on Prostitution, Human Rights and Feminism; (1986); European Parliament; Brussels; 1st-4th October

20) Rosen, Ruth; (1982) *The Last Sisterhood; Prostitution in America 1900-1918;* Baltimore MD; Johns Hopkins University Press.

21) Rozario, M. Rita R.G.S; assisted by Mr. Rasool Javed and Mr. Kesari Pradeep (1988) *Trafficking in Women and Children in India: Sexual exploitation and Sale:* A Joint Women's Programme Publication, Uppal Publishing House; New Delhi.

22) "Sex Tourism to Thailand"; (1979); The article appeared in Dutch in *Onze Werald* in March 1979; available from NOVIB, Netherlands;

translated by ISIS.

23) Silbert, Mimi; (1981), Principal Investigator "Sexual Assault of Prostitutes"; San Francisco.

24) Slide show and discussions with forensic expert Pritam Phatnani; Bombay.

25) "The Tragedy of Tulasa"; (1983); Special Report; *Probe India;* January.

26) "Tourism: Selling South East Asia'"; (1981); *South East Asia* Chronicle; April.

27) "U.S. Military Bases in the Philippines"; (1983); *South East Asia Chronicle,* April.

28) Werlhof, Claudia Von; (1980); "Relation between Sexuality and Economy"; *Sexual and Economic Review;* IV; Summer.

29) "World Charter for Prostitutes' Rights"; (1988); International Committee for Prostitutes' Rights; Amsterdam; February.

Part V

Chapter-7: Experience in Various Countries with Legalized Prostitution

Introduction

Prostitution has existed as a legal activity for a long time in several parts of the world. The 19th century traffic in women and children for sexual exploitation in Europe, was directly linked to legalization of prostitution by the state, the existence of which can be traced back to ancient Greece and Rome.

There was a renewed interest in state legalized prostitution in 19th century Europe. The spark that set aflame this renewed concern was the rampant spread of VD in the French Army during the French Revolution. This was said to adversely affect military efficiency. The state perceived legalization of prostitution as the official weapon to combat the VD menace, without preventing the army man's access to prostitutes.

In due course the regulation of brothels spread from the military to the general public. By the middle of the 19th century, individualized and isolated efforts of the French medicos and police at identifying public prostitutes, registering and examining them and subjecting them to periodical medical examinations, evolved into a well-defined system of state legalization of prostitution through brothels. Brothels were the only places in which prostitutes were permitted to work legitimately (Barry, Kathleen; 1979).[1]

From its inception in France and Germany, state legalized prostitution spread throughout Europe. In 1871, at the

International Medical Congress in Vienna, an international law was proposed to make legalization uniform throughout the world. While state legalization of prostitution was considered a 'progressive' welfare measure to 'promote public health', in practice, it sanctioned sexual exploitation and bondage of women and girls in prostitution.

In the mid - 19th century, It was introduced in Britain through the Contagious Diseases Acts (C.D. Acts), enforced between 1864-1869. The same Acts were imposed in 19th century British India. They have since been repealed in both Britain and India.

Several countries still continue with the system of legalized prostitution. While most of the United States of America is governed by the Prohibitionist system of law, Nevada is the only state in the U.S. that has state legalized prostitution. Contemporary Germany is another example of the system of legalized prostitution.

Any examination of legalization as a system of state control must seriously consider and draw on the experiences of those countries that have legalized prostitution, so as to better assess not only its desirability, but also its feasibility as a system of law governing prostitution.

GREAT BRITAIN : THE CONTAGIOUS DISEASES ACTS 1864 - 1869

As mentioned earlier, state legalized prostitution was introduced in Britain between 1864 and 1869, in the form of the Contagious Diseases Acts. These Acts were primarily enforced in 11 garrison towns, military stations and sea ports of Britain. They were especially tailored to protect the health of military personnel. The Acts empowered the 'Special Morals Police' to subject any woman that they identified as a prostitute, for surgical and special vaginal examinations. An amendment to the Contagious Diseases Act of 1864 required that every woman who was identified by the 'Special Morals Police', as a prostitute should submit to a medical examination. If she was found clear of VD, she would be officially registered and issued a certificate stating that she was a 'clean prostitute' (Barry, Kathleen; 1979).[1]

By contrast, however, customers of prostitutes were outside the control of the Acts.

Conditions for the Emergence and Rational for the Acts

The Contagious Diseases Acts were a post - Crimean war reform of the 1860's and 70's. Social commentators in Britain attributed the disappointing military performance of the British in the Crimean wars, to the moral and physical degeneration of the male soldiers. Sex was seen as a panacea for revitalizing the lives of British soldiers. Military reformers were confronted with the problem of reconciling the soldiers' presumed male 'sexual drive' with military efficiency. An uncontrolled natural sex drive, in their opinion, led to indebtedness, drunkenness, illness and poverty. Permission to satisfy this natural sex drive with 'greedy and unclean' women would lead to a decline in the country's military capabilities. The Victorian Army, therefore, began to foster a certain kind of man, the creation of which, had implications for treatment of women with whom a male was permitted to consort (*Militarization of Prostitution;* p. 2).[3]

As mentioned earlier, the crucial issue facing the military or naval hierarchy was the problem of reconciliation between sex appetite and its threats to military efficiency. To exemplify the issue, commanders sending sailors on long sea voyages, feared homosexual relations between men confined to each others' company in close quarters. This would reduce their efficiency. Alternatively if male soldiers sought sexual relations with women, the military man's loyalty would be diluted, his health ruined and finances drained (*Militarization of Prostitution;* p. 22).[3]

So, while commanders believed that women drained male vigour, they justified the Contagious Diseases Acts on the basis of protection of the military man's health from the 'vicious scourge of VD' (*Militarization of Prostitution;* p. 23).[3]

Health Checks on Military Men Prior to the Acts

Prior to the Contagious Diseases Acts of 1864, military men were subject to a compulsory medical examination for VD by the military medical officer. Married soldiers were exempted as they formed a small proportion of the force. It was also believed that marriage divided loyalties and married men were not as tempted by prostitutes as their bachelor comrades. Moreover, in Victorian England, married men were considered more respectable and spared the humiliation of a medical examination for VD (*Militarization of Prostitution;* p. 23).[3]

However, this system of medical checks was discarded. This was because British Officers, as men, felt that a compulsory medical examination of their subordinates for VD was a demeaning and humiliating experience for the latter and an embarrassing experience for the former. The system of health checks on military men, was therefore replaced by the Contagious Diseases Acts. What is obvious is that male bonding and a shared male identity cutting across class, ethnic and rank divisions played a major role in determining attitudes to male sexuality and official policy towards the military man's sexuality (*Militarization of Prostitution;* p. 23).[3]

Comments On The Acts

1) Sexist Assumptions With Respect To Women

With the introduction of the Contagious Diseases Acts, women were supposed to serve men and male institutions, not just by providing cheap unpaid labour, but 'clean' sex. The Acts implied that only if women were sexually healthy could men's presumably uncontrollable sexual drives be allowed full rein, without society's male institutions being put in jeopardy (*Militarization of Prostitution;* p. 25).[3]

2) Control of Prostitutes and all Women

The Contagious Diseases Acts, designed to repress Contagious Diseases *i.e.* V.D. was ostensibly formulated for a certain class of women but to reach them all women residing in districts to which it applied were brought under its provisions. The 'Special Morals Police' who were specially assigned to identify prostitutes were invested with unlimited power and control over women. They could take any woman to court, where she was required to prove that she was not a common prostitute. The Magistrate could condemn her even if the policeman only swore that he had good cause to believe her to be one. If condemned, she was to be thoroughly examined periodically by a surgeon for 12 months. Resistance on her part led to her imprisonment with or without hard labour - an imprisonment which was to be renewed for her whole life, unless she submitted periodically to the brutal requirements of the law (Barry, Kathleen; 1979).[1] This indicated the measure of power and control that male law enforcing and interpreting agencies exercised over women.

Legalization therefore did not eliminate police harassment of prostitutes. It also extended such harassment to any and every woman, and put all women in fear of arbitrarily being identified as prostitutes and sent for compulsory VD examinations. Stereotyped conceptions of how a prostitute walked, talked and dressed played a role in this identification.

Apart from this, these innocent women were also compulsorily detained for days, for VD examinations in hospitals by examining surgeons.

The following example bears testimony of how innocent women were arbitarily picked up and detained for medical examinations. "It appears from the evidence of Dr. Wolferstan, a Civil Surgeon formerly attached to the Certified Hospital in Davenport, given to the Royal Commission of 1871 that 609 women who had been sent to the Hospital by Mr. Sloggett, the state appointed Examining Surgeon, had been discharged within 10 days of their admission between October 1866 and December 1869, as free from disease. Copies of letters signed by the four civil and independent surgeons of the Hospital, and addressed to the Lords of the Admiralty, stated that "numerous cases" had been sent to the Hospital by the Government Surgeons for compulsory detention; and they added that "some of the women had been purposely kept a few days, without specific treatment, and still were found to be, after repeated examinations, perfectly free from the diseases". (The Congagious Diseases Acts; p. 17).[2]

The well documented case of a 19th century English woman, Mrs. Percy, cited by Kathleen Barry in her book, *Female Sexual Slavery*, is another piece of evidence of harassment of 'straight' women.

Mrs. Percy supported her family by working in a musical theatre, on a military base. Her 16-year old daughter accompanied her each evening and they were always escorted home by a military officer. On one evening, the police approached the woman and her daughter calling them public prostitutes and ordered them to report for the required medical examination. According to an account given by the daughter, Mrs. Percy said that she would rather sign her death warrant than the paper given to her by the police. Both mother and daughter refused to submit to the medical examination and Mrs. Percy made her outrage known through a letter to the *Daily Telegraph*. The police avenged this by forcing her employers to fire her. She and her daughter moved out of town, but were persuaded by one of her co-workers to return and work under a false names. The police relentlessly pursued her and warned lodging houses that if they took her in, they would run the risk of being cited for running a 'Disorderly house'.

In desperation with no place to live or work, Mrs. Percy threw herself into a canal (Barry Kathleen; 1979).[1]

The Contagious Diseases Act, thus not only regulated and controlled prostitutes, but they showed the rest of the women, that to venture out of their homes, was to risk being identified as a prostitute.

3) Demanding Nature of Medical Examinations

Further, the character of the medical examinations was demeaning. Besides the use of crude medical instruments, doctors were callous and insensitive in their attitudes to and their treatment of prostitute women.

4) Client Uncontrolled

While other laws controlling other contagious diseases, applied to both men and women, these Acts were applicable only to women. This laid bare the sexist bias in these Acts, as they viewed professional prostitutes as the source of infection.

5) Inability to Cure VD

Also, in failing to direct health measures and services to the whole population, the spread of VD could not be arrested, thus defeating the purpose of the Acts. In England there was recorded a steady increase of VD during the operation of these Acts as can be seen from the following extracts from the British Medical Journal, May 18, 1970:

In the Army

"The latest return as to disease in the Army is Parliamentary paper 325, House of Commons, August, 1885, giving statistics from 1860 to 1884 inclusive, as to all three forms of contagious diseases. The benefit of the Acts to the Army, if they had existed, ought to have manifested themselves, during the years of their administration, in a reduction of those forms of the diseases, which some of the highest medical authorities admit to be the only ones of consequence to the community, namely, secondary or constitutional diseases. But, if the figures in this return, commencing with 1869, are divided into four equal

series of years, the ratios per 1000 of troops admitted to
hospital, for constitutional diseases in the districts subjected to
the Acts, are respectively 21.25, 22.25, 21.26 and 24.50. Each
period usually shows an increase upon its predecessor, or, in
other words, the proportion of these forms of diseases had
increased by over 15%, during the full administration of the
Acts! The figures in this return for the only complete year since
the partial suspension of the Acts (1884) show 'no increase' in
the most serious form of disease" (Contagious Diseases Acts;
1888; p. 11).[2]

Among Registered Women

"The same parliamentary paper also classifies disease among
registered women; and the result, as regards the form of disease
alleged to be chiefly influenced by the operation of the Acts,
must be extremely disappointing to those who supported the
Acts. If the 12 years for which the requisite information can
be obtained, is divided into 2 equal period, the ratio of
admissions in the second is 33.64 per cent higher than that of
the first; if into three periods of four years each, the ratio for
the second is 7.09 per cent higher than that of the first, and
the ratio for the third 35.93 per cent higher than that of the
second; if into four periods of three years, the ratio for the
second, is 4.07 per cent higher than that for the first, the ratio
for the third is 15.17 per cent higher than the second and the
ratio for the fourth is 35.71 per cent higher than that of the
third. This result cannot be surprising to those who know that
no effort whatever is made to prevent access to registered
women by diseased men and it goes some way to prove the
statement in the Report of the Royal Commission (paragraph
VII, p. 10) that, "there is no distinct evidence of any dimunition
of disease among the men of the Army and Navy, which may
have taken place, is attributable to a dimunition of disease
contingent upon the system of periodical examination among
the women with whom they have consorted. Your memoralists
are able to supply a table showing the fluctuations of disease,
amongst registered women and troops in subjected districts.
The contrasts in it are very striking, and being calculated from
the police returns up to 1881 (the latest issued), substantiate
still further the views of the Royal Commission" (Contagious
Diseases Acts; 1888; p. 12).[2]

In the Navy

"In regard to the Navy, contagious diseases of all kinds increased to a very large extent in spite of the Acts, being 52 per cent higher in 1882 than in 1886, when the first Act was passed; and higher by 18 per cent on average over the whole 16 years during which the Acts had been in force. And the loss of service in consequence of men being in hospital from these diseases had steadily risen from an average of 172 per 1000 in 1866 (previous to the Acts) to an average of 230 per 1000 in 1882, the last year of the unhindered operation of the Acts, the average strength of the Navy being 20,000 men throughout". (Contagious Diseases Acts; 1888; p. 12).[2]

6) Segregation of Prostitutes

The Contagious Diseases Acts led to the segregation of prostitutes into isolated areas which only resulted in publically identifying a woman as a prostitute and locking her into a situation which drastically reduced her social mobility.

Historian Judith Walkwitz in her well known book *Prostitution in Victorian England* points out that prior to the Contagious Diseases Acts, prostitution in the English working class community was casual. Prostitutes were part and parcel of the community in which they lived and grew up. They were not a specifically identified group and there was some degree of social mobility outside prostitution. The Acts, however, separated them form their neighbourhoods and made them move into red-light areas. This identified them as prostitutes and decreased their social mobility. As evidence of this, Judith Walkwitz states that in the early years of the Act prostitutes were young and single. But by the later 19th century thr rigidity of the social role led to the women remaining longer in the profession possibly indicating a declining social mobility. (Barry Kathleen; 1979).[1]

7) Double Standards of Morality

The Acts reinforced the 'madonna-whore' standards. They encouraged prostitution, but simultaneously tried to preserve a hypocritical semblance of morality by condemning street prostitution while allowing 'invisible' prostitution in brothels.

8) Traffic in Women and Girls for Prostitution

Finally the Acts licensed and legalised the obnoxious practices of brothel-keepers, pimps and procurers, who forced women into prostitution and sexual bondage. This led to an increase in traffic in women and girls for prostitution.

In fact it was observed that the legalization of prostitution was directly responsible for the increased activity in traffic of women and children for prostitution in 19th century Europe. Investigations conducted by Alfred Dyer, an English writer, on traffic in English women in the 19th century, revealed that they were being freely and increasingly exported to Belgium, Holland and France for prostitution. The conditions of English prostitutes were at their worst at the time of the repeal of the Contagious Diseases Acts. Trafficking in women and children for prostitution and heinous crimes against them were at its peak (Barry Kathleen; 1979).[1]

Movement or Repeal of these Acts

In 1869, an English woman, Josephine Butler, formed the National Ladies Association to demand the repeal of the Contagious Diseases Acts. She vociferously attacked brothel-keepers, pimps, procurers, and the state who exploited and forced women and girls into prostitution and demanded stringent action against prostitution racketeers.

She emphasized the exploitation of all women in prostitution and made no class or racial distinctions between prostitutes; nor did she separate her rescue and rehabilitative work from her political campaigns. She wanted to bring about a change in values leading to liberty based on individual freedom and self-respect. Her campaign grew from a small town organisation to an international movement called The International Abolitionist Federation (Barry Kathleen; 1979).[1]

Impact of the Movement

The protest originally launched by Butler unleashed massive public opinion and action. Research and documentation on the traffic of English girls to Continental brothels became a widespread activity. People became especially concerned about the increasing incidence of child prostitution.

The movement demanded that the age of consent for girls be raised from 12 to 18 years as a measure to curtail procuration of children for prostitution.

In 1881, the research findings on traffic in women and girls provoked an inquiry into legislation, to curtail such traffic. However, the demand to raise the age of consent was hotly debated and delayed.

However, due to massive public pressure, the government finally repealed the Contagious Diseases Acts in 1886. (Barry Kathleen; 1979)

References

1) Barry Kathleen; (1979); *Female Sexual Slavery*; Prentice Hall, Inc. Englewood Cliffs; New Jersey.

2) *Contagious Diseases Acts;* (1888); Records of Debates on Contagious Diseases Acts in India discussed by the Bombay Medical Union; Printed at the Anglo-Jewish Vernacular Press; Bombay.

3) "Militarization of Prostitution"; Copy of monograph obtained from Women and Development Programme; Institute of Social Studies; The Hague, The Netherlands.

Chapter - 8: The Contagious Diseases Acts in 19th Century India

In 1869, the Contagious Diseases Acts were imported to India by the ruling British Government. The provisions of the Acts could be introduced in places specified by a local government with the sanction of the Governor-General in Council. These provisions included compulsory registration of brothels and prostitutes, periodical medical examinations and compulsory treatment of prostitutes found to be infected. The medical examinations and treatment were conducted and provided respectively at Lock hospitals. Prostitutes could be forbidden to live in specified areas. Also, for the purpose of discipline, they were placed under the supervision of a small police force and matrons paid by the Government (Ballhatchet, Kenneth; 1987).[1]

The Acts were staunchly supported and defended by the government and military authorities and surgeons. The declared objectives of the Acts were to protect the health of the British soldiers in India and thus maintain the efficiency of the Indian army, prevent veneral diseases from being transmitted to the offspring of those affected by it and thus prevent the physical deterioration of future generations.

The principle on which these Acts was based was more economic than humanitarian or philanthrophic. The argument that underpinned the Acts was that though the State prohibited marriage in the army, the sexual instinct was too prevalent to be denied. The State was therefore justified in providing illicit sexual indulgence to soldiers, so as not to jeopardise their health and efficiency (The Contagious Diseases Acts; 1888; p.3).[2]

Though the primary object of the Acts was to limit their operation to the army and the navy, they were later extended to the civilian population of military and naval stations and the Presidency towns.

A study of various aspects of actual operation of these laws clearly reveals their true intentions and biases.

Encouragement of Procurement and Exploitation of Girls

The Contagious Diseases Acts directly encouraged the procurement and exploitation of women and girls for prostitution.

Evidence in Bombay suggested that young soldiers on landing at Bombay were sent directly to the Deolali military camp, from where they were moved to their various stations. The Deolali camp was deliberately supplied with licensed prostitutes. On account of a large influx of soldiers, subordinate officials received an increase of pay to go out into villages within five miles of Deolali and arrest native women who were known or were supposed to be living 'immoral' lives, and bring them into the camp so that the supply might be adequate to the increased number of soldiers (Contagious Diseases Acts; 1888; p. 18).[2]

Circulars were passed exhorting *'dhais'* (matrons) to be alert and furnish them with authority to visit the neighbouring villages in order to procure young girls of "attractive appearance and tender age" and place them in the prostitutes' quarters for the use of British soldiers. British officers even recommended that the 'dhai' should receive a commission for every girl she induced to leave her native village and become a prostitute.

The Officer commanding the Connaught Rangers wrote to the Assistant Quarter Master General saying:- "The Cantonment Magistrate has already, on more than one occasion been requested to obtain a number of younger and more attractive women, but with little or no success. He will again be appealed to, and as there is no lack of money in the cantonment funds, much might be done. The Major General Commanding should invoke the aid of the local government by instructing the Cantonment Magistrates whom they appoint, that they give all possible aid to commanding officers in the procuring of a sufficient number of young, attractive and healthy women".

The Officer commanding the Cheshire Regiment at Solon issued the following instruction to the Cantonment Magistrate at Umballa: "Please send young and attractive women". Further on, in connection with this requisition he wrote to the Assistant Quarter Master-General as follows, "Some of the women are not very attractive. Application has been made to the Cantonment Magistrate of Umballa for others, but as yet none have arrived. Therefore, it is presumed, a great difficulty exists in procuring the class of young women asked for. The present strength of officers and men is 600 and the number of women at their disposal is 6. Therefore, the number of extra women now required is 6, but up to date none have arrived".

The 'dhai' was empowered to recruit fresh girls and was helped by the Magistrate (or the village patel as he was called) who on receipt of an official document gave every facility to the 'dhai' to carry out her pursuits of decoying women on false pretexts of lucrative employment or of marriage, often with the consent of parents or guardians, who being in abject poverty, would part with their daughters.

There have been several instances of death even on the first or second morning of the arrival of many young girls because of consorting with several soldiers at the time and due to the outrages inflicted on them. (Contagious Diseases Acts; 1888; pgs.47-49).2

There was severe abuse of the intentions of the Acts. The Acts failed to accomplish their objectives.

2) Failure to Control VD

The Acts failed to control VD. The investigations of the Committee of the House of Commons in 1882 stated that proponents of the Contagious Diseases Acts averred that there were about 200 more soldiers and sailors on active service, instead of in hospital, because of the operation of these Acts, at a cost of £40,000 a year.

The opponents of the Acts, some of whom were on the committee in the House of Commons, did not believe or agree that there was any improvement in the efficiency of the army resulting from the operation of the Acts. They argued that during their operation, the decrease of disease had been less marked than before the Acts were introduced.

According to the report of the minority Committee of the House of Commons, the majority report stated that there was a saving to the army of 5.38 men per 1000 daily, on parade, instead of in hospital, due to the operation of the Acts. The data on which this computation was based was incomplete. The conclusions were hence misleading. By inserting the omitted data the result was a loss of 1.47 men per 1000, instead of a daily saving of 5.38 per 1000 (Contagious Diseases Acts; 1888; pgs.4-5).[2]

With regard to Lock hospitals in the cantonments, available evidence shows that from the time the Cantonment Acts (rules for prevention of VD) came into force in Bengal to the end of 1879, the general returns for the Presidency showed no real improvement in the ratios of admissions from venereal diseases". (Contagious Diseases Acts; 1888; pgs.4-5).2

There was a lot of other evidence adduced to show that there was no decrease in the incidence of VD in India.

This is also seen from the following:-

("Enclosure 2 to No.1, N 3603 Lock Hospital dated Simla 9th October 1884; From Sir A.D. Home, KCB VC Surgeon General Her Majesty's Forces to Colonel G. Chesney, Secretary to the Government of India, Military Department, Simla".)

Para ; 2 -"With reference to the comparative statistics of the prevalence of venereal diseases at stations which have Lock hospitals and those which have not, taking the statistics for the period 1864 - 1883 as an illustration, it will be seen that of the 42 protected stations there are 26 stations at which the rate of prevalence of veneral diseases has increased, whilst there are only 16 stations at which it has diminished". (Contagious Diseases Acts; 1888; pgs.12-15).2

Para -3 -"Full significance of the statistics is now shown by bare comparison made above. Taking the group of important stations, that is, those stations have not less than the strength of the one battalion, it is seen that the rate of venereal diseases is higher in 1883 than 1884 at 17 stations, whilst it is lower at only 5; and further, that every one of the very largest stations shows an increased rate of prevalence". (Contagious Diseases Acts; 1888 pg.15).2

Further, the Army and Sanitary Commission of 1882 - '83 said "The Contagious Diseases Acts have failed in India to protect the health of the troops from venereal diseases and there are no facts on which the measures could be sustained".

The Surgeon General, H.M.'s Forces, Bengal, in reply to the information sought by the Director-General, Army Medical Department, London, as to the efficacy of the Acts wrote a strong protest saying, "In my judgement the measures taken for protecting the troops in the Bengal command from venereal diseases have failed. It is surely obvious that failure of seventeen years' application means nothing more or less than the hopeless inadequacy of the measures to effect the purposed end". (Contagious Diseases Acts - 1888; pg.24-25).2

The Chief Secretary of the Government of Madras, in reply (Feb 1888) to the information required by the Government of India said, "Although it has undoubtedly been of some service to the troops, its beneficial effect cannot be said to have been very marked, since the average number of admissions to the hospital for venereal diseases has gone up, i.e. during the five years ending with 1886 there was a 386 per 1000 of strength against 395 per 1000 for the five years 1863-1867". (Contagious Diseases Acts - 1888; pg.25).2

His Excellency, the Commander-in-Chief of Madras, while minuting on the feasibility of the Acts, said, "It will be observed that the increase in venereal diseases in the Madras Presidency in 1885, as compared with the previous ten years, was far greater both in the protected and unprotected stations than in other Presidencies. (Contagious Diseases Acts; 1888; pg. 26).2

3) Non-Registration by Prostitutes and Causes for Increase in V.D.

A large percentage of prostitutes were known to desist from registration. In Calcutta, with a population of about 4 lakhs of people, the number of registered women was 3000, and it was reckoned that there were as many clandestine prostitutes as well. In Bombay, the population was about 8 lakhs and the number of registered prostitutes was only 1,800 on average. It was reckoned that judging from Calcutta, the number of clandestine prostitutes in Bombay was 4 times greater than in Calcutta. (Contagious Diseases Acts; 1888; pg. 43).2

Prostitutes avoided registration as surgical examinations were an outrageous violation of their persons. Besides, registration openly identified them as prostitutes and left them vulnerable to harassment. (Contagious Diseases Acts; 1888; pg.13).2

When infected with VD, prostitutes went to private practioners, if they could afford it. Alternatively, they let the disease run its course and kept working. They did not seek relief in public hospitals for fear of forcible registration and imprisonment. (Contagious Diseases Acts; 1888; pg.14).2

As a result, a vast amount of VD remained concealed and untreated. The Acts thus offered help and treatment to only 1/10th of the portion of the sufferers from VD and prevented the larger remaining portion from seeking relief. (Contagious Diseases Acts; 1888; pg.43).2

It is obvious from the above data that, despite the operation of the Acts, a significant number of women consciously dodged registration and detection. But the public, relying on the word of the Government that all prostitutes had clean bills of health and were therefore free from disease, visited prostitutes in larger numbers. If the place of those detained in Lock hospitals was not filled by women free of VD, and the number of frequenters remained the same, there would have been a greater rush on those remaining, who were not clean, plus the infected women who had escaped. This arrangement might or might not have caused a diminution of disease among frequenters and if there was any diminution at all, it would have been very slight.

But the chances were that the number of frequenters would increase when the Acts were in force and the increased number would more than counterbalance any slight good that may have been produced. (Contagious Diseases Acts; 1888; pg.10-11).2

Lastly, another important reason for the failure of the Acts to decrease VD was that measures were unfairly directed only against the prostitute population, while preventive and curative measures for clients and the general populace wer absent.

4) Harassment of Prostitute Women by the Police and Military Surgeons

The Contagious Diseases Acts placed a tremendous amount of power in police hands - power which they greatly used and abused against powerless prostitute women.

That these Acts were held in great horror by the helpless women can be seen from the following extract from a letter to Mrs.

Josephine Butler (Founder of the International Abolitionist Forum) by a citizen Mr. Sadoba Aandurang (June 28, 1870) - "The great terror in which the Act is held by these helpless women on account of the galling disgrace and oppression to which they are subjected at the hands of the executive, is well exemplified by a simple fact which has come to light, viz. that no sooner was the news of the introduction of the Act spread in the town of Bombay, than about 3,000 poor souls at once left the city and dispersed into the country, where they starved and died unknown and uncared for. (Contagious Diseases Acts, 1888; pg.15).[2].

Dr. Pesikaka of the Bombay Medical Union, quoted instances from the Indian Spectator of June, 1888, showing how police officers used their authority:- "Some years ago I saw a Panjabi woman, made dead drunk and then raped by three or four sepoys. Though more dead than alive under the influence of arrack, she was still goraning piteously. Had she appealed to the police, she might have been locked up, perhaps to be further outraged. They insist upon an examination before accepting the word of a woman, and this even a prostitute woman is loath to submit to. I have known cases in Girgaum, Chowpatti and elsewhere, in which girls were first betrayed to military or naval clients and then made over to the "tender mercies" of the police because of the C.D. Acts. It need hardly be added that the poor things were done for".

"Again, where a woman has two lovers, the one discarded may, because he's jealous, induce the police to watch her movements and get her arrested. The police in plain clothes will track her and ask her, even in the presence of her husband, parentsand children, to go up to the State Surgeon for an examination. On refusing she is threatened to be placed before a magistrate. The woman, with her already wounded honour, fears to be exposed to public obloquy, and to avoid it, feels compelled to go up to the State surgeon, to be outraged again. Surgeon-General Cunningham rightly remarked that the apprehension in Calcutta of 12 women on average, every day in 1879, was of grave danger to the State. There were many instances of women who have through wretchedness and desperation sought relieff from the cruel persistence of police tormentors in death. There is evidence of two girls killed by a fall from the roof of their house to escape the clutches of a government official. A girl of twenty named Brown drowned herself after a previous attempt to cut her throat. Another named House threw herself out of a window; a third named Mulcarty drowned herself. The widow of an actor committed suicide at Aldershot. These incidents rarely came to light as they relate to a class of women who have no resources of any kind to make their gievances heard. (Contagious Diseases Acts; 1?888; pg.49-50).[2]

The police 'zoolum' did not rest with unlicensed women only, but affected the class of licensed women as well. If the women after registration refused or neglected to go for an examination at the stated hour and place, they were liable to be punished with imprisonment. If found or even suspected of being diseased, they were to be locked up in the special hospital for a period varying from one to several months, depriving them of all their liberties as if they were government slaves. No public hospital authorities had the right to force confinement to patient even for a minute against his/her wishes, but here unfortunate women were locked up for being diseased by men and the Acts did not seek to regulate men who infected and propagated the disease. (Contagious Diseases Acts; 1888; pg.50).[2]

So severe was the abuse against women, that women perfectly free from VD were also picked up and detained in hospital. An incident in Bombay in 1880 is an illustration of this. The cry was raised that there was a large outbreak of a well known disease, and that as the hospital for women was full, a much larger hospital was necessary. This induced one Surgeon General Beatty to personally examine the reports sent in by the State apointed examining surgeons. The result was the appointment of a Medical Committee which after careful inspection of the women who were being forcibly detained and medicated, discovered that of the nearly 200 alleged cases of contagious diseases, 90 of the women were not suffering from VD at all, and the surgeon in charge practically admitted this view of the case by tendering his resignation. (Contagious Diseases Acts, 1888; pg.17).[2]

Apart from this, the severest censure should fall upon those surgeons who for years have performed disgusting and undescribable instrumental examinations upon the unwilling bodies of young girls, sometimes under 12 years of age, and even upon pregnant women, for the sole object of protecting men in the army and navy, from the physical risk of prostitution. (Contagious Diseases Acts; 1888; pg.18).[2]

One of the arguments advanced against the Acts was that it did not yield results. According to an Explanatory Memorandum by Surgeon General Cunningham (Member of the Committee assembled at Calcutta, under the orders of the Government of India, as conveyed by the Resolution in the Home, Revenue and Agricultural Department 1881), the results which were gained, imperfect and unsatisfactory as they were, seemed altogether insufficient to justify the expenditure of money and the interference with the people in their most intimate social relations, which they necessitated. the cost had fallen a little short of Rs. 5000 per month. The arrest on average of 12 women every day per year for a breach of the rules represented a state of things which was a very grave risk. The people disliked the Acts very much. The municipality could ill-afford to bear the full cost of implementing the Acts. Apart from this, the evil effects of diseases like fever, dysentry and other common diseases were far greater than that of VD. (Contagious Diseases Acts, 1888; pgs.5-6).[2]

The above arguments which applied primarily to Calcutta, applied with even greater force to Madras and Bombay. In both of them, it was quite evident, from the small number of women on the register that the Acts were merely a waste of public money. The Madras municipality was poor and could ill-afford the charge. The Bombay municipality had openly declared its opposition to the Acts, and had declined to contribute towards the expenses of working them. (Contagious Diseases Acts; 1888) pg.6).[2]

Ideological Criticism of the Acts

Even at that time various medical authorities and social commentators strongly opposed the Acts and questioned the validity of their basic assumptions. It is interesting to examine their argument

1) Irrepressible male sexuality

To begin with, the much propagated irrepressibility and uncontrollability of male sexuality is a patriarchal assumption. Medical testimony, great in quantity and much of it of the highest quality was opposed to the idea that the sexual instinct was too imperious to be denied. (Contagious Diseases Act; 1888; pg.10).[2]

2) Argument against incontinence

According to Dr. Katrak of the Bombay Medical Union, there was no excuse for the soldiers incontinence, particularly under the short period system of military service. Many of the civil population had to defer marriage until they were as old as those doing the first term of military service. There were therefore, no grounds for protecting incontinence in the army. (Contagious Diseases Acts; 1888; pg.4).[2]

3) Interference in the Civil Population: Class & Racial Oppression of Indians

The system necessitated an interference with the people in their most intimate social relations, which was most objectionable in any country, but especially in India, where owing to indigenous habits, all such interference involved a constant risk of oppression and injustice. (Contagious Diseases Acts, 1888; pg.92).[2]

Prostitutes were divided into classes. The first class consisted of 'public prostitutes frequented by Europeans', the second, of 'public prostitutes not so frequented'. Certain brothels were reserved purely for European clientele and others only for local clientele.

Lambert, the Deputy Commissioner of Police, testified that the Acts were very unpopular with 'all classes of natives'. They had no sympathy with them as they considered they were introduced to benefit the European male. (Ballhatchet, Kenneth; 1878; pg.49).[1] Not only were the Acts reflective of patriarchal oppression of women, they were also indicative of class and racial oppression of Indians.

The state could interfere to prevent the spread of disease, if the presence of an infected person/persons in a locality/assemblage could infect others and produce an epidemic or if a healthy person was forced to come into contact with a diseased person, thus incurring risk of infection.

As the transmission of VD falls into neither of these categories, state interferene to prevent it, in the form of the CD Acts in India, severely jeopardised individual and collective liberty.

It is questionable as to whether the State in order to boost its paltry economy was justified in depriving unfortunate women of liberty and forcing them to submit to medical examinations, which, unless urgent, was a wanton outrage of modesty. (Contagious Diseases Acts; 1888; pg.7).[2]

4) Unconstitutional anti-women bias

The Acts were politically unconstitutional as they sided on the liberty of one sex in suppression of the other. The real objective was not just to stamp out disease but make prostitution safe for men, as the Acts applied to one class of contagious diseases, and one sex only, without bringing every infected subject under regulation. (Contagious Diseases Acts; 1888; pg.45).[2]

5) Unjustifiable on Political Considerations

Regulation of prostitution was unjustifiable on political considerations, because instead of challenging a patriarchal and exploitative institution like prostitution, the State accepted, regulated and helped perpetuate it as a state establishment. The attitude of the state amounted to this because it was a partisan of procurers and abetted the act of procuring; and also, by supplying prostitutes with a clean bill of health, it actually aided prostitutin.

Conclusion

From the foregoing information about the actual implementation of the Acts, as well as the arguments of the opponents, it is clearly evident that the Acts were a failure in India.

They were finally repealed in 1888, partly as a consequence of local distaste and displeasure and largely because they were repealed in England, because of intense public pressure against the Acts.

References

1) Ballhatchet, Kenneth; 1979; *Race, Sex and Class under the Raj: Imperial Attitudes and Policies and their Critics (1793-1905);* Vikas Publishing House, Delhi.

2) *The Contagious Diseases Acts;* (1888); Records of the debates on the Contagious Diseases Acts discussed by the Bombay Medical Union; Printed at the Anglo-Jewish Vernacular Press, Bombay.

Chapter - 9: Legalized Prostitution in Nevada (U.S.A.)

Prostitution is illegal in the United States, except in the State of Nevada.

However, in many other cities a quasi-legalized brothel system has evolved under the aegis of the Police Department. The city of San Francisco is an example of such a system. In the early 1970s, the San Francisco Board of Supervisors passed an Ordinance regulating massage parlours. The Ordinance required the owners of the massage parlours, as well as the massage workers employed therein, to obtain licenses from the Police Department's Permit Bureau. Licenses would be denied on grounds of a prostution-related offense in the previous three years. Similarly, a conviction subsequent to obtaining the license was a ground for revocation. In 1981, the San Francisco Board of Supervisors passed a similar ordinance regulating escort services (Alexander, Priscilla; 1987; p.5). [1]

To all intents and purposes, it would appear that the Ordinance was designed to prevent prostitution. However, according to police pronouncements, the Ordinance was really designed to "regulate and control prostitution and not to prevent it". It effectively ensured a turnover of workers, because the police raided parlours and escort services at intervals, and revoked the permits of the women they arrested. The Board of Permit Appeals in San Francisco usually upheld the revocation, even when the charges were dropped or a judge dismissed them for

lack of evidence. This was generally followed by advertisements
by the massage parlour for new staff.

The same massage license is required by all the other states
except Nevada, whether the work is 'legitimate' or a 'sexual
massage'. When a woman applies for a license, the police
assume she is a prostitute and treat her so. When the police
raid massage parlours and escort services, and arrest all the
women working there, the latter are usally arrested for minor
infractions of the massage parlour licensing code, such as failure
to wear identity badges, instead of on charges of prostitution.
These cases are often dismissed the next morning by the judges
who believe that such arrests are a mere waste of the tax
payers' money and the courts' time. Despite the absence of a
conviction, the arrested women lose their licenses and hence
their jobs. However, women who have been arrested do not
stop working as prostitutes. They engage in one form of
prostitution or another and may even move to another city
where they have no arrest record, to apply for another license.
(Aléxander, Priscilla, 1987; p.6).[1]

Nevada

In Nevada in the U.S.A., prostitution is either legal or openly
tolerated.

In a paper by Richard Symanski, based on his field work in
1973. reported that there were thirty-three brothels in rural
and small-town Nevada with about 225 to 250 prostitutes
operating therein (Symanski, Richard; 1974; p.246).[4] More
recent reports indicate this number is now 37. Legal,
quasi-legal and brothel-owner regulations shape the location of
brothels and activity spaces of prostitutes. Statutes and
ordinances at the State, County or City levels define the legal
context within which the brothels have to operate. Madams
and girls also obey written and unwritten rules of questionable
legal validity formulated by City Councils and law enforcement
authorities. Madams also lay down their own rules to regulate
prostitutes and control house and community behaviour. The
net effect of this plethora of regulations has turned brothels
into prisons. "Occasionally even prostitutes describe themselves
as prisoners, although they emphasize the voluntary nature of
their confinement" (Symanski, Richard; 1974; p.248).[4]

According to the Nevada Revised Statutes of 1971, a county

with a population of 200,000 or more, at the national census couldn't grant a license to operate a house of "illfame or illrepute', or any other business employing a prostitute. Only Clark County (which includes Las Vegas), with a population in 1970 of 272,288 was excluded by this statute. The second largest county, Washoe, which includes Reno and Sparks, had a population of 121,068. The Statute empowered the Board of County Commissioners to license, tax, regulate or prohibit brothels in cities and unincorporated towns. Four Nevada counties, Storey, Lincoln, Lyon and Esmeralda licensed brothels by Ordinance. In other places where brothels could be illegal outside towns, they were licensed not as brothels but as bars and boarding houses which were specifically regulated by prostitution Ordinances. Washoe (Reno), Ormsby (Carson City), Churchill and Douglas counties prohibited brothels. The four counties which licensed brothels did so to avoid any possibility of brothels being defined as common law nuisances and thereby subject to abatement. (Symanski, Richard; 1974; p.249).[4]

adhered to, and are framed to protect customers and the public at large from venereal disease and from women who have criminal records and are addicted to drugs. These rules and regulations are vociferously touted by ardent proponents of legalized prostitution. They are also accepted by brothel managements, despite their questionable legal validity, as any challenge would jeopardize the very existence of brothels. It is these rules that rigidly restrict the areas where prostitutes can operate, (Symanski, Richard; 1974; p.253).[4]

The Ordinances of Lyon and Esmeralda counties provide a striking contrast in the exten to which rural brothels are regulated. Esmeralda County requires brothels to have permits designating the areas where they may be located. They must be uninhabited areas at least five miles from cities, towns, mobile home parks or places where people normally dwell. No gaming or narcotics are permitted on the premises, and prostitutes must have weekly and monthly medical examinations, (Symanski Richard; 1974; p.253;254).[4]

In contrast, the 1972 Lyon Ordinance tries to ensure that brothels will not be a public nuisance, by including elaborate sections requiring data on the financial conditions of the owners, addresses of the owners and prostitutes during the previous ten years and detailed information concerning previous convictions of the owners. A prostitute who has been convicted of a felony' cannot be employed. The sheriffs can limit the working time of brothels, the number of prostitutes that can be employed and the size of the buildings. They are to receive weekly reports on the health of the girls, and the girls must have regular examinations. Males can be employed by the houses only for maintenance and repair of brothel premises, and no male is allowed to live on the property on which the brothels stand, (Symanski, Richard; 1974; p.254).[4]

Brothels in the Lyon county must be at least three miles away from incorporated and unincorporated towns, and they must be more than 300 yards from any public street, road, highway, private residence or business establishment, although they may be closer to a business establishment if they receive the written consent of the owner. Brothels are prohibited from advertising and can only have three-foot by five-foot signs, which must read, "GUEST RANCH - MEN ONLY". Signs on public roads may indicate only the name of the operation, approximate distance to the brothel, a single arrow pointing in the direction of the operation, and others where the road may divide. Finally brothels must be enclosed by a fence at least six feet high, with an entrance that can only be opened from the inside, (Symanski, Richard; 1974; p.254).[4]

The Brothel Set-up

Size of Brothels and Amenities

Nevada's brothels can be categorized by the number of girls in a brothel. The largest houses are closest to major cities, major 'feeder' regions or are in the largest towns permitting prostitution. Brothels of intermediate size are on the major tourist and truck route traversing the state, the Interstate 80. The smallest brothels are in small places away from large cities or in remote inaccessible rural areas.

While the larger houses have several women employed and have the most attractive interior settings and decor, the smallest houses tend to have sparsely decorated bars. They have a dirty and unkempt appearance and are without other amenities. Also, they occasionally only have one girl.

Further, while in the larger houses business is brisk, in the smallest houses, business is often slack and a client is in a much better position to bargain, (Symanski, Richard; p.259-260).[4]

Background of Prostitutes

Symanski found that data on the background of prostitutes was difficult to obtain. Some of the women said that they had been street-walkers or call girls; others had worked as waitresses, secretaries, sales women or had been at university. Money or quick financial gain was often the main motive for entry into prostitution, (Symanski, Richard; 1974; p.261).[4]

In both rural and town brothels, blacks constituted at least twenty-five to thirty per cent of the prostitute population. An equally high percentage of house or bar maids was also balck. Though the high proportition of black prostitutes was well above black representation in the total population, it is not surprising when compared to their incidence in the total prostitute population, (Symanski, Richard; 1974; p.261).[4]

Poverty may be attributed to being the main cause of black women entering prostitution. Black women are also an important element in the 'diversity and variety mix' of services which brothels offer.

Working Conditions of Prostitutes

Parlour Dynamics, Clients Hours of Work, Earnings, Restrictions on Prostitutes, Mobility

In the parlour, a client makes a quick choice, usually from a line up of girls called by the madam. If the house does not insist on an immediate choice, he can relax, drink, 'inspect' one or more girls or talk to her/them before making a decision. Physical contact is rarely allowed in the parlour. If a client is not attracted to a prostitute, the madam and girls try to make him change his mind, (Symanski, Richard; 1974; p.269-270).[4]

Madams and girls waste no time in making explicit the nature of their business, especially at peak hours. They explicitly tell anyone who idles or seems unfamiliar with brothels that they are not selling love and companionship, and not even really drinks, though most brothels have liquor licenses. If it is obvious that a client is not interested in buying sex services, he may not be permitted to enter and prostitutes may leave the parlour and return to their rooms. Quick purchases are demanded as clients who waste time, reduce the turnover rate, which adversely affects the earning capacity of the women, as they get only a percentage of what they make. Also most prostitutes have only a financial interest in their clients. The fewest financially unrewarding demands on prostitutes, and the least time spent with them leads to the client paying the smallest amount, (Symanski, Richard; 1974; p.270).[4]

Parlour dynamics, however vary from brothel to brothel depending on the attitudes and regulations of the madam. But the above pattern changes as the atmosphere becomes more relaxed which is in the late morning or early afternoon, when business is slack and the women as well as the madam, may just be rising, as they work until 4 or 5 a.m.

What is also pertinent to note is that most Nevada brothels have 14-hour shifts, with girls entertaining 10 to 15 clients a day or more. The women have little or no right to refuse a client, though brothel managements try to keep out potentially dangerous clients. Prostitutes are not allowed to protect themselves from STDs by insisting on condom usage by clients, but now at least two houses in Nevada have become "all-condom-houses" to prevent the spread of AIDS. Because of the gruelling aspects of the long work shifts many women use drugs which are given by the same doctor performing the regular health checks. The drugs are used to keep them awake and alert or for sleep. (Alexander Priscilla; 1987; p.18).[1]

The case of Mustang Ranch, one of the biggest brothels in Nevada, is an illustration of the exploitation prostitutes face. "Located in a deserted area, it has a prison-like atmosphere. Fifty women from different racial backgrounds work there at a time.

The women attired in body stockings and bikinis are not permitted to talk to each other or read. They sit around till the buzzer sounds; then they line up in front of the door and wait mutely till they are chosen by a client. Each woman is made to work for a minimum of tree weeks before she is allowed out of the premises. She must earn at least $ 100 a week in the summer or $ 500 in the winter, otherwise she is thrown out. Fifty per cent of her earnings go to the house; with the remaining 50 per cent, she pays for boarding, for clothes, weekly VD checkups, written prescriptions, etc. The women are thus left with less than 40 per cent of their earnings. They work for 14-16 hours a day with three weeks on and one week off. They are not permitted to go out unless they have a man to take them out or they get permission to leave for 2 hours of shopping. Even medical treatment is perfunctory and callous since any drug may be prescribed", (Barry Kathleen; 1979).[2]

Parlours in Winnemucca are unique in Nevada. Several of the houses have large bay windows, behind which the girls sit facing the street to attract passing clients or to be inspected by them. When business is slow or when girls sense that those at the bar are present to socialize but not to buy, they often return to their window seats to watch for others, or if bored read a novel or newspaper, (Symanski, Richard; 1974; p.271).[4]

Restrictions on Prostitutes: Local Authorities/Madams

Brothel prostitutes are required to observe a number of regulations established by local authorities. Some are nearly universal and relate directly to their work; others exist primarily in urban areas and place restrictions on personal relationships and mobility and are only occasionally work-related. The latter restrictions blatantly define prostitutes as people of questionable social standing who cannot be trusted. As mentioned earlier, the legal or quasi-legal limitations placed on mobility result in socially sanctioned restricted activity spaces, (Symanski, Richard; 1974; p.266).[4]

Restricted activity spaces are off-limits during certain times. Prohibited spaces are either permanently off-limits, or off-limits as long as one remains a member of a particular class. For example, when a woman leaves prostitution, changes houses from one county to another, or permits herself to be 'bought' out of a house for a day or more, the nature of her activity space may be redefined. Prostitution in Nevada provides examples of these concepts, (Symanski, Richard; 1974; p.266).[4]

Prostitutes are permitted outside the brothels, with a few exceptions, only between the hours of 10 a.m. and 5 or 6 p.m. In Wells, the hours are from 1 p.m. to 4 p.m. Winnemucca allows girls in town after 4 a.m. and until 7 a.m., if the brothel is closed and the police department is notified of intentions and areas to be visited. Lander County prohibits leaving brothels on Sundays. Activity within these permitted hours is confined to visiting certian establishments or sections of the town, and to particular interactions. Places which can be visited include doctors' and dentists' offices, beauty parlours, shopping areas,

and, perhaps, movie theatres.   Girls are explicitly prohibited
from going to bars, gaming houses and residential areas; they
are not permitted to rent rooms in town.   The then Sheriff of
Wells once made an uncommon exception by permitting a girl
to go to a hotel with a 'bottle' and a customer.   Ely allows girls
to eat in restaurants with bars during shopping hours if they
are unaccompanied by male escorts.   Until recently there was
an additional provision that the restaurants had to have side
entrances, (Symanski, Richard; 1974; p.266).[4]

The rule that no girl may solicit business outside the house is
rigidly enforced.   Written regulations usually state that a girl
may not be accompanied by a male escort in town.   The twenty-
three point list in Winnemucca goes further.   Prostitutes are
not allowed to have friends within the town including pimps,
boy friends, husbands and others defined by the police
department.   Girls in three different counties report that they
cannot talk to anyone when out of the brothel, or, at most, can
only exchange salutations.   To obviate problems after a girl's
official status changes, Ely requires that the girls who have
been terminated or fired must leave town on the first available
transportation, (Symanshi, Richard; 1974; p.266).[4]

There are exceptions and house variations in the way activity
spaces are defined.   If a girl has a birthday or if there is special
occasion such as Thanksgiving, the madam may obtain
permission to escort the girls as a group to a bar in town.   Wells
permits only three girls to accompany the madam.   One brothel
in Winnemucca with six or seven girls avoids these problems
by permitting each girl to shop and attend to medical needs
on different days of the week.   In rural areas, where most of
these issues do not arise, prostitutes often go for their medical
checkups in a group, accompanied by the madam, (Symanski,
Richard; 1974; p.266).[4]

Local rules and regulations also place restrictions on family
proximity, dates with clients and employment changes.   A
prostitute cannot be employed in a brothel in Winnemucca or
Battle Mountain if a member of her family lives in the same
county. The rule on outdates varies. Some towns require that
a client meets a girl at the town limits or dates her beyond the
town limits. Others stipulate that the girl and client must leave
the county.   In either case, the intent is the same to avoid

embarassment to those in the community. If a girl leaves or is fired from a house, she usually has to leave the county for a period ranging from 15 days to three months before she can be hired by another house in that county. Violation of these or other rules results in revocation of the work permit and perhaps banishment from the county, (Symanski, Richard; 1974; p.267).[4]

Most brothels permit their girls to leave for a week, once every three or four weeks. Bogus Christian names by which clients know girls and equally bogus surnames on police records are temporarily shelved while the girls return to their previous identities as respectable mothers, daughters, students or workers. Likewise, the names of cities, towns and even states are discarded for real places and remembered neighbourhoods. One can only speculate on the effect of constant shifting between real and work-designated identities, or between restricted and open activity spaces on those who remain for a long time in prostitution, (symanski, Richard; 1974; p.267).[4]

The madams place other restrictions on activity, especially during work hours. They may limit the number of telephone calls a girl can make, or specify that there may be no calls at all during certain hours. Many houses permit girls to drink only sugar water, tea or nonalcoholic beverages during working hours. Also, children of prostitutes are not allowed to live on the premises with their mothers. (Private discussions with prostitutes at the Brussels Conference).[3]

In general, there are fewer restrictions on madams compared to those placed on prostitutes. Madams are respected entrepreneurs simply making a living. Restrictions on their activities seem to be limited to the entry of bars. They are, of course, prevented from hiring pimps, pimping themselves, permitting pimps, ex-felons, or felons on the premises and in most places, hiring males, (Symanski, Richard; 1974; p.267-268).[4]

However, almost all women in Mustang Ranch have pimps; pimps are, in fact, necessary to get into Mustang Ranch or into any other eros centre. Pimps come weekly to take what is left of the woman's earnings after the houses have taken their cuts, (Barry Kathleen; 1979).[2]

Further, the crime and violence against women in these brothels including murder is often ignored. This is due to the legal existence of these brothels outside the scope of law, the tight links between prostitution, organized crime and the law enforcing authorities and the dependence of prostitutes on pimps and the brothel management, (Barry Kathleen; 1979).[2]

Mobility Between Jobs

There is frequent, variable and seasonal turnover and horizontal mobility between jobs. Different classes of prostitutes seem to have different mobility potentials and patterns that they may even be immobile near the end of their careers.

Reasons given by girls for movements were usually limited to three or four principal factors. The most important was house atmosphere, a general rubric which included the nature of house rules, approach to clients, and the number and kinds of girls in the house. In the small houses particularly there was often mention of how easy it was for a girl to explode emotionally in the confined atmosphere. Other rasons for moving were boredom, the opportunity to make more money elsewhere, particularly during the expensive season, and the absence of a friend, (Symanski, Richard; 1974; p.263-264).[4]

Concluding Comment

The experience of legalization in Nevada, clearly shows that this system of law has only served to rigidly control prostitute women. Defining activity spaces for prostitutes curbs their movements. It isolates prostitutes into segregated areas thus ghettoising them and reinforcing the 'straight-woman'-'whore' divide. More importantly such segregation reflects a hypocritical morality, in so far as 'main street' or 'visible' prostitution is cleaned up, while the invisibility and oppression of prostitution in back alleyand within the 'prison walls' of a brothel is endorsed. Further, the provisions for finger- printing, photographing and compulsory medical examinations of prostitutes, not only violate their freedom and dignity but also serve to publically identify them and render them more vulnerable to harassment and impede their social mobility.

Conditions in brothels are appalling. Appropriation of a large percentage of prostitutes' earnings by the house, strict control by the brothel management over prostitutes' relationships, interactions amd movements, the firmly entrenched institution of pimping and violence against prostitutes speak little for the prostitutes' conditions of work. Legalization in Nevada has brought few benefits for prostitutes.

References

1) Alexander, Priscilla; February (1987); "On Prostitution"; Paper for the National Task Force on Prostitution; San Francisco, USA.

2) Barry Kathleen; (1979); *Female Sexual Slavery;* Prentice Hall Inc., Englewood Cliffs, New Jersey.

3) Private Discussions with Prostitutes at the Brussels Congress on Prostitution, Human Rights and Feminism; (1986); European Parliament, Brussels, 1st - 4th October.

4) Symanski, Richard; (1974); "Prostitution in Nevada"; Annals of the Association of American Geographers; Vol. 64; No.3; September.

Chapter - 10: Legalized Prostitution in Imperial and Contemporary Germany

Prostitution had existed in Germany, as elsewhere, before the late 19th century. It was however localized and on a small-scale, a temporary phenomenon which arose in times of famine and want. The late 19th century, however, saw prostitution appearing to be both large-scale and endemic - a phenomenon that social critics of that period attributed to the rise of industrial capitalism and bourgeois social values (Evans, Richard; 1976; p.108).[2]

More explictly, poverty, decline in artisanship, unemployment, low wages, decreasing level of demand for female labour and meagre and discriminatory wages for female labour led many women into prostitution. These women were largely from working class backgrounds - factory workers and poor peasants.

As in the middle ages, prostitution in the mid-19th century was carried on in well-known streets and areas, reserved largely or exclusively for prostitution. They were usually the back alleys in the oldest parts of towns away from the main streets and shopping centres, but close enough to them to be of easy access for customers. While towns were still relatively small in size, authorities found it easy to regulate prostitution, forcibly confining prostitutes to these streets and exercising a rigid control over them. With the growth of prostitution in the late

19th century, these methods of control continued to be used by the 'Special Morals Police', but tended to be inadequate (Evans, Richard; 1976; p.109).[2]

Prostitution Prior To 1871 and After

Prior to the foundation of the German empire in 1871, local authorities, *i.e.*, the police, were expected to maintain law and order. Maintenance of public decency, health and morality were also seen as police work. So, prostitution in Germany was not regulated by law, but by the police. After the unification of Germany the police had to obey the laws of the Imperial Criminal Code whose regulations derived to a large extent from Prussian Law which replaced the existing laws. The Imperial Code contained certain clauses relating to prostitution empowering the police to arrest and subject to medical examination anyone they suspected of being a prostitute. But another clause contradicted this because it "decreed that anyone who provided through his own agency any opportunity for the exercise of prostitution and so countenanced and furthered it, would be imprisoned. This clause related to procurers and brothel keepers, but it also made police - controlled brothels illegal and exposed the police who controlled them to the risk of prosecution for procuring." (Evans, Richard; 1976; p.110).[2] The Imperial Code led to the closure of controlled brothels in many towns in Germany. Hamburg was the only large city which continued to have a system of police - controlled prostitution, despite fierce opposition.

Failure of the System of Regulation
1) Inadequate Strength of the Police Force

The failure of this system of regulating prostitution, however, became more obvious in the post - mid-19th century. The woefully inadequate strength of the Moral Police Force in most cities was apparently one of the causes of the failure. However, the subsequent increase in the number of the force, failed to deal with the increasing number of prostitutes and the emerging problems. In petitions to the authorities for an increase in their strength, the police maintained that it was to deal with the emergence of large-scale endemic casual prostitution - a new form of prostitution - that an increase was required.

2) Failure to Keep Prostitutes Off the Streets

By the 1890s it was quite evident that the police had failed both in tackling the phenomenon of casual prostitution and maintaining control over the then existing system of regulation. They failed in their own hypocritical objective of keeping street prostitutes away from the public eye.

3) Problems in Registering Prostitutes

Also, the system of control was thwarted as prostitutes rarely stayed long in one official brothel. "In Hamburg every year, well over one thousand changes of addresses were officially registered. According to official estimates, every officially-controlled prostitute changed her address twice a year. Moreover, several prostitutes also took up other employment and were de-registered. In 1862, for instance, 610 prostitutes were added to the official register, while 573 were withdrawn. Of these 573, 234 returned to their families, 159 left to register themselves as prostitutes elsewhere, 82 remained in Hamburg but were removed from the register, 78 absconded, 9 married, 10 died and 1 entered a home for reformed prostitutes, thus revealing the ineffectiveness of "rescue work" as far as registered prostitutes were concerned. These conditions hampered proper supervision. The police, too, were unwilling to enforce regulations too stringently, because the more unpleasant they made the situation for controlled prostitution, the more the latter would evade control altogether (Evans, Richard; 1976; p. 113).[2]

In fact registered prostitutes formed an insignificant proportion of the total number of prostitutes. The overwhelming number of public complaints against prostitution and the response of the police to this in the form of raids and arrests provide some indication of the magnitude of illegal prostitution.

For example, in 1898, the residents of Niedernstrasse and Steinstrasse complained that the locality was becoming overrun with prostitutes. The Hamburg police set up a special watch in the area and made 769 arrests of illegal prostitution in the first eleven months of 1899. The total number of arrests made in the whole city in the year 1897 was 1654 which was a much smaller number in proportion to the area covered, but the number of illegal prostitutes probably ran into several thousands - perhaps well over three thousand in Hamburg alone (Evans, Richard; 1976; p.113).[2]

In the harbour area of St. Pauli district which then came under

Prussian jurisdiction, authorities were forced to admit that they had failed miserably. The police gradually reduced the number of officially controlled brothels both in St. Pauli and Hamburg. The ineffectiveness of regulations was becoming apparent in other cities besides Hamburg. According to the American investigator, Abraham Flexner, few prostitutes stayed in their profession long and most managed to avoid control. "In most cities", he concluded "....... regulation is moribund and in many, quite dead". In 1909, for example, 140 women were enrolled in Munich; during the same year, the Munich police were keeping track of 2,076 'clandestine' prostitutes; the enrolment was thus 7 per cent of those actually known - and these were itself only a part of the whole. The truth was, as one prostitute told Flexner, "only the stupid are enrolled". (Evans, Richard; 1976; p. 114).[2]

Notwithstanding the failure of the regulation system, the Morals Police still tried to maintain the regulations. They decreased the number of police - controlled brothels and employed more police to deal with clandestine prostitution. They were very sensitive to public criticism concerning the regulation stystem as can be seen in the following incident. In a speech to the Reichstag in 1894, August Bebel denounced the controlled brothels in the city state of Hamburg as centres of the white slave trade. Following this, all registered foreign prostitutes in Hamburg were arrested and deported by the Morals Police. (Evans, Richard; 1976; p. 115).[2] Several other raids, arrests and purges of a similar nature were carried out on receipt of public complaints or in response to public agitation. However this did not improve the system of regulation.

Arguments Advanced by Policemen in Favour of Regulation

1) *Control of VD*

Trapped by a patriarchal value system, the perceptions and the objectives of an administrative system, the police still adhered to the system of regulation of prostitutes. They gave three main reasons for their desire to continue with it. Firstly, they believed that it was easier to supervise prostitutes and maintain a close check on the latter's health when they were concentrated in one place. There would then be controlled medical checks and in their opinion that would curb the spread of VD. However, by the end of the 19th century, it was obvious that this claim was erroneous. Some opponents of regulation even argued that the system spread disease by encouraging men to believe that all regulated prostitutes were 'safe'. (Evans, Richard; 1976; p. 117).[2]

2) *Preservation of Public Morals*

Secondly, authorities were concerned about immorality becoming a public spectacle, but most regulations curbing the movements and activities of prostitutes were directed towards this end. "In Hamburg not only were prostitutes strictly forbidden to go to certain theatres, places of entertainment, the botanical gardens, the zoo and the town hall, they were also banned from the Jungfernsteig and other main thoroughfares and were not allowed out at all in the afternoons. Similar regulations existed in Berlin, where dire penalties threatened registered prostitutes who strolled along unter den Linder or drove through the city in an open carriage. Vice could flourish in the back streets and dark alleys of the older parts of the great cities; but no self-respecting police force could allow the newer and more respectable parts of its city to become a market-place for trade in human flesh, if it wished to maintain its reputation as the guardian of public decency and the protector of the respectable classes. Yet the failure of the regulation to encompass more than a tenth of those actively engaged in prostitution ensured from the start that this object stood no chance of being achieved". (Evans, Richard; 1976; p. 118).[2]

3) *Maintenance of Public Order*

The need to preserve public order was the third argument advanced by the police in defence of regulation of prostitution. They believed that unregulated prostitution would give rise to networks of pimps, procurers, hangers-on and organised crime and violence associated with prostitution - all prostitutes being drawn from the ranks of the poor and destitute. They said no reservation of public order would lead to social disequilibrium.

While this was undoubtedly an extreme and hysterical point of view, it reflected the middle class phobia of social disorder and unrest in the wake of mass unemployment and casual employment in large cities - above all, perhaps, in Berlin were police control over prostitution was very lax.

These fears were greatly increased when there was a

sensational murder case in 1891. It became thé focus of national attention and there were public outbursts against prostitution. "In 1891 one Heinze and his wife were convicted of breaking into a Berlin church to steal the silver and of murdering the watchman who intercepted them. It was revealed that Heinze was a pimp and his wife whom he had married purely for professional purposes, was a prostitute with forty previous convictions for violating vice regulations. To add to the scandal, Heinze insisted on refreshing himself in the dock with a bottle of champagne, and his defence was conducted to the enthusiastic approval of his underworld friends who gathered in the public gallery to watch him." (Evans, Richard; 1976; p.119).[2]

So intense was public furore over this case that the Kaiser himself openly condemned the leniency of the courts and urged the Government to introduce more stringent measures against prostitutes and procurers. The Prussian cabinet subsequently amended its Imperial Code and allowed police authorities to re-establish regulated brothels in the hope of finding the procurers.

Debates in Germany on the Regulationist System

Morality Association

Fiery debates were sparked off by the aforementioned case on the issue of regulation of prostitution. At one end of the spectrum were the Morality Associations dominated by Evangelical clergymen, with a few Catholics. They were mainly men from the middle class especially school teachers. They were supported by several other organizations including the Association for the Protection of Young Persons. They perceived prostitutes as instruments of the devil, immoral seductresses and a major threat to society and morality. It was therefore the duty of the state to persecute and not control them. The Morality Associations propagated a host of moral and legislative reforms such as abolition of state regulated brothels, deportment of foreign prostitutes, imprisonment of all other prostitutes, reformation of women's prisons and establishment of special departments to impart moral education to prostitutes and the life. Prostitutes were thus regarded as criminals.

Abolitionists

Vociferously opposing this section was Josephine Butler's

International Movement for the suppression of state-regulated vice, which consisted of a group of radical feminists in Berlin and Hamburg. They saw state regulation of prostitution as an official sanction of the double standards of male sexual morality and a symbol of sexual enslavement of women as a whole. Despite their vociferous campaigns, the heated debates raised and public opinion created, they failed to achieve their aims of abolishing the system of state regulated prostitution. This was perhaps because prostitution as an issue had ramificatins far wider and deeper than immediate concerns of public morality, health and order. The abolititionists not only perceived in prostitution the exploitation and enslavement of women, but also the product of an immoral aristocratic and militaristic system of values. They presented a challenge to the German state. This was in sharp contrast to the Morality Associations who also saw the social and political dimensions of prostitution but were mainly troubled by the status of the prostitutes and only urged changes in methods to deal with prostitution.

The Social Democratic Party

Even more radical than the Abolitionists were the Social Democrats, who mounted a fierce attack on the system of regulating prostitution. They saw prostitution as a product of capitalism and the symbol of degeneration of the bourgeois society. It could, in their opinion, only be eliminated by a socialist revolution. Later reformist tendencies which developed within the party led to the formulation of specific reforms to deal with prostitution, rather than just speculate on its elimination after a socialist revolution.

In a desperate bid to assert its control over society, the government responded to these groups and the fast moving forces of change that were taking place in German society by passing a great deal of legislation against subversion, industrial and social unrest, moral degeneration and revolution. At the local level, the police vigorously maintained the system of regulation of prostitution and were very wary of any criticism.

This system continued till the outbreak of the First World War, when military authorities introduced an even more rigid system of regulated prostitution for the troops. "The system was extended during the war with even more drastic regulations brought in, providing for the forcible incarceration in mobile brothels of any woman suspected of indulging in sexual intercourse with more than one man (even without demanding payment) and of all women suffering from veneral disease, and mandating severe punishments for anyone, male or female, who knowingly spread veneral disease (Evans, Richard; 1976; p. 128).[2]

Measures to regulate prostitution failed in the revolution of 1918-19. Controlled brothels were closed down in 1922 and 1927, when the Social Democrats, left wing liberals and women activists came to power occupying important positions at every level in the legislative assemblies and government. The system was once again revived with Hitler's ascendance to power in 1933. The regulationist system of prostitution still exists in the Federal Republic of Germany.

It is quite obvious from the history of regulation of prostitution in Imperial Germany that the system was a failure. Not only did the police fail to keep prostitutes off the streets, but effectivity was also hampered by prostitutes refusing to register themselves with local authorities. Further, the group against regulation argued that V.D. was not reduced by this system. Also, the system of regulation worked in the interests of the male client and community at large, but was detrimental to the interests of prostitute women. Prostitutes were segregated, publically identified, restricted in their movements, harassed by the police and subjected to demeaning compulsory medical examinations. The system of regulating them only served to control them..

This author was unable to procure detailed information on the system of law governing prostitution that existed in Germany between 1933-1974. However, a West German researcher, Barbara Yondorf, in her article, "Prostitution as a Legal Activity: The West German Experience", states that prostitution has always been a legal activity in West Germany.

Legalized Prostitution in Contemporary Germany

Prostitution has always been a legal activity for a greater part of West German history with some regulations controlling prostitutes. Till 1974, West Germany imposed criminal sanctions for breach of these regulations. Since 1974, however, prostitution laws in West Germany have been revised and updated. Criminal sanctions for violation of regulations have been replaced by civil and administrative sanctions. (Yondorf,

Barbara; 1979; p.420).[4] (Barbara Yondorf is a German researcher studying prostitution in Germany).

Current Federal Law in West Germany

The following are the principal features of current West German Federal Law on prostitution and related activities.

Prostition is permitted in towns with a population exceeding 20,000. Each city regulates prostitution by means of its own local ordinance.

Zoning Laws

Zoning laws restrict the activity spaces of prostitutes. They are localized and vary from city to city. There are three forms of zoning laws in operation in West Germany: The multiple zoning policy, no-zoning policy and single zoning policy.

a. Multiple Zoning Policy

The City of Munich has the multiple zoning system. Street walking here is restricted to 9 designated areas of the city. In two areas, street walkers are permitted to operate at any time of the day. In the remaining 7 areas, street walking is only allowed between 8 p.m. and 7 a.m. Prostitutes who solicit and negotiate off the street may practise at any time of the day in any part of Munich, except the city centre and cemetry, where all forms of prostitution are prohibited (Yondorf, Barbara; 1979; p. 421).[4]

b. No-zoning Policy

In West Berlin, where there is a no-zoning policy, prostitution can be practised in any part of the city (Yondorf, Barbara; 1979; p. 421).[4]

c. Single Zoning Policy

The single zoning policy stringently restricts all prostitution to a single area. The St. Pauli district in Hamburg, the adult entertainment zone (measuring 1/2 sq. km.) is an example of such a system. Sex shows, bars, striptease joints, bordellos and prostitution houses are all concentrated in this zone (Yondorf, Barbara; 1979; p. 421).[4]

Prostitution in Germany is also prohibited in the vicinity of schools, churches, cemetries or in houses where people are less than 18 years of age.

Age and Nationality of Prostitutes

Prostitutes must be 18 years of age or older. They must be citizens of West Germany.

Boys between 14 and 18 years of age may only visit prostitutes with parental permission.

Registration and Health Regulation

Each of the eleven states of the Federal Republic of West Germany is responsible for public health control, including VD control. This means that the West German health department is responsible for regular VD checks on prostitutes, the cost of which is borne by the government.

To facilitate the health department's monitoring of prostitutes, prostitutes are required to register themselves as prostitutes with the local health departments and must be medically examined for V.D. at regular intervals as stipulated by the local law. In some cities, prostitutes are required to undergo compulsory medical examination once a week, in others twice a week and in still others, once in 2 weeks. After registration and a medical examination, each woman is given a special health card which she must carry with her, indicating among other things, her last visit to the doctor. The police, social workers, and health officers, may at any time ask to see the health card. If as a consequence of such checks, it is discovered that a woman has not been for a medical examination, she is sent to a hospital for one; Resistance to undergoing such an examination incurs penal measures. (Yondorf, Barbara; 1979; p. 421).[4]

4. Taxation of Incomes

Income from prostitution is subject to taxation (Yondorf, Barbara; 1979; p. 420-421).[4]

5. Illegal Pimping and Procuring

The Federal Republic of West Germany has made pimping and procuring illegal.

An Evaluation of the System of Legalized Prostitution in Contemporary Germany

Zoning Laws and Restrictions/harassment of Prostitutes

Zoning laws have two primary functions, both of which only

serve to oppress and exploit the woman in prostitution. Firstly, they serve to regulate the times of business and activity spaces of prostitutes, so as to avoid public nuisance and preserve public morals. This segregationist policy is a crude manifestation of the double standards of male sexual morality.

Prostitution is legalized and hence legitimized by society largely on the basis of the patriarchal assumption of its universality and inevitability. But while the institution is allowed to flourish, the individual prostitute is ironically condemned for nuisance value and for corrupting public morals and hence unjustly isolated geographically and socially.

Secondly, zoning renders the police department's task of patrolling the areas to identify and regulate prostitutes easier, as all prostitution has to be concentrated in certain areas. However, prostitutes complain that such a system places excessive power in police hands and makes a prostitute more vulnerable to police harassment. The police are known to arrest and fine prostitutes whom they identify outside the zone, even if the woman has not been soliciting, but has only gone shopping. This is undoubtedly a serious restriction on the free movement of prostitutes (Private discussions with German prostitutes at the Brussels Congress).[3]

Zoning laws have also been partly responsible for a recession in the prostitution business in Frankfurt. The laws have decreased the areas of prostitution activity and have led to a greater concentration of women in a smaller area, resulting in severe competition and underpricing.

Existence of Pimping and Crimes Against Prostitutes

Moreover, concentration of prostitutes and prostitution in zones gives power to the pimp and creates problems of crime linked to prostitution. As prostitutes are to be in particular zones, it is obvious that when a new prostitute enters, a pimp can easily identify her and pursue her. A pimp may even be necessary for a prostitute to gain entry into and operate within a zone.

This is despite the fact that pimping is illegal in West Germany. Interestingly, about 80-95 per cent of prostitutes in West Germany have pimps. In a small, but significant number of cases, pimps are lovers, boyfriends and husbands. A conviction of a pimp becomes difficult, unless the prostitute turns against him (Yondorf, Barbara: 1979; p. 427).[4]

While few cities in West Germany maintain statistics on crime related to prostitution, both the Hamburg and West Berlin police report that only a small number of prostitutes are involved in crime and mainly in petty crime (Yondorf, Barbara; 1979; p. 423).[4] By contrast, however, crime and violence against prostitutes by pimps and clients and the like are very common. In Munich, the police estimate that 90 per cent of crime agaiondorf Barbara; 1979; P. 423).[4]

Researcher Joseph Sharbert in an article on prostitutes in Munich stated that between 1962 and 1972, 20 prostitutes were victims of violent deaths. Between January and December 1973, 30 Munich prostitutes were victims of armed robbery and 80 prostitutes were victims of theft (Yondorf Barbara; 1979; p. 425).[4] In West Berlin the police estimated that between 1st October 1974 and 15th July 1975, there were 9 cases of procuring minors (8 of whom were part of the white slave trade) and 127 cases of procuring adult women (85 of whom were cases of pimping) for prostitution (Yondorf, Barbara; 1979; p. 424).[4] Confirming this, Barbara Yondorf states that there were widespread pimp-related crimes in brothels and eros centres in West Berlin between October 1st 1974 and July 15th, 1978. White slave traffic, pimping and procuring of minors and women for prostitution was rampant as a result of legalization of prostitution in Germany (Barry, Kathleen; 1979).[1]

Registration of Prostitutes

Runaways, women who were wanted by the police and those not wanting to be known as prostitutes refrained from registration. When a prostitute registers herself she has to furnish information concerning her name, age, address, health status, when she usually goes for a holiday, etc. This publically identifies and labels a woman as a prostitute, renders her vulnerable to blackmail and other forms of harassment, hampers her social mobility and is above all a violation of her human rights. According to local police authorities, in December 1976, there were 3,000 registered prostitutes in West Berlin, 2,400 in Hamburg and 800 in Munich. While exact estimates are difficult to obtain, the Hamburg police maintain that there are around 2,500 unregistered prostitutes in Hamburg while according to the Munich police there are about 300 unregistered prostitutes in Munich (Barry Kathleen; 1979; p. 422).[1]

As registration is one of the means used to identify prostitutes for medical examinations and treatment for VD, Refusal to register only renders efforts to curb VD in this manner farcial.

Age, Conditions of Prostitutes, Especially Foreign Prostitutes

While the law stipulates that no female engaging in prostitution should be less than 18 years of age, the age range of prostitutes in West Germany is anywhere between 14 and 60 years. The average age of a German prostitute is 24 years, (Yondorf, Barbara; 1979; p. 422).[4]

According to Health Clinic social workers, there is a significant proportion of juvenile prostitution. Most juvenile prostitutes are runaways.

The majority of them work the streets and have pimps, as prostitution establishments avoid hiring underage girls for fear of the law. It is, however, difficult to give accurate estimates of the magnitude of juvenile prostitution, as this form of prostitution is forbidden in Germany and hence young girls do not register themselves with the local authorities (Yondorf, Barbara; 1979; p .427).[4] A large proportion of German prostitutes work in small houses with anywhere between 7 and 20 women. Prostitutes often rent rooms in houses for between 20 and 40 a day and are turned out of the house if they are unable to pay their rent. Alternatively, they can pay the owner a percentage of their income per client. Interviews with German prostitutes reveal that prostitutes give around 40 per cent of the income per client to the owner. (Private discussions with German prostitutes at the Brussels Congress).[3] They work for around 8 hours or more a day, earning around $ 12 for straight sex in times of slack business, $ 24 being the typical base price index in December 1976 (Yondorf, Barbara; 1979; p. 422).[4]

German prostitutes also work in clubs. Clubs have stringent rules which affect prostitutes adversely. Prostitutes cannot choose a client. They have to submit to the clients, sexual preferences, lest they are beaten or fired. The submission to perverted sexual demands like oral sex and sadomasochism in clubs has become even more in demand because of the severe competition from Asian and black prostitutes and the German clients' preference for 'exotic' Asian or black women. Further, clubs are not governed by laws which stipulate minimum wages, work limits, number of clients and so on (Private discussions with German prostitutes at the Brussels Congress).[3]

Conditions of Foreign Prostitutes in Germany

Although it is illegal for a foreigner to work as a prostitute, in West Germany, there is a large number.

Interviews with a German prostitute revealed that more than 1/3 to 1/4 of the prostitutes in the city of Frankfurt alone were foreigners with more than half of them being of Thai origin. Most of these women have fallen prey to international trafficking networks, the use of trickery and deceit, to ensnare them into prostitution. The promise of lucrative jobs and luxury in Germany or fake marriage contracts are three of the means used by these networks to recruit women from developing countries into prostitution in Germany, as they promise elsewhere.

Women are often brought on 3-month tourist visas to Germany. After the 13-month period has lapsed their stay is illegal but there is no way in which they can return to their home countries because their travel documents are, from the outset, kept with the agents, traffickers and the like. Ignorance, inability to speak German and the knowledge of the illegality of their stay inhibit them from approaching concerned authorities (Private discussions with German prostitutes at Brussels Congress.[3]

According to a recent amendment to the Foreigners Act in the Federal Republic of West Germany any woman who marries a German has to produce, on demand, proof of her marriage and evidence of the fact that she resides with her German husband. This amendment was introduced in the wake of a spurt in the number of people who sought political asylum in Germany, and therefore married Germans but never lived with them. Pimping and procuring networks in Germany use this Act to marry foreign women, bring them to Germany and force them into prostitution. These women are thus not only in a sense forced to engage in marriage with these men, but they must live with them and move wherever they go because they would necessarily have to show that they are not only married to them but also live with them. They are enslaved (Private discussions with German prostitutes at the Brussels Congresss).[3]

The conditions of foreign prostitutes in Germany is pathetic.

The fear and trauma of being sold into prostitution, the distance from home, the lack of money, the absence of travel documents, the inability to speak German and the alien cultural setting cause a tremendous feeling of powerlessness.

The vast majority of Third World women in the sex industry, live and operate in low grade brothels and eros centres. Clubs do not hire them for fear of the law. Conditions in these brothels are appalling. They are dark, dingy and insanitary. Women must entertain numerous clients a day. They have no right to choose clients and more than half their earnings are appropriated by brothel managements. With increasing client demand for 'exotic' Third World women and more perverted forms of sex, these women have no choice but to give in to demands for anal sex or sadomasochism. Refusal to comply meets with verbal abuse or being beaten up. Movements and interactions of these women are watched carefully. Even the more seasoned among them do not risk venturing out much, in case the police detect them.

Another problem peculiar to these women is the problem of racism. Brothels may be several storeyed buildings with 7 to 10 or more girls from a particular country occupying a specific floor. For example, one therefore encounters a situation where they may be German prostitutes on the ground and first floors, Asians on the second and third floors and blacks on the fourth floor. Clients can go to the women of their preference. To begin with there is little communication between women of different racial groups. Also, German prostitutes complain of a decline in their business because of the 'AIDS hysteria'. They pin the blame for the emergence and spread of AIDS on black prostitutes.

Racism and ethnocentricism thus complete the life of alienation for Third World prostitutes (Private discussions with German prostitutes at the Brussels Congress).[3]

Taxation of Incomes from Prostitution

Public coffers burgeoned with taxes collected from bars and brothels. One Munich brothel of 100 women paid $ 400,000 per year in taxes. Taxing individual incomes of prostitutes was more difficult because of the problems involved in the accurate determination of their real incomes, the mobility of the prostitutes, and the consequent difficulties in tracing them

(Yondorf, Barbara; 1979; p. 426).[4] Although incomes from prostitution were taxe, prostitutes did not have the right to receive pensions, social security benefits, public health insurance and the like. Taxation of incomes from prostitution thus had two deplorable aspects. Firstly, it was one of the crudest manifestations of state endorsement of prostitution, the state actually living off the earnings of a patriarchal and exploitative institution. Secondly, such taxation exhibited double standards of morality and a discriminatory stance towards prostitutes because while their incomes were taxed like any other citizen's, they did not have the same rights and did not enjoy the same benefits.

Like all other countries that have legalized prostitution, the experience of Imperial and contemporary Germany reveal that, legalization severely controls prostitutes. The work conditions of prostitutes, particularly those forcibly induced into prostitution from Third World countries are horrendous. Lastly, despite the taxation of incomes from prostitution, prostitutes receive none of the benefits that other normal tax-paying citizens are entitled to.

References

1. Barry Kathleen; (1979); *Female Sexual Slavery:* Prentice Hall Inc; Englewood Cliffs, New Jersey.

2. Evans J. Richard; (1976); "Prostitution, State and Society in Imperial Germany"; Revised and extended version of a paper first delivered to the Volkswagen-Stiftung Conference at St. Anthony's College, Oxford, in July 1972 and subsequently at a Research Seminar at the University of Stirling.

3. Private discussions with prostitutes at the Brussels Congress on Prostitution, Human Rights and Feminism; (1986); European Parliament, Brussels, 1st/4th October.

4. Yondorf, Barbara; (1979); "Prostitution as a Legal Activity: The West German Experience"; *Policy Analysis;* Vol.5; No.4.

Conclusions

From the foregoing discussion on the experience of those countries that have legalized prostitution it is evident that far from working in the interests of prostitutes, legalization has only served to regulate and control them. Any breach of restrictions imposed on these women under this system of law, leads to sanctions like fines and imprisonment, the revoking of their work permits and banishment from the area. Brothel-managements are usually unaffected legally.

The patriarchal arguments advanced in favour of legalization in these countries are its necessity to curb the spread of V.D. among military men (and all males) and thus preserve their efficiency, the need to preserve public morality and public order are unacceptable.

(a) Patriarchal Assumptions

Firstly, legalization of prostitution is based on the patriarchal assumption of the "uncontrollability of the male sexual drive. Prostitutes are that category of women set aside to give full rein to this 'uncontainable' male sexuality. But prostitute women must be sexually clean and healthy to prevent any hindrance to the efficiency of males and male institutions. Hence the sexist bias against prostitutes to legalize prostitution. Prostitutes have to be checked medically in order to curb the spread of VD.

Secondly, this system of law reveals the double standards of male sexual morality because while it accepts and legitimizes prostitution in society, it ironically tries to maintain a facade of morality by cleaning up visible street prostitution.

(b) Failure of Legalization to Meet its Objectives

Inability of the Police to Keep Prostitutes off the Street

The police have been unable to control visible prostitution in all the countries regulating prostitution.

(c) Non-Registration of Prostitutes

Prostitutes have been known to evade registering themselves as prostitutes, for fear of destroying their anonymity and being harassed. Registration is also known to be avoided as prostitutes resent the demeaning health checks which they perceive as a blatant violation of their persons.

Evasion of registration has thwarted efforts to identify prostitutes for health checks.

(d) Failure to Curb VD

Inability to identify prostitutes, coupled with the unfair direction of health measures against prostitutes alone, while exempting clients from such regulations, has rendered efforts to control the spread of VD futile.

VD has not diminished in countries that have legalized prostitution.

(e) Control over Exploitation of and Discrimination against Prostitutes

The experience of countries that have legalized prostitution reveals that restrictions on business hours and activity spaces of prostitutes and the requirement to register themselves as prostitutes has affected prostitutes adversely.

It has restricted their freedom of movement.

Geographical isolation and registration has reiterated the'madonna-whore' division among women and has resulted in the identification of prostitutes as public women, stigmatized them and decreased their social mobility.

The police who have been empowered to identify prostitute women for compulsory medical examinations are known to have harassed and abused prostitutes, driving many a woman to suicide.

The spatial definition of prostitution areas appears to have led to an increase in pimping activity and crime in these areas, most important of which are crimes by pimps and clients against prostitute women.

While certain countries that legalized prostitution did not ban the practices of pimping and procuring women and girls for prostitution, countries like West Germany have made pimping illegal. Regardless of the legal position on pimping and procuring, those countries with legalized prostitution have seen an increase in pimping activity and traffic in women and girls for prostitution. Trade in women and girls for prostitution reached an all time high in England during the operation of the Contagious Diseases Acts, which legalized prostitution.

(f) No Benefits ro Prostitutes

Moreover, legalization has brought no real benefits to prostitutes. Brothel-attached prostitutes are known to be rigidly controlled by the brothel-management who not only appropriate a significant proportion of their earnings, but also maintain a close watch on their movements, interactions and relationships. Further, despite paying taxes, prostitutes are not entitled to the benefits that any other tax paying citizen is entitled to.

(g) Control over the Entire Female Population

Finally, the experience of countries that have legalized prostitution reveals that arbitary police identification of prostitutes for compulsory health checks has put all women in fear of being identified as prostitutes. Police are known to arrest and harass any woman whom they believe to be a prostitute according to stereotyped conceptions of a prostitute's mannerisms.

Thus, apart from controlling prostitutes, legalized prostitution has served to control the entire female population residing within the jurisdiction of such a system of law.

Chapter-11:Recommendations for Change

The foregoing discussion makes it obvious that the present legalization of prostitution is not working. Nor will legalization work in the interests of women in prostitution.

This chapter suggests certain amendments to the current law, as well as the creation of structures which would enable stringent implementation of the existing provisions. Apart from legal reform, the suggestions also deal with measures for rehabilitation of prostitutes and the setting up of safeguards for women who have entered prostitution as a result of socio-economic vulnerability.

From the long-term point of view it is only structural change that can eliminate patriarchal institutions like prostitution.

While it is necessary to continue with the existing tolerationist system of law, the SITA/ITPPA need to be further amended as follows:

Decriminalization of the Act of prostitution

It is time that the law and society at large, perceived the prostitute as a human being, a victim of exploitation and an active survivor.

It is, thereofre, necessary to decriminalise the act of prostitution by deleting all sections in the ITPPA and other local laws, which criminalize and penalize the prostitute. This must be applicable to all categories of prostitutes. The measure would remove the focus and punishment from the individual in prostitution. It could substantially curb police harassment of prostitutes.

(D'Cunha, Jean; 1986).1

Tightening of the Law Against Clients And Prostitution Racketeers

The law must also be tightened up against clients and prostitution racketeers in the following ways:

1. Acts warranting penal sanctions for clients

Because one has to understand the complex structural context of client demand for women in prostitution and view the adverse effect penal provisions against the client might have in the short run, on the life and earnings of the women in prostitution, penal sanctions should only be incorporated for the following acts by the client: non payment to and/or rape of woman, violent or kinky sex, demand for child prostitutes and the like (D'Cunha, Jean; 1988).[2]

2. Comprehensive penal provisions for landlords and traffickers

While amending the existing section No. 3(b), the burden of proof that the landlord did not know that his premises or part of it was being used for prostitution, must be placed on him/her. "Ignorance is no defence".

3. In order to effectively prevent traffic in persons for prostitution, the Act must incorporate explicit provisions for disciplinary action at the point of buying and selling persons for prostitution.

4. Penal provisions against corrupt enforcement authorities

Provisions must be introduced to penalize police officers who extort sex favours from prostitutes and bribes from prostitution racketeers. Similar penal sanctions must also be incorporporated against magistrates indulging in the aforesaid activities (D'Cunha Jean; 1988).[2]

Implementation and Reinforcement of the Law

The police and courts are the primary implementing and enforcing agencies under ITPPA (like the SITA), and are invested with immense power. Although the provisions for non-official advisory boards and committees exist under the Act to assist the special police officer and magistrate, the scope and functions of these bodies is far too limited. They are not mandatory and are, in many cases, not actually constituted.

In view of the tardy implementation of the Act - largely a result of corruption and sexist attitudes rife amidst implementing/enforcing authorities - and with a view to curbing the power of these authorities, alternate structures must be found for it to be effective. This will also help the new amendment raising the number of penalties under the ITPPA.

*Citizens' Committees:*The efficacy in implementation could be enhanced by the constitution of statutorily recognized mandatory citizens' committees, area-wise, to oversee its implementation.

The committees must consist of not less than five full time paid women social workers or lawyers or representatives of women's organisations or researchers who must be appointed by the State Governments.

The jurisdiction of the proposed citizens' committees should coincide with that of the administrative authorities constituted to implement the Act in each particular area.

The female social workers must be trained and must possess Master's Degree in Social Work.

The women's organisations must have at least one year's experience in helping women in distress or of performing agitation and propaganda concerning women's rights.

Lawyers must show evidence of having taken up cases of women's rights and social scientists (researchers) must also show evidence of doing research and writing on women's issues from a pro-woman point of view.

Powers and Functions: The committees must be empowered to detect, report, and put pressure on the police to raid, arrest and follow up the prosecution and conviction of prostitution racketeers.

The committees must also be empowered to give evidence against prostitution racketeers in court and combat police harassment of women in prostitution.

Social workers in these committees must be empowered to verify the antecedents of persons claiming guardianship rights of girls under the Act.

The committees may also function as outreach teams that spot runaway children and refer them for rehabilitation. They must also rescue and refer for rehabilitation those women and girls wishing to leave prostitution.

The State Government is empowered under the Act to set up Special Courts for the quick hearing of cases. Such courts must be set up. (D'Cunha, Jean; 1986).[1]

Training for implementing authorities on legal provisions and attitudinal changes: Special legal education on the provisions of the law governing prostitution and other related laws must be imparted to the implementing authorities.

Similarly, workshops must be organised for the latter to discuss the structural roots of prostitution and question the sexist attitudes towards prostitutes and prostitution.

Rehabilitation

The orientation to rehabilitation under the Act is one of 'correction or reformation'.

Therefore, the perception towards prostitutes must change. They must be seen as victims of and survivors in an exploitative social system, rather than as offenders, delinquents, and nymphomaniacs. Understanding and affection must replace discipline and punishment in rehabilitation.

Number of Homes: As mentioned in Chapter 3, there are only three protective homes set up under the Act for the whole of Maharashtra.

Given the tardy implementation of the Act, the gross inadequacy of the homes is probably not evident. But with tighter implementation, the need will be obvious.

An adequate number of protective homes must be set up, taking into consideration the approximate number of prostitutes in the area.

Finances: Adequate finances must be provided by the Government for the maintenance and administration of the homes and for the maintenance of the staff.

Staff: The number of staff in such institutions must be in proportion to the number of inmates in the home.

The post of Superintendent and Assistant Superintendent must be residential.

Staff members must be appointed after an interview for an advertised post. Appointments must be made on the basis of social work experience, orientation and qualifications.

A full-time counsellor and psychotherapist must be appointed.

The Superintendent, Assistant Superintendent, social workers and matrons must hold Master's Degrees in Social Work.

The above mentioned staff must know about the provisions of the law and must impart this knowledge to the rest of the staff.

Staff salaries must be adequate and paid from Government grants.

Orientation of staff: In their training the staff must be given an analysis of the structural roots of prostitution and must also be oriented to perceiving women in prostitution as human beings, victims and survivors in an exploitative social system.

Facilities and Administration of the Homes

*Amendments to the inmates' register:*The inmates' register required under the Act must be amended to include information about family history:

(a) Name, occupation and age of each family member

(b) Family income

(c) Address

(d) Nature of inmate's relationship with the family members

Background of the woman/girl in prostitution

(a) Details of how the woman entered prostitution

(b) Names, descriptions and addresses of individuals inducing and keeping her in prostitution

(c) Conditions under which she carried on prostitution

(d) Section of the Act under which she was rescued from prostitution.

This information could help the authorities track down those involved in prostitution.

Progress Records: Apart from the need to maintain detailed progress records concerning the physical conditions of the inmates, as specified in the rules, records of the emotional states of the individuals should also be maintained.

Language Panels: Panels of people conversant with various Indian languages must be constituted as interpretative liaisons between the individuals and the social workers. This would facilitate rapport building and might lead to more accurate records of case histories and progress records.

Health Facilities: A full time medical practitioner should be appointed for each home.

Facilities for treating VD and other ailments should be available in the homes.

Isolation rooms for contagious diseases and rooms for counselling must be maintained in the homes.

A rule must state that a staff member must stay with an inmate in hospital, if the latter is admitted there, as this could safeguard the girl from prostitution racketeers who might meet the girl in hospital and coerce her into returning to prostitution.

Counselling and Psychotherapy: Counselling and psychotherapy sessions must be held every day if possible. In these sessions inmates must be helped to understand the social roots of prostitution and perceive themselves as victims and surviving subjects, rather than as 'scum'.

Similar sessions must also be held with the family members.

Psychological, Intelligence Quotient and Aptitude tests must be carried out at each institution. They must be devised and administered by experts bearing in mind the Indian situation, the socio-economic status and the traumatic emotional experiences of the inmates. Such tests must be administrated at periodic intervals to record change and progress.

Vocational and Occupational Training: The Act states that every institution must run literary classes, vocational and occupational training. However, this must be based on the aptitude of the individual and the market value of the job. Such training must not reinforce sex role stereotypes.

The institutions must procure job contracts; for example, with factories, for those staying for a long term. Inmates must be encouraged to bank their wages.

The institutions must create links with job placement agencies to secure jobs for inmates.

Preparatory education in family living, marriage, banking and savings must be given to all inmates.

Recreation and socialization: The institutions' staff must organize regular outings, films, picnics and socials for the inmates every month. Gatherings and socials must be organized with the opposite sex in order to facilitate normal socialization.

Participation in Home Management: All inmates must be encouraged to democratically participate in the running of the homes.

Marriage: Marriage must not be perceived by the staff as the only alternative to prostitution. The choice of being a single working woman should also be discussed with the inmates.

As suggested in the rules under the SITA, the social workers must probe the family background, economic status and character of the proposed grooms. Time and opportunity must be given for the couples to get to know each other. Short marriage preparation courses must be held and the grooms must be informed of the girls' past in order to avoid complications after marriage.

After-care Homes and Hostels: Half-way homes and government subsidized hostels for women and their children must also be set up to house them when they leave.

Follow up: The SITA rules state that there must be checks on girls discharged and those married for at least 3 years after the discharge from the homes, by the home staff.

Board of Visitors: The provisions for a Board of Visitors under Rule 41 of the SIT Act must be adhered to. The Board must include representatives from women's organisations who are taking up issues concerning women's rights.

They must discuss institutional problems with and make suggestions for change to the Superintendents of the homes. They must also present their reports concerning the institutions to the Citizens' Committees once a month (D'Cunha, Jean; 1986).[1]

Other Measures

While the task of providing adequate support structures to women desiring to give up prostitution is an urgent need, it is equally important to set up adequate safeguards to prevent women from entering prostitution.

The following measures need to be undertaken to help accomplish this:

Public Education: There must be widespread public education through different forms of mass media and educational institutions on the structural roots of prostitution, the public's responsibility (direct or indirect) in sustaining the institution of prostitution, in order to make the public aware that the moral and legal isolation of prostitutes is artificial and conceals many tragedies. Such education must also emphasize the need for gender equality and human values.

For women in the entertainment industry: Health facilities and legal aid must be provided to women workers in the entertainment industry to protect them from abuse and exploitation which often lead to their entry into prostitution (Thanh-Dam, Truong;1985)[3]*For victims of sexual violence*: It is necessary to create shelters for women who are victims of sexual violence, where legal aid and counselling can be provided and where advice on alternative employment can be given, so that they are not forced into prostitution (Thanh-Dam, Truong; 1985).[3]

Health facilities for working prostitutes: Different forms of media must be used to alert working prostitutes about health issues and issues related to their work which contribute to the quick deterioration of their life-style and therefore decrease the seemingly advantageous rewards of the profession (Thanh-Dam, Truong; 1985).[3]

Education and employment for women: Pressure must be brought to bear on the government to effectively implement its policy of free and compulsory matriculate education for policy measures must be formulated to upgrade employment alternatives to prostitution. More jobs must be reserved for women. Wages and other facilities for employed women must equal those for men doing the same work.

Review existing and planned policies on tourism: Existing and planned policies on tourism must be reviewed in order to find alternative forms of tourism from the prevailing one which tends increasingly to incorporate prostitute services in various forms as a component of the tourist package (Thanh-Dam, Truong; 1985).[3]

End discrimination in other laws: Government must reform personal laws and work towards legislation and practices that guarantee equal rights in marriage, divorce, custody, inheritance, maintenance and employment.

Laws on the use of women's images in advertising which often promote women as available and exotic temptresses must be reviewed. Images in advertising are not simply beautiful photographs. They constitute particular ideological products produced by the media to condition human behaviour. The advertising industry is very significant not only in terms of its size, but also because it has become an indispensable adjunct of global corporate capital (Thanh-Dam, Truong; 1985).[3]

The link between women researchers and activists must be strengthened to fill gaps in knowledge and correct bias by involving prostitutes or ex-prostitutes in research for policies and action (Thanh-Dam, Truong; 1985).[3]

Long-term measures: From the long term point of view, it is only the recognition and acknowledgement of the material and sexist roots of prostitution, coupled with a determined struggle to restructure our unjust social system and change our male oriented values, that will help towards eliminating a patriarchal institution like prostitution (D'Cunha, Jean; 1986).[1]

References

1) D'Cunha, Jean; (1984); "The Suppression of Immoral Traffic in Women and Girls Act, 1956: A Critical Review"; Research Project for the Research Unit on Women's Studies, S.N.D.T. University.

2) D'Cunha Jean; (1988); "The Law in India: Biased against Prostitutes, while Racketeers and Clients go scot free - Critique and Proposals for Change"; Paper presented at the Asian Regional Conference on "Exploitation of Women and Children", New Delhi, 17th-19th November.

3) Thanh-Dam, Truong; (1985): "Virtue, Order, Health and Money: Towards a Comprehensive Perspective on Female Prostitution in Asia"; Paper prepared for Workshop of Experts on Prevention and Rehabilitation Schemes for Young Women in Prostitution and Related Occupations; ESCAP, Bangkok, 17th - 21st June.

Bibliography

1) Alexander, Priscilla; (1986); "Customer Violence against Prostitutes"; Paper for the National Task Force on Prostitution; San Francisco, (U.S.A.); June.

2) Alexander, Priscilla; (1987); "On Prostitution"; Paper for the National Task Force on Prostitution; San Francisco, U.S.A.; February.

3) Alexander, Priscilla; (1987); "Prostitutes are being scapegoated for Heterosexual AIDS", Paper for the National Task Force on Prostitution; San Francisco, U.S.A.; February.

4) Association of Anti-Prostitution; (1984); *Anti-Prostitution Activities in Japan.*

5) Association for Social Health in India; (1987); Paper on "The Immoral Traffic Prevention Act: A Resume".

6) Ballhatchet, Kenneth; (1979); *Race, Sex and Class under the Raj: Imperial Attitudes and Policies and their Critics (1793-1905)*; Vikas Publishing House Pvt. Ltd., New Delhi.

7) Barnett, Harold; "The Political Economy of Rape and Prostitution"; *The Review of Radical Political Economics;* Vol.8, No.1.

8) Barry, Kathleen; (1979); *Female Sexual Slavery;* Prentice Hall, Inc., Englewood Cliffs, New Jersey.

9) Ed. Barry, Kathleen; Bunch, Charlotte; Castley, Shirley; (1983); "International Feminism - Networking against Female Sexual Slavery"; Report of the Global Feminist Workshop to organize against Traffic in Women; Rotterdam, The Netherlands; April 6th - 15th.

10) Barse, Sheela; (1982); "The Right to a Profession"; *Indian Express,* 21st November.

11) Barse, Sheela; (1983); "Brothel Blues"; *Bombay Magazine,* July.

12) Barse, Sheela; (1984); Article on Prostitution published in *Hindustan Times,* 22nd July.

13) Bill No. XXF of 1986; (1986); "The Suppression of Immoral Traffic in Women and Girls Amendment Bill 1986"; (as passed by the House of Parliament); An Act.

14) "Cases of AIDS in India: A Future Scenario"; (1988); Projected by the Centre for AIDS Research and Control (CARC); *Bulletin of the Centre for AIDS Research and Control;* No.3; September-October.

15) "Contagious Diseases Acts"; (1888); Records of Debates on Contagious Diseases Acts in India discussed by the Bombay Medical Union; Printed at the Anglo-Jewish Vernacular Press; Bombay.

16) Correira, Alberto. S. and Germano C.; (1939); "Indian Portuguesa: Prostitutione Profilaxia, Anti-Venera-historica; Demografia, Ethnographe, Higiene and Profilaxia - Tipographia Rangel Bastora".

17) "Crime in India"; (1980-82); Bureau of Police Research and Development; Ministry of Home Affairs; New Delhi.

18) Davis, D.E.; (1971); *Physiological Factors in Aggressive Behaviour in Animal Aggression"*; ed. Southwick Van Nostrand Runhold; New York.

19) D'Cunha, Jean; (1984); "Voices in the Dark"; *Eve's Weekly;* 19th to 24th May.

20) D'Cunha, Jean; (1984); "The Suppression of Immoral Traffic in Women and Girls Act 1956: A Critical Review"; Research project for Research Unit on Women's Studies, SNDT University, Bombay, India.

20.a) D'Cunha, Jean; (1985); "No this can never be a profession like any other"; *Femina Controversy.*

21) D'Cunha, Jean; (1987); "Children of the Night"; *Indian Express*; 19th April.

22) D'Cunha, Jean; (1987); "Prostitution in a Patriarchal Society: A Critical Review of the SIT Act"; *Economic and Political Weekly;* 7th November.

23) D'Cunha, Jean; (1986); "The Law in India: Biased against prostitutes, while racketeers and clients go scot free - Critique and Proposals for change"; Paper presented at the Asian Regional Conference on "Exploitation of Women and Children"; New Delhi; 17th - 19th November.

24) Dhar, Lekha; (1985); "The Madam who stirred Bombay's Politics"; *Telegraph;* 24th August.

25) Draft statement on Prostitution and Feminism; (1986); International Committee for Prostitutes' Rights; European Parliament, Brussels; 1st-4th October.

26) D'Souza, A.A.; (1973); "Prevention of Prostitution: A strategy of Social Change"; *Social Action;* Vol. 23.

27) Dutta, Nilima; (1986); "Trafficking in Women"; *The Lawyer;* September.

28) Evans, J. Richard; (1976); "Prostitution, State and Society in Imperial Germany"; Revised and extended version of a paper first delivered to the Volkswagen - Stiftung Conference at St. Anthony's College, Oxford in July 1972 and subsequently at a Research Seminar at the University of Stirling.

29) Ghosh, J.N.; (1923); "Social Evil in Calcutta"; Booklet; City Press; Calcutta.

30) Gokhale B.B.; (1955); "Study of Prostitution in Pune"; Paper published in *Samaj Seva;* January.

31) Gough, Kathleen; (1984); "The War Against Women: Prostitution in Vietnam". *Manushi;* Vol. 4; March-April.

32) Harrod, J.; (1985); *The Unprotected Worker: The Social Relations of Subordination;* New York; Columbia University Press.

33) Hooja, Swarnalatha; (1970); "Prostitution in Rajasthan: Then and Now"; *Indian Journal of Social Work;* Vol.XXXI; No. 2, July.

34) Interview with Dr. I.P. Gilada; Secretary of the Indian Health Organization, J.J. Hospital, Bombay (1984).

35) Interview with Mr. Prabhakar Sawant; Public Relations Officer, Maharashtra Police; (1984).

36) Interview with Shiraz Bulsara, Activist, Kashtakari Sangatna; Dahanu Taluka; Thana District (1986).

37) Interview with Shalinitai Kurade; Devadasi Sangatna, Pune; (1987).

38) Joarder, B; (1974); "A Social Study of Prostitution in Vizag"; *Bulletin of Anthropological Survey of India,* Govt. of India, Vol.XXIII; Nos. 1-2.

39) Joarder, B; (1976); "A Study of Prostitution in the Industrial Area in West Bengal".

40) Khorshed, Pavri; (1988); "Epidemiological Features of AIDS: A Global Public Health Problem"; *CARC Calling;* Bulletin of the Centre for AIDS Research and Control; Vol.I, No. 1; May-June.

41) Khorshed, Pavri; (1988); "AIDS and You: An Indian Point of View"; *CARC Calling;* Bulletin of the Centre for AIDS Research and Control; Vol. I, No. 1, May-June.

42) Kapur, Promila; (1978); *Life and World of Call Girls of India;* Vikas Publishing House Private Limited; New Delhi.

43) Lagerberg, C.S.I.J. and Wilms, G.P.; (1972); "Profiel Van Cenhandelstad in West Cameroon'; Verslagen en verant woording van een social antropologisch Onderzock in Kumba" (Tilburg Development Research Institute).

44) Leonard, B. Eileen; (1982); *Women, Crime and Society: A Critique of Theoretical Criminology;* Longman; New York and London.

45) Liddle, Joanna and Joshi, Rama; (1985); "Gender and Imperialism in British India"; *Economic and Political Weekly;* Vol.XX; No. 43; 6th October.

46) Macmillan, Jackie; (1976); "Rape and Prostitution"; *Victimology International Journal;* Vol.1; No.3.

47) Mathur, A.S. and Gupta, B.L.; (1965); *Prostitutes and Prostitution;* Published by Ramprasad and Sons.

48) Mayo, Katherine; (1927); *Mother India;* New York.

49) Mcleod, Eileen; (1982); *Working Women Prostitutes Now.*

50) "Militarization of Prostitution"; Copy of Monograph obtained from Women and Development Programme; Institute of Social Studies; 251 Badhuisweg; The Hague, The Netherlands.

51) Mukherjee, S.N.; (1933); *Prostitution in India.*

52) Narayan, Uma; (1981); "Feminism and Psychoanalysis"; Term paper; Ph.D. Course Work; Department of Philosophy; I.I.T., Bombay.

53) National Task Force on Prostitution (N.T.F.P.) Policies; (1984-86); San Francisco, U.S.A.

54) National Task Force on Prostitution (N.T.F.P.); (1986); Paper on "Health Issues for Prostitutes"; San Francisco, U.S.A.

55) News Item; (1983); "Prostitute bashed to death"; *Daily;* 11th Jan.

56) News Item; (1983); "Prostitute done to death"; *Indian Express;* 29th September.

57) News Item; (1988); "Delhi a Major Transit Point for Trafficking Women"; *The Hindu;* 3rd February.

58) Omvedt, Gail; (1983); "Devadasi Custom and the fight against it"; *Manushi;* No. 19.

59) Ong, Aihawa Dr.; (1984); "Industrialization and Prostitution in South East Asia); Paper for U.N. NGLS Invitational consultation on "Female Sexual Slavery and Economic Exploitation' .

60) Phongpaichit, R.; (1980); "Rural Women of Thailand: From Peasant Girls to Bangkok Masseuses". Geneva; ILO World Employment Programme; Research Working Paper 14.

61) Phongpaichit, Pasuk; (1981); "Bangkok's Masseuses: Holding up the Family sky"; *South East Asia Chronicle;* Issue No. 78.

62) Prabhu, Uma; (1987); "Suburbia Sees Red"; *Bombay Magazine;* 22nd June - 6th July.

63) Private Discussion with Prostitutes at the Brussels Congress on Prostitution, Human Rights and Feminism; (1986); European Parliament, Brussels; 1st - 4th October.

64) Punekar, S.D. and Rao Kamala; (1962); *Study of Prostitutes in Bombay;* Lalwani Publishing House; 2nd Edition; 1967.

65) Ramesh, Asha and Philomena H.P.; (1985;0 *Devadasi System in North Karnataka;* Preliminary report of the study conducted by the Joint Women's Programme Team in North Karnataka.

66) Ranga Rao M. and Rao R.; (1969); *A Study of Prostitutes and Prostitution in Hyderabad City;* Published by the Association for Social Health in India; Andhra Pradesh Branch.

67) Records of Vigilance Cell, Crime Branch, CID, Bombay; (1980-1987).

68) Reynaud, Em'manuel; *Holy Virility: The Social Construction of Masculinity;* Pluto Press.

69) Rosen, Ruth; (1982); *The Last Sisterhood: Prostitution in America 1900-1918;* Balimore MD. Johns Hopkins University Press, 1982.

70) Sr. Rozario, M. Rita R.G.S. assisted by Rasool Javed and Kesari Pradeep; (1988); *"Trafficking in Women and Children in India: Sexual exploitation and sale;* A Joint Women's Programme Publication; Uppal Publishing House, New Delhi.

71) Sabharwal, Jyothi; (1985); "The Girls of G.B. Road"; *Sunday Observer;* 20th October.

72) Sadasivam Bharathi; (1987); "False Beacons in Kamathipura"; *Indian Post,* 27th December.

73) Sadasivam, Bharathi; (1988); "Wooing Kamathipura"; *Indian Post;* 22nd December.

74) Savli; (1985); "Devadasis: Victims of Social Slavery"; an article presented to the Working Group of the Human Rights and Anti-Slavery Commission of the U.N., Geneva; 29th July—2nd August.

75) "Sex Tourism to Thailand"; (1979); The article appeared in Dutch in *Onze Wereld* in March 1979; Available from NOVIB Netherlands; translated by ISIS.

76) Silbert, Mimi; Ph.D; Principal Investigator; Sexual Assault of Prostitutes; San Francisco; Delancey Street Foundation.

77) Slide show and discussion with forensic expert Pritam Phatnani, Bombay.

78) Srinivasan, Amrit; (1985); "Reforms and Revival - The Devadasi and her dance"; *Economic and Political Weekly;* Vol. XX; No. 44; 2nd November.

79) Symanski, Richard; (1974); "Prostitution in Nevada"; *Annals of the Association of American Geographers;* Vol. 64; No. 3; September.

80) *Telegraph;* (1985); "Prostitutes' Union Chief Arrested"; 21st March.

81) "The Tragedy of Tulasa'; (1983); Special Report; *Probe India;* January.

82) Thista, K.F; (1980); "Providence and Prostitution"; London; Change.